NOTRE DAME vs. THE KLAN

NOTRE DAME

VS.

THE KLAN

How the Fighting Irish Defeated the Ku Klux Klan

TODD TUCKER

LOYOLAPRESS.

CHICAGO

LOYOLAPRESS.

3441 N. ASHLAND AVENUE
CHICAGO, ILLINOIS 60657
(800) 621-1008
WWW.LOYOLABOOKS.ORG

© 2004 Todd Tucker

Cover photo of cross burning used by permission of the Indiana Historical Society, Bass Photo Co. Collection, 86797. Cover photo of the Golden Dome used by permission of the University of Notre Dame Archives.

Jacket and interior design by Megan Duffy Rostan

Library of Congress Cataloging-in-Publication Data
Tucker, Todd, 1968-
  Notre Dame vs. the Klan : how the Fighting Irish defeated the KKK / Todd Tucker.
    p. cm.
  Includes bibliographical references.
  ISBN 0-8294-1771-0
  1. University of Notre Dame—History—20th century. 2. Ku Klux Klan (1915-)—
Indiana—History. 3. Anti-Catholicism—Indiana—History—20th century. I. Title:
Notre Dame versus the Klan. II. Title.
  LD4113.T83 2004
  378.772'89—dc22

                                                                    2003027927

Printed in the United States of America
04 05 06 07 08 RRD 10 9 8 7 6 5 4 3 2

To my parents, Ken and Laura Tucker,
two of the world's great readers

The [Irish] are by nature full of faith, respect, religious inclinations, and are sensible and devoted; but a great defect often paralyzes in them all their other good qualities: the lack of stability.

—Edward Sorin, CSC
founder of the University of Notre Dame[1]

CONTENTS

ACKNOWLEDGMENTS

FIRST AND FOREMOST, I WOULD LIKE TO THANK SUSIE, MY wife. Susie proofread every chapter before I sent it to Loyola and endured ten anecdotes about the Klan and Notre Dame for every one that I included in the final text. Thank you for believing in this book and in me.

Many other family members deserve thanks. My mother-in-law, Beth Reising, acted once again as my unpaid research assistant. My father-in-law, Ken Reising, gave me long-term loans from his extensive Notre Dame library, including a hard-to-find edition of Arthur Hope's *Notre Dame: One Hundred Years* as well as Marvin O'Connell's expansive (and expensive) biography of Edward Sorin. My parents provided me with a love of books, endless encouragement, and free child care. Thank you all again.

I am lucky to have two good friends who have listened to me talk about this book and have advised me about it from its earliest stages. Professor Tom Buchanan of the University of Tennessee at Chattanooga, a loyal friend since third grade, was the first to hear about this idea, on a rainy day in Cincinnati three years ago. He has had to listen to me talk about it ever since. Also deserving of thanks is Doug Bennett of New Albany, Indiana, a talented writer in his own right who now knows more about the Klan than he probably ever wanted to. Thank you both, gentlemen. I promise to talk about something else now.

Many in the Notre Dame family helped me. Sharon Sumpter in the archives was a joy to work with, hospitable even in the earliest stages, when my credentials were the thinnest. Charles Lamb was a huge help with photographs and deserves special mention for locating the photograph of William Foohey in his Klan robe. Professor David Smith overwhelmed me with his hospitality, having photocopied and collated relevant articles for me in advance of our meeting. Finally, I have to thank Fr. Monk Malloy and his secretary, Joan Bradley, for making the time to see me in the middle of reunion week.

Barb Holleman of the South Bend Police Department put me in touch with the department's historian, Don Cornelius. They helped me track down some interesting information at the last minute about Chief Lane. Susan Sutton of the Indiana Historical Society helped me navigate through the wealth of material held by that fine facility. John Straw did the same at Ball State University. Thank you all.

I would like to thank two of the surviving riot participants who spoke with me at length about their memories of May 1924: I. I. Probst, class of 1926, and George Scheuer, class of 1928. It was a privilege to speak with you. The book helped me get back in touch with several old friends from Notre Dame. My classmate Tony Troup helped me launch a Web site for the book. I also have to thank Mark Foohey, Sean Foohey, and Jim Foohey, all of whom shared with me the Foohey family saga, a classic Irish American success story.

Jim Manney at Loyola Press was the editor I have been promised since I started writing: kind, insightful, and enthusiastic about this book. Others at Loyola who have my gratitude are Chrissy Kolaya, Matthew Diener, Heidi Hill, and Melissa Crane.

Finally, I would like to thank Joe Durepos for actually reading the proposal I mailed to him, seeing its potential, and calling me on my cell phone while I was getting a cup of coffee at the Steak n Shake in Valparaiso, Indiana. We've called it the "Good News Steak n Shake" ever since. Thanks for everything, Joe. Without you, none of this would have happened.

PROLOGUE
MAY 19, 1924

BILL FOOHEY WAS IN HIS DORM ROOM STUDYING chemistry when the call to arms sounded again. It was a Monday night, around 9:15. After Saturday's thrills, the young men of Notre Dame were settling back down into the weekday routine of classes and studying. Sophomore Hall had been quiet until the telephone at the end of the hallway rang, setting off a burst of activity. Doors slammed open and shut and feet pounded excitedly up and down the hall. Foohey closed his textbook, walked to the door of his room, and stuck his head into the hallway. The sounds of frenzied young men reverberated off the thin walls of the drafty building they called the "Cardboard Palace."

"They've got one of the boys downtown!" shouted his friend I. I. Probst, who had apparently taken the report on the dormitory's only phone. He seemed more ecstatic than upset. *Who could they have?* Foohey wondered. Most of the men who lived on campus were probably getting ready for the next day's classes or heading to bed. Maybe it was one of the many upperclassmen who lived in town. Even though they were technically subject to the same lights-out rule as the men on campus, everyone knew they went out most nights to play pool and smoke cigarettes, which was forbidden on campus. The Ku Klux Klan might have grabbed a random Notre Dame man off the street to avenge the whipping they had taken on Saturday. Foohey could see his peers through their open dorm-room doors hurriedly tying their shoes and throwing on jackets. Through the window at the end of the hallway, he could see the shadows of men from Freshman Hall running across the quad toward town. It appeared that the freshmen had a head start. The men of Sophomore Hall were getting ready in a panic, terrified that they might miss the fight.[1]

"We're going to have to teach them another lesson!" someone yelled as he flew down the stairs. A general cheer of support followed. Probst punched Foohey on the arm as he ran past him.

"You're coming, aren't you?" Probst asked. Foohey had been a hero of Saturday's donnybrook. He looked over his shoulder at the Klan robe and hood that he had seized on Saturday afternoon—they hung on his wall like hunting trophies.

He had already recounted the incident to his friends a hundred times, in the dining hall, between classes, and on the quad as he posed for photographs in the stolen robe on Sunday afternoon. Foohey and two friends from Sophomore Hall had followed three Klansmen into an alley. They were easy to identify, with their robes in bundles at their sides. They had innocently asked some Notre Dame students on the train platform for directions to Island Park, the site of the Klan's tristate rally. The Notre Damers had helpfully directed them to the alley that Foohey and his friends were guarding.

The Klansmen got about halfway down the alley when they realized it was leading them nowhere. They turned around, only to find Foohey and his friends blocking their exit. Two of the Klansmen immediately tried to run past the students, but Foohey's accomplices tackled them to the sidewalk with a precision that Rockne would have admired. The Klansmen's bundled robes landed next to them on the ground. When Foohey's friends jumped after the robes—their real target—the two Klansmen took the opportunity to hastily abandon their comrade.

The remaining Klansman made a weak attempt at running around Foohey, who slammed him into a door. In the weeks leading up to the Klan's rally in South Bend, many of Foohey's friends had worked themselves into a righteous rage over the Klan's lies. Copies of the Klan's newspaper, the *Fiery Cross*, had made their way onto campus, and the students had read with disbelief its stories of secret papal armies and the un-American nature of Catholicism. Some of them had gone into town to heckle a Klansman who spoke about the menace of Catholic education during a speech he gave.

The Irish were another favorite target of the Klan, who portrayed them as subhuman goons or drunken degenerates. Foohey could take those insults personally: his father, Timothy, had left County Cork, Ireland, at the age of seventeen in 1859. Still, Foohey might have been able to laugh off the Klan's ridiculous accusations, at least until early May 1924, when the Klan's slate of candidates swept Indiana's Republican primary. The Republicans were the dominant party in the state. It seemed very likely that Foohey would soon be living in a state run by a Klansman governor.

The Klansman standing in front of Foohey in the alley was not the muscular soldier of the Invisible Empire that he had imagined. He was a wide-eyed hillbilly, a slack-jawed rube venturing into the big city for a picnic and a parade.

"What do you want?" he asked Foohey.

Foohey pointed to the bundle at his side.

The man shook his head weakly. "I don't want a fight," he said, but he did not hand over his robe.

Foohey pushed him into the door again, harder this time, rattling the door in its frame. The Klansman dropped his robe and raised his fists. He managed to throw one feeble punch. Foohey dodged it easily and then countered with his left hand, just as the brothers had taught him in boxing class. "You're skinny," Br. Francis had told him, "but, my God, you've got big hands." One of those giant hands, curled into a fist, connected solidly with the Klansman's chin.

The Klansman fell to his knees. He managed to get up and stagger out of the alley, suddenly less attached to the robe that was now crumpled up at Foohey's feet.

Saturday's experience had left Foohey with a sense of satisfaction: the Notre Dame men had shown the Catholic-hating Klan that they wouldn't back down. So Foohey was surprised to learn just two days later that the men they had routed had come back for more.

He looked at Probst and decided he couldn't miss another fight. "Yeah," he said. "I'm coming." He followed his friend as the men of Sophomore Hall poured onto the quad.

The group of young men grew as it crossed the campus to Angela, the road that would take them into town. It was mid-May, and there was still just a touch of coolness in the air. To Foohey, the crowd of Notre Damers seemed bigger than Saturday's group—maybe those few students who had obeyed Fr. Walsh, the school's president, on Saturday and remained on campus were determined not to miss out on the fun a second time. They were definitely a more cheerful crowd than the one that had charged into town on Saturday. The men on Saturday had been angry, indignant, and maybe just a touch afraid—until, that is, they got to the city and put the Klansmen on the run. Their mood had then changed from anger to jubilation, and by early Saturday afternoon, Notre Dame students were running the streets of South Bend while the Klansmen were cowering in their headquarters at the corner of Michigan and Wayne streets. This time, the Notre Damers were ebullient from the start. They ran shouting and chanting to the Klan's headquarters, the site of much of Saturday's action.

The Klan's weekly meeting had just let out. Men were standing in the doorway of the headquarters and on the sidewalk and street in front of the building. Unlike on Saturday, the Klansmen were not wearing or carrying their robes, nor did they appear surprised in the least by the appearance of the Notre Dame men. The students ran up to the building. A fiery cross of red lightbulbs shone in the third-floor window. Destroying that cross had been one of the Notre Damers' early victories on Saturday; putting it back up was a clear provocation on the part of the Klan. The students were right up against the building now, standing together in a tight group. Foohey looked around. The Klansmen who had seemed to be leaving the meeting were standing firm in their positions on both sides of the street. The cheering Notre Dame men were surrounded.

The Klansmen charged. This time, it was the Notre Dame students who were caught by surprise. Foohey put his fists up instinctively. Many of the attackers, their breath smelling of whiskey, identified themselves as sheriff's deputies. Uniformed South Bend city police officers were also in the mix. Bottles were flying through the crowd. They were indiscriminate missiles; Foohey saw a bottle smash the nose of a deputy next to him who was grappling with a freshman. Blood and broken glass covered the ground.

"We're the law here!" shouted one of the deputies as he beat a Notre Dame man to the ground with an ax handle. Foohey reached into the tussle with his long arms, tying the deputy up long enough for the Notre Damer to get away. The young man lurched down Wayne Street, spitting out blood and teeth.[2]

As Foohey clashed with the deputy, something hit him in the back of the head; he fell to the ground, stunned. *These guys are trying to kill me*, he thought. One of them kicked him hard in the ribs. He rolled over, crawled away, and stood up. He raised his fists, groggily ready to defend himself. By then, though, the deputies had moved on to another student.

Standing there dazed, Foohey saw a group of Notre Dame men running into Hullie and Mike's, a student hangout across the street. He fought his way to the edge of the crowd and followed them in.

There were about twenty of them inside. Most were groaning, pointing bloody noses in the air, or holding towels over their wounds. The most seriously injured had been laid out on the two pool tables and were receiving rudimentary medical attention from George Hull and Mike Calnon, the owners of the establishment. Calnon looked up from the leg he was bandaging as Foohey entered. With a cigar clenched between his teeth, he grunted, "Looks like the bastards were ready for you this time." Through the window,

Foohey could see that the Notre Dame students who could escape the clubs and the bottles were in full retreat. He ran back outside to see if he could stop them.

He chased after them for about three blocks. At the courthouse, a safe distance from the club-wielding Klansmen, they stopped. They milled around on the lawn, gasping for breath and nursing their wounds. Few of them relished the idea of going back into the fight, but none of them wanted to continue running all the way back to campus like cowards. They would wait on the courthouse lawn and see what happened next.

Foohey looked around him. Everywhere there were men with purple-black eyes, fat lips, and bloody gashes, men limping and groaning. They had been ambushed. The men they had all been ridiculing were going to have the last laugh. It enraged Foohey.

"Let's go back!" he shouted. "We can't let them get away with this!" He heard a few hoarse, unenthusiastic shouts of approval. "We can take them," he said. "There might still be some of us over there!" A number of the men moved toward him, ready to continue the fight. "Come on!" he screamed. "Are you afraid?" More students came toward him. "Are you afraid?" he yelled again, to a group of Notre Damers who had not moved. They reluctantly limped forward. Saturday had been a robe-stealing bit of fun compared to this—now they were in a real fight. Well, they could play that game too. From three blocks away, Foohey heard the thoughtless, hollow roar of a victorious mob, a sound he knew from football games and Saturday's fray. He was eager to take his battered squadron back to Michigan and Wayne to squelch it.

Just then, car headlights shone onto the courthouse. At first, Foohey thought it might be a police car. Then two priests in full-length robes stepped out. Even in the darkness, Foohey knew who they were: Fr. J. Hugh O'Donnell, the prefect of discipline, and Fr. Matthew Walsh, the school's president. A curious thought crossed his mind: *Now we're in real trouble.*

Fr. Walsh walked authoritatively across the courthouse lawn, surveying his wounded men. He looked disgusted but not surprised—it was the disaster he had been predicting since the Klan first announced its rally in South Bend. He looked more at home in this strange scene than any of them, thought Foohey, remembering the legends he had heard about Walsh's wartime service. Fr. O'Donnell hurried behind him, trying to keep up.

Directly in front of the largest part of the group, Walsh stopped and began to speak, but he couldn't make himself heard over the distant cheers, the closer sirens, and the groaning of the crowd. He looked around for a better position. Directly behind him was South Bend's Civil War memorial. He climbed with surprising agility atop a cannon, spreading his arms briefly to gain his balance. Standing there motionless, his arms outspread, he could almost have been part of the monument, a tribute to the Notre Dame chaplains who had served in the Civil War. Walsh began to speak again, and this time a few of the men on the lawn could hear him. Foohey wanted desperately to return to the fight, but he could not bring himself to turn his back on Fr. Walsh.

"Whatever challenge may have been offered tonight to your patriotism, whatever insult may have been offered to your religion, you can show your loyalty to Notre Dame and South Bend by ignoring all threats," Walsh began.[3]

Bill Foohey moved closer.

Bill Foohey's grandson was a friend of mine. His name was Mark Foohey, and we both arrived at Notre Dame in the summer of 1986. We both lived in Cavanaugh Hall, where our rector was Notre Dame's dean of rectors, Fr. Matthew Micelli, CSC, a man who had witnessed more than twenty years' worth of undergraduate depravations from his small dorm room on the first floor. The University of

Notre Dame, in his eyes, had made only two mistakes in its history. First, it had never selected an Italian president—almost all of the priests who had served in that capacity were Irish. Second, the school had admitted women in 1972. Fr. Micelli frequently threatened to write a book entitled *The Emasculation of Notre Dame*.

Mark was a much more typical Notre Dame man than I was. Like the vast majority of the student body, Mark was Catholic—I was Protestant. This caused some concern for Fr. Micelli. He would periodically ask me if I wanted to come aboard and offer to sponsor me, having perceived correctly that my Protestantism was of the vague, unaffiliated variety. His evangelism was never heavy-handed. Fr. Micelli suggested that I become Catholic with the same tone that you might use to tell a friend to renew his expired license plates—a tone that says it's just something you really should do.

Like many Notre Damers, Mark had the school in his blood—two uncles and a grandfather were graduates. I was from a family and a town that had never sent anybody to Notre Dame. Mark was from the East Coast; I was from southern Indiana. Mark was the first person I ever saw playing lacrosse. Despite our differences, Mark and I became friends in the way that men living in close quarters during eventful times do. We were never roommates, but we saw each other nearly every day for four years.

Mark and I came to Notre Dame at a good time. The legendary Fr. Hesburgh was still president when we were freshmen. Our first year was also the first year for football coach Lou Holtz. Our sophomore year, Tim Brown—a fellow Cavanaugh resident—won the Heisman Trophy. Our junior year, 1988, the football team won the national championship.

Like all Notre Dame students, Mark and I were thoroughly indoctrinated in Notre Dame lore from our first day. We learned about Rockne, First-Down Moses, and Touchdown Jesus. We memorized the names of the Four Horsemen and the six Heisman Trophy winners. We learned about the annual snowball fight, the annual spring

festival—called An Tostal—and Circus Lunch, a dining-hall extrava-
ganza complete with cotton candy and staff members in clown cos-
tumes. We memorized an obscene version of the Michigan fight song.
We learned about campus history, catching snippets of the stories of
Fr. Sorin and the Log Chapel and Old College.

One bit of campus history Mark and I never learned anything
about was the riot between Notre Dame students and the Ku Klux
Klan in 1924. It is not an event that the university brags about.
Neither do its participants. Mark's grandfather never mentioned it to
him. He died when Mark was young, but it doesn't seem as if Bill
Foohey made a point of talking about the riot to anyone, even in the
years immediately following the incident. He never said a word
about the riot to his brother, James Foohey, who arrived at Notre
Dame in 1932.

I discovered again and again as I researched this book that participants in the riot rarely reminisced about those violent days in
1924. Maybe they were ashamed of themselves for lending credence
to the stereotype of the belligerent Irishman, a stereotype that was
frequently bandied about by the Klan. Maybe they didn't like to
recall an era when vicious anti-Catholicism was very much a mainstream philosophy. Maybe they remained quiet because of the long
shadow cast by Fr. Matthew Walsh, who had ordered them to stay
away from the Klan's festival in South Bend. I talked with many
descendants of Notre Dame men who had been at Notre Dame at the
time of the riot. Most of them had never heard of it.

Mark and I, Catholic and Protestant, were only superficially aware
that there had ever been a time when Catholics were a feared and
hated minority in the United States. Catholics were so assimilated to
our minds that it was impossible for us to imagine that kind of widespread prejudice. I was a lifelong resident of Indiana, yet I had no
idea that the Klan had briefly owned the state, claiming a majority
of the state's legislators, the governor, and one out of three white
Hoosiers as members. The Ku Klux Klan is Indiana's family secret.

The echoes of that riot and that era, though, resonated down through the years to Mark and me, affecting us in ways that we could only vaguely perceive. Mark and I lived in Cavanaugh Hall for all of our four years at Notre Dame. The university strongly encouraged students to live on campus.

Mark and I lost touch with each other immediately after graduation. I was not on his short list of friends to keep in touch with through moves and career changes; he was not on mine.

While working on this book, I tracked down the handful of Notre Dame men who had been present at the riot and are still alive. There are precious few—a man who was eighteen years old at the riot, a freshman, would be ninety-eight today. One of them was I. Irwin Probst, currently of Fort Pierce, Florida. "I. I.," as he likes to be called, gave me his own priceless account of the May 1924 riot. He also sent me the names and numbers of other surviving rioters. Finally, along with a stack of relevant papers, I. I. sent me a crude, photocopied picture of a Notre Dame man posing in a Klan robe after the riot. The resolution was extremely poor, but I could see the young man's smile, his slightly wrinkled robes, and his intimidating large hands. He was standing in front of Sophomore Hall, a building that no longer exists. I. I. told me that the original photograph was somewhere in the Notre Dame archives. He also told me the student's name. It was a friend of his, Bill Foohey, class of 1926.

With the help of Charles Lamb, one of Notre Dame's indefatigable archivists, I got my hands on the original. Looking at the picture, linking the name and the suddenly clear face, I made the connection. The man had to be related to my friend Mark Foohey— they could have been twins.

I wanted to call Mark to see if he had ever heard any stories about the riot at his grandfather's knee. I was relieved that Mark remembered who I was after such a long time—we hadn't spoken since 1990. He was obviously surprised to hear from me, surprised that I had gone to so much trouble to find him. Not really knowing where to begin, I described for him the photograph that I had of his grandfather.

"How did my grandfather end up in a Ku Klux Klan robe?" Mark asked me.

"Well, Mark," I said, "it's a long story."

———

Author's note: When I set out to write this story, I knew I wanted to tell it from the point of view of Matthew Walsh, of D. C. Stephenson, and of a Notre Dame student who had participated in the riot. I had extensive written records of the thoughts and feelings of Walsh and Stephenson— letters, speeches, and the like—but I had very few firsthand accounts of the riot from the young men who had taken part in it. I had some oblique mentions of the riot, a few handed-down memories, and the stories of two eyewitnesses. This made it difficult for me to describe exactly what it felt like to throw a potato at a fiery cross, or how Walsh sounded from atop the cannon.

For the sake of the story, I have taken a great liberty. I have attributed thoughts and emotions to Bill Foohey in this story, all of which are based on accounts of others, the historical record, and reports of the riot, of which we know he was a part. His thoughts and feelings in this story are also based, I suppose, on my own experiences as a hotheaded young man at Notre Dame. Bill is, in other words, a composite character. In recounting the stories of Matthew Walsh and D. C. Stephenson, I have also assigned them thoughts and feelings, which I have taken from their own personal letters and speeches. In some places, I have extrapolated historical events in order to bring out the drama of the situation. Again, all of this is based on the historical record.

I have researched the events of May 1924 to the best of my abilities. I believe that I have made accurate suppositions about the thoughts and feelings of Bill Foohey and others, but they remain suppositions.

1

THE ANTAGONISTS

I N JUNE OF 1893, THE HOLY CROSS BROTHERS WHO RAN
St. Columbkille's School in Chicago lined their boys up and
marched them by a tired-looking priest. Their distinguished visitor
was Fr. Thomas Walsh, the president of the University of Notre
Dame, the most esteemed Catholic school in the country. He suffered from Bright's disease and was visibly ill; in fact, he would live
less than a month longer. The brothers hoped that a parade of their
youngsters might cheer him up.[1]

Like the rest of the boys, young Matthew Walsh concentrated on
becoming invisible as he marched past the priest. It was not to be.

"Come here, Matthew," said Br. Marcellinus. Walsh reluctantly
stepped forward. As the school's most promising student, he was frequently called on to recite for visitors the five sorrowful mysteries,
the seven dolors of Mary, the fourteen stations of the cross, or any of
the other memorized lists that characterized his religious instruction.
Such performances were usually followed by teasing and taunts of
"teacher's pet" on the playground.

"Fr. Walsh, this is Matthew Walsh," said the brother, seeming
amused by the coincidence of their last names. The priest smiled
weakly as he patted the boy's head. He looked as if he barely had the
energy to stand.

"Pleased to meet you, Father," said Walsh. The priest nodded.

"Fr. Walsh is the president of the University of Notre Dame," said Br. Marcellinus to the entire class. He swept his hand dramatically across the room, stopping at a picture of Notre Dame's famous Golden Dome hanging on the rear wall. The brothers of St. Columbkille's, as Walsh and the other boys well knew, belonged to the Congregation of Holy Cross, the same order that ran Notre Dame. Good behavior in the classroom—often by Matthew Walsh— was rewarded by the compliment that there might someday be a place for such a youngster at the great Catholic university.

Although the teasing kept him from saying so aloud, the young Walsh hoped the prophecy would come true. His parents hoped so too. For a boy from a family like theirs—immigrant and poor—to go to college at all would be a great achievement.

Matthew Walsh's father, David Walsh, was born in Mitchellstown, County Cork, Ireland. His mother, Joanna Clogan, born in Troy, New York, was also of pure Irish stock. Walsh's father was part of the vast human wave that left Ireland in the nineteenth century, fleeing famine, British oppression, and economic hopeless- ness. In the years between 1845 and 1855, more Irish left their coun- try than had previously emigrated in the country's entire recorded history.[2] The Irish had few illusions about ever returning to the mother country. Of all the ethnic groups streaming into America, only the Jews had a lower return rate than the Irish.[3] In nearly every large city in America, the Irish claimed neighborhoods as their own by crowding the tenements, building churches, and winning political offices. The Walshes settled in West Town, Chicago, a neighborhood where it was not at all remarkable to find people named Walsh—or Murphy, or Kelly, or Sullivan, for that matter, the only Irish surnames more common.[4] Even the parish's patron, St. Columbkille, was an Irish import, a rash prince who became a holy man in exile.

An array of stereotypes followed the Irish to the New World, most revolving around the twin activities of drinking and brawling. No one knew better than the Irish themselves that there was a grain of truth to these prejudices. Irish boys did tend to become wilder as they got older and were quick to fight. There was unquestionably an element among them that did more than its share of drinking. The Walshes encouraged the quiet studiousness of Matthew, the seventh of their ten children, in part because it was so rare.

Walsh was born on May 14, 1882, in Chicago. From the start, he impressed every adult in his life. His parents hoped that his academic achievements might earn him a place at Notre Dame. To get into college, though, Matthew would need more than stellar grades and scholastic performance. He would have to fulfill an even greater dream of his parents, neighbors, and teachers: he would have to become a priest. Joining a religious order was just about the only avenue to a higher education for children of immigrants in America at the time.

The Walshes believed that such a life brought great spiritual rewards. Priests dealt with "sacred matters in a sacred language."[5] They welcomed babies into the church with baptism and administered the last rites to the dying. By virtue of having been called to a life in Christ, parish priests had unequivocal authority within their communities. Their authority was rooted in the fact that they could do something that no one else on earth could—they could celebrate Mass.

For a family like the Walshes, there were considerable earthly rewards to the priesthood as well. Not only would the door to higher education be opened for a young man who wanted to become a priest, but his family would also be treated with great respect and admiration within their community. Large Catholic families like the Walshes were not unusual at the turn of the century, nor were their priorities. Seminary applicants were plentiful, and thus the seminaries could afford to be highly selective in choosing whom they committed to feed, clothe, educate, and employ for a lifetime. Matthew Walsh's acceptance into the seminary would bring great credit to his parents and teachers. In addition to being educated and esteemed as a priest, Walsh would enjoy a standard of living that would be a measure higher than what his siblings experienced; he'd perhaps even have a laundress, a cook, and a housekeeper.[6] Matthew Walsh's family and teachers made sure that he knew from a very young age to listen closely for a call to the priesthood.

The center of Walsh's community, both literally and figuratively, was St. Columbkille's Church. Division Street, Lake Street, Hoyne Avenue, and May Street formed the boundaries of the parish, an area roughly fifteen city blocks on a side.[7] The Catholicism that Walsh learned there was as rigidly defined as the parish boundaries. Families in the parish were expected to rent pews. The pews were reserved until just after the first Gospel reading, by which time everyone could see which families were absent. The pews were then made available to nonrenters in exchange for a "voluntary" offering of ten cents. No marriage ceremony would be performed after 5:00 PM. Funerals had to be arranged by family members, not by the undertaker. Parishioners wishing to donate money to Catholic causes outside the parish needed written permission from the pastor. Every aspect of church life was regulated with cheerful fervor by the church's rector, Fr. Nathan Mooney, Notre Dame class of 1877.[8]

In 1896, at the age of fourteen, Walsh completed grammar school and moved up to the brothers' high school. As the rest of the boys in school got louder and bigger, his reticence grew even more conspicuous. Unlike his swearing, brawling peers in West Town, Walsh was becoming a young man who could absolutely swim in silence. Walsh's grades, demeanor, and piety all seemed to confirm what religious men had been telling him all his life: he was different. At the dawn of adolescence, his self-awareness became acute. In 1897, after completing a single year of high school, Matthew Walsh fulfilled the expectations of everyone around him. He announced to his family that he would like to join the priesthood. The choice of orders was clear. The Holy Cross brothers of St. Columbkille's scurried to enroll him in the seminary at Notre Dame. He was fifteen years old.

Walsh left for Notre Dame in the summer of 1897. He and his mother took the train from Chicago to South Bend, Indiana, the home of Notre Dame and Walsh's home for the next six years. To Walsh, who had been a city boy all his life, the trip was like traveling into a great wilderness—he watched out the window as the northern Indiana forests and the shore of Lake Michigan rushed by him. It was a quiet trip. Walsh's mother would occasionally clear her throat or gather her breath as if she was about to speak, but she never did. At the train station in South Bend, they boarded a horse-drawn carriage for the two-mile trip to campus. Walsh recounted his arrival at Notre Dame years later to his friend and Notre Dame historian Arthur Hope, who included the story in his book *Notre Dame: One Hundred Years*.

"We need to go to Notre Dame," his mother told the driver. "My boy is going to be a priest."

"Very good," said the driver as he snapped the reins and started them forward. Walsh could tell that his mother had expected a more energetic response.

The carriage soon pulled up to the steps of the domed Main Building, the same building pictured in the photograph that hung on the wall of Walsh's grammar school classroom. The breathtaking architecture was offset by the appearance of a rotund, unremarkable-looking priest standing on the building's front porch with his hands in his pockets.

"These people want to see Fr. Corby!" the driver shouted to the priest. Walsh remembered that Fr. William Corby was the provincial, the head of the Holy Cross order at Notre Dame.

"He's in the presbytery," said the priest.

As they continued on their way, Walsh's mother asked the driver about the priest on the porch.

"That's Fr. Morrissey," he said, surprised that she didn't know. "The president." He stopped the carriage at the door of a small gray building.

It was easy to find Fr. Corby's office in the deserted building. Through his open door they could see him working at a tiny desk. He looked up as the mother and son he had been expecting appeared in his doorway. With his gray hair and long, flowing beard, Fr. Corby looked every inch the aging Civil War hero. He stood and introduced himself. Both Walshes were trying hard not to show any fear; he was proud of them for that. After a brief conversation about the train ride, he put his hand on the boy's shoulder. Corby had been a part of many good-byes, in the army and at the seminary. In his experience, it was best to make them quick.

"I'm on my way to see Dr. Linneborn at the seminary," he said to the slight, quiet boy. "You can go with me." Walsh, his mother, and Fr. Corby all exchanged looks. It dawned on Walsh's mother that Corby did not expect her to travel any further with her son. He was in Corby's hands now.[9]

"Oh," she said. She took a deep breath. She kneeled and kissed her son on his forehead. "I'll see you at Christmas."

Walsh muttered, "Good-bye," and then she was gone.

"Let's go," said Fr. Corby gently, not allowing a pause. He placed his hand on the boy's shoulder and led him out a different doorway into the blinding summer sunshine.

They walked the short distance to the seminary along a lake. Fr. Corby introduced Walsh to the man at the door.

"This is Dr. Linneborn," he told him. Walsh could hear the importance that Corby placed on "Dr." in his introduction. "He is the rector of the seminary."

"Pleased to meet you," said Walsh.

"I have a job for you already," said the rector, with a strong German accent. "I need you to bring down all of the mattresses from the attic to air out here on the lawn." Dr. Linneborn paused, raising a bushy eyebrow at the young seminarian. "I hope you are not too little."

Over the next two days, Walsh tackled his first project in the seminary, wrestling every mattress outside into the brief South Bend summer air.

Walsh steadily built on the reputation for earnestness and efficiency that he earned in those two summer days. He did what he was told to do and never complained, whether the project was studying the mysteries of the Catholic Church or moving mattresses. As he worked his way through high school and the seminary, that set of attributes gained him the favor of his superiors.

When Walsh completed his high school work in 1899, he began his college studies. The school was rife with conflicts at the time, conflicts that Walsh observed but avoided getting personally involved in. Two camps of priests were at odds, both believing that their goal for the university was most advantageous. One group of priests, led by Fr. John Zahm, argued that Notre Dame needed to do away with its prep school and its trade school and focus on becoming a great university. Zahm's own academic credentials were impeccable. In addition to having a PhD, he had written a book on evolution—a book eventually banned by the pope for its progressive theories.[10]

The other school of thought was led by the university's president, Fr. Andrew Morrissey, nicknamed "the Kilkenny Chieftain" after the Irish county of his birth. Fr. Morrissey maintained that energy invested in making Notre Dame a great research university was misspent. He believed that their little Catholic school would never be able to compete with the likes of the University of Michigan or Ohio State University. Notre Dame should concentrate on remaining, as he put it, a "compact, tidy little boarding school."[11] The debate turned personal at times. By arguing for faculty with advanced degrees, Fr. Zahm implied that Fr. Morrissey, who did not have a PhD, was not qualified for his position. In fact, no Notre Dame president up to that point had ever held a doctorate.

Matthew Walsh kept his head down and avoided the debate in part because of his natural reticence and in part because he could clearly see both sides. He didn't go to Notre Dame because it was a great university—he went there because it was a great Catholic university. If improving the academic status of Notre Dame meant watering down its Catholic identity, as many in the Morrissey camp argued, then he wasn't interested. In addition, if the trade school and the prep school provided the university with a steady stream of much-needed income, then why should the university close them down?

On the other hand, Walsh agreed with the Zahm loyalists that college professors should have PhDs. He could see in his own teachers a subtle but discernible difference between those few with doctorates and those without. It was the difference, he thought, between learning from those who had read the books and those who had written the books. He appreciated Zahm's argument that the pursuit of knowledge led to a better understanding of God's creation—and how could that be un-Catholic? Walsh was certain that an advanced education was part of God's plan for him.

At Notre Dame, seminarians were kept somewhat isolated from the rest of the student body, and Walsh was comfortable with that. He wanted to become a priest—not join the rowing team or the chess club or attend the brutish football games, whose increasing popularity convinced him yet again that he was fundamentally different from the rest of the crowd. He did write the occasional article for *Scholastic*, Notre Dame's student magazine, but even these have the cool tone of a lecture, not the lightheartedness of a young man joking with his chums. In only one article—"A Leap Year Ride," published in January 1903—does Walsh give the impression that he ever had anything to mention at confession during his youth. In the article, Walsh recounts a dangerous horse ride his friends took on a dare on a frozen February 29 in Chicago. The article confirms another pattern in Walsh's life: while he had no obvious wild side of his own, he sometimes enjoyed the company of those who did. And they enjoyed his.[12]

Walsh received his bachelor's degree from Notre Dame in 1903. Fr. Morrissey then selected him to go to the Holy Cross house of studies in Washington, D.C., a mission founded by Fr. Zahm to enable Notre Dame priests and seminarians to study at the recently founded Catholic University. The leader of the house of studies at the time of Walsh's arrival was Fr. James Burns, a chemistry PhD and Zahm protégé. While Fr. Zahm had established the mission to advance his liberal ideas, it also served a practical purpose for Notre Dame's conservative administration. If their own priests obtained advanced degrees, they could then teach at the university, saving the administration money it would have spent to hire lay faculty. Priests and brothers, after all, worked without salary. In addition to the expense of lay professors, the administration was also uncomfortable with their independence and was always looking for ways to reduce their numbers. Sending bright young seminarians to Zahm's house of studies was an effective way of decreasing lay faculty jobs—even if it did appear to validate Zahm's progressive theories.

Walsh worked toward his PhD in American history at Catholic University. He wrote his dissertation on the political status of Catholics in Colonial Maryland and received his doctorate in 1907. His star was on the rise with the Notre Dame leadership; they appreciated a highly educated seminarian who wasn't a radical. Morrissey was so comfortable with Walsh that he allowed him to take courses in economics during the summer after he received his doctorate—at Columbia and Johns Hopkins. Sending seminarians to non-Catholic institutions had been considered unthinkably progressive by Notre Dame's leadership, even by Zahm. Matthew Walsh, though, was non-threatening enough to gain such latitude. In the process, he established himself as Notre Dame's wunderkind.

To Walsh, however, the degrees, the grades, and the praise he earned for his academic efforts paled in comparison to the honor he would soon receive. On December 21, 1907, Walsh was ordained a priest in Washington, D.C. Afterward, he boarded a train in Washington and made the long, uncomfortable trip home to Chicago. He was an old hand at trains now, much changed from the boy who had traveled with his mother to Notre Dame ten years earlier. On Christmas Day, in front of his mother, father, nine siblings, and proud parish family, Matthew Walsh sang his first Mass at St. Columbkille's Church.

He was allowed only a two-day vacation in his hometown. Notre Dame had accepted Walsh as a ninth grader, paid for his education all the way through postdoctoral work, and trained him for the priesthood. Now it was time for the school to recoup its investment. Walsh was named a professor in both history and economics. In the 1908 yearbook, his first as a faculty member, Walsh was notable for his youthful appearance as well as for the rare "PhD" after his name.

The Notre Dame that Matthew Walsh returned to in 1907 was quite different from the university he had left four years before. For seven years, the defining dynamic of the institution had been the feud between Fr. Andrew Morrissey, the school's president, and Fr. John Zahm, who had been appointed provincial of the order at Notre Dame in 1898. In 1905, the battle had reached its inevitable conclusion: Zahm, with his authority as provincial, forced Morrissey out of office and installed Fr. John Cavanaugh as president of the university.

Morrissey engineered his revenge during a yearlong exile from Notre Dame. He traveled extensively with Fr. Gilbert Français, the superior general of the Holy Cross order, who had named Zahm provincial. Over the course of their travels, Morrissey gently convinced the superior general that his appointment of Zahm, while well-intentioned, had turned out to be a mistake. The man, Morrissey told Français, was a renegade. Morrissey's numerous friends in Holy Cross houses throughout the American province corroborated the story. Morrissey had always been the more skilled politician of the two adversaries. In the end, his lobbying worked. When Zahm's term as provincial expired in 1906, Français appointed Morrissey to the position. The Kilkenny Chieftain promptly banished Zahm from campus.

Zahm became a well-known priest-adventurer in exile, at one point even venturing to South America with Theodore Roosevelt. He would not return to Notre Dame until he was buried in the community cemetery there in 1921.

The lesson was not lost on Walsh. Fighting openly with others was not the way to settle disputes. It was best to leave it to others to fall on their swords. Walsh knew that he would never be a visionary like Fr. Edward Sorin, the founder of the school, a man destined to have buildings named for him. But he would never end up like Fr. Zahm, either, banished from a place he loved because of a personal dispute.

Walsh quickly became a favorite professor at Notre Dame. Even though his style was a little formal, he was always exceedingly well-prepared and his lectures were interesting. He had a natural talent for working with young men, having grown up with the rambunctious boys of St. Columbkille's School and West Town. He knew instinctively when to assert his authority and when to cut the men a little slack. The men of one senior class liked Walsh so much that they dedicated their yearbook to him, "whose scholarship has elicited our admiration, and whose simplicity, earnestness, and quiet dignity have endeared him to us."[13]

The Notre Dame administration noted with pleasure that Walsh was dependable and absolutely loyal to the university. The school's president, Fr. John Cavanaugh, was especially impressed with Walsh. A Zahm protégé, Cavanaugh was committed to raising Notre Dame's academic standards. To his credit, he went about doing this without declaring open warfare on the established order. When the position of vice president came open in 1911, he decided it was time to put someone in the university's front office who had a PhD, although he himself did not have one. Matthew Walsh, while young, was the perfect vice presidential candidate. The Zahm camp admired him for his sterling academic credentials, the Morrissey camp appreciated his noncontroversial personality, and his superiors praised his loyalty. Just four years after Walsh became a professor at Notre Dame, Cavanaugh asked him to be his vice president. The twenty-nine-year-old Walsh accepted.

Fr. Cavanaugh's personality was a striking contrast to his stoic vice president's. When a campus priest began writing sonnets in memory of every member of the Holy Cross order who had died, Cavanaugh said that the poet had "added a new terror to death."[14] When a young boy wrote to Cavanaugh asking what he needed to study in order to become a cowboy, Cavanaugh replied with a light-hearted note that outlined a course of studies.[15] Such frivolity was unimaginable from the pen of Matthew Walsh. Likewise, Cavanaugh's bellicosity regarding his homeland occasionally horrified his young vice president. On the subject of Irish home rule, Cavanaugh's playful rhetoric veered toward reckless. When the war in Europe began, three years after Walsh became vice president, Cavanaugh openly cheered every British defeat. In a speech he gave in New York City, Cavanaugh declared that Germany was only doing to Belgium what England had been doing to Ireland for seven hundred years.[16]

Despite their personality differences, Walsh and Cavanaugh were united when it came to developing and nurturing the young men in their care. This nurturing could be challenging, as it was one night in 1916 when the young men of Notre Dame decided to right a wrong committed by the South Bend Streetcar Company.

There was a long-standing feud between the students and the streetcar operators on the route from the Notre Dame campus to South Bend. The students were convinced that the cars on that route were the oldest and least comfortable in the system and that the operators were deliberately rude to Notre Dame students. The streetcar operators complained that the Notre Dame students didn't pay their fares, smoked on the cars, and were generally obnoxious.

Things got so bad that the streetcar company hired a couple of enforcers to rough up two Notre Dame students in an attempt to teach them some manners.

Later that week, a student mob, planning to set things right, stormed a streetcar as it headed toward campus. To their embarrassment, one of the passengers on that streetcar happened to be Fr. Cavanaugh, who was traveling back to campus with two professors. Cavanaugh stepped out of the car to assess the situation.

Nearby, another group of students had commandeered a different streetcar and were in the process of destroying it. Shocked, Fr. Cavanaugh ordered them to stop, which they did immediately. He then had them march back to campus while he and the professors returned on their streetcar.

When he arrived back at campus, Fr. Cavanaugh went immediately to his vice president's room in Corby Hall and proudly recounted the incident. "You know, Matt," he said, "they're fine boys. All I had to do was tell them to go back to their halls!" As he said this, something caught his eye outside Walsh's window. The smile on his face disappeared.

Walsh joined Cavanaugh at the window. A streetcar at the edge of campus was in flames.

The students had waited until Cavanaugh had walked out of sight before recapturing the doomed car. After ejecting the operator, they had poured gasoline over the car's rattan seats and set it aflame. They cheered and shook their fists as it burned to the tracks before the fire department could save it.

While officially horrified by the behavior of the students, Fr. Cavanaugh thought the streetcar company was at least partially responsible for the incident and refused to pay the five thousand dollars in damages.[17]

For Walsh, it was merely an introduction to a young man's capacity for violence.

World War I had been raging in Europe since 1914, but the United States had steadfastly stayed out of it. U.S. interests did not seem to be in imminent danger, although there were occasional disasters, such as the sinking of the *Lusitania*, with 128 Americans aboard, in 1915. Certainly, U.S. territory was not threatened. Many Americans felt that God had blessed their nation with its geographic distance from Europe. The natural tendency of Americans to stay clear of "European entanglements" was strengthened by the presence of two diverse and enormous immigrant groups. Most German Americans did not want the United States to take up arms against the fatherland, and most Irish Americans did not want the United States to do anything to help the British. The immigrant sentiment was not out of the mainstream. When President Woodrow Wilson campaigned for reelection with the slogan "He kept us out of war" in 1916, he won. As long as the vast majority of Americans felt safe, this convenient pacifism held sway.

Gradually, though, events eroded Americans' sense of security. The sinking of the *Lusitania* in May 1915 was the first to cause a breach. American indignation over this and additional submarine attacks during the next few months led Germany to restrict its submarine operations to military targets. On January 31, 1917, however, convinced that it would win them the war, the Germans announced to the United States that they were resuming unrestricted submarine warfare. President Wilson ended U.S. diplomatic relations with Germany a few days later, but it wasn't until the publication of the Zimmermann Telegram in March 1917 that public opinion solidified on the idea of going to war. The intercepted telegram revealed that the German foreign secretary had conspired to strike a deal with the Mexican government: if the U.S. went to war against Germany, Mexico would become Germany's ally, and Germany would in turn recover Texas, New Mexico, and Arizona for Mexico. Once the American public learned of this plan, they were ready to fight. Wilson went to Congress and received a declaration of war on April 6, 1917.

At Notre Dame, Fr. Cavanaugh and Fr. Walsh moved to immediately and conspicuously support the war effort. Cavanaugh's hatred of the English evaporated with the declaration of war—no one would accuse him or Notre Dame of being anything less than 100 percent patriotic. After all, even the Irish in Ireland were enlisting in droves; many thought it would help them gain concessions from a grateful England after the war. Like Cavanaugh and Walsh, their students were eager to demonstrate their patriotism. The president and vice president agreed to let seniors in good standing graduate early in order to enlist.

Cavanaugh and Walsh didn't want their young men going to war alone, so they encouraged their staff to enlist as well. Eighteen Notre Dame priests volunteered immediately. When Fr. Morrissey, still the provincial, looked at the list of names, he said, "As long as we're in this thing, let's give the best!"[18] Six of the eighteen were designated to go first. They were a diverse group, including a prefect of discipline, a professor of chemistry, and a professor of rhetoric. The most prominent member of the group by far was a professor of history who also happened to be the school's vice president. On a cold day in January 1918, Fr. Matthew Walsh left for Camp Sheridan, Alabama.

Around the time that Matthew Walsh was preparing to embark on an academic life at Notre Dame, another young boy was struggling against poverty and circumstances to obtain an education. A thousand miles away from Chicago in Houston, Texas, David Curtis Stephenson, born the youngest son of a sharecropper on August 21, 1891, was showing academic promise at his Catholic grammar school. Although not Catholic, Stephenson's family had sent him to the school because it was near their home. His mother was thrilled when the sisters at the school reported that young Stephenson was an energetic student, an avid reader who devoured histories of Caesar and Napoleon. Stephenson's father, Andrew Monroe Stephenson, embittered by a lifetime of sharecropping, made a point of remarking within earshot of the boy that such learning wouldn't do him a lick of good behind a plow.

Already in his fifties, Andrew Stephenson longed to leave the sharecropping life and farm his own land. In 1901, he moved his family—including his wife and their other two children, Clara and Arizona—to Maysville, Oklahoma, during the last great Oklahoma land rush. Maysville was a tiny, dusty town about halfway between Oklahoma City and the Texas state line. To the children, the higher social position achieved in land ownership was not immediately apparent. Their first home in Oklahoma was a dugout house, a hole in the ground with a straw roof. Andrew Stephenson hoped that he might save enough money in a year or two to build a sod house. For ten-year-old David, the worst thing about Maysville was not living in a hole, or the screaming winter wind, or the backbreaking farm work—it was the lack of a school. His father didn't mind this; his son's education in Texas had served only to distract him from work, and he needed David's help as he tried to scratch a living out of Oklahoma's hard prairie.

For two long years, David Stephenson worked at his father's side on their isolated piece of land. Now that he didn't have to ride his son about the uselessness of an education, Andrew Stephenson took to ranting against the boy's good looks. Blond-haired, blue-eyed David bore an attractive softness despite the family's hardscrabble existence. Andrew Stephenson linked his son's "pretty" face and aversion to farm work to overall laziness. David in turn enraged his father by carefully combing his hair in front him and by reporting for chores doused in cheap cologne from the Maysville drugstore. "A farmer doesn't need to smell like a whore!" Andrew Stephenson would scream at David. "And we're farmers. That's what you will always be." He might have been right had a rail line not cut through Maysville in 1903.

The railroad brought with it people and ideas that would change David Stephenson forever. To serve its increased population, the town opened a school in a new Methodist church. David enthusiastically resumed his studies despite the grumblings of his father. He graduated from the eighth grade at the top of his class in 1907, the same year Oklahoma became a state. Maysville had no high school. Stephenson's formal education had come to an end, but his on-the-job training was about to begin.

Among the people who came to Maysville with the railroad was a man named John Cooper. Short and broad shouldered, with a bushy mustache and twinkling eyes, Cooper was a successful farmer, but his real love was politics. Statehood had sparked countless political debates across Oklahoma, and in Maysville, Cooper—a proud Socialist—was almost always at the center of those debates.

In 1910, Cooper bought a controlling interest in the town's only newspaper, the *Maysville News*. He gave Arizona Stephenson, D. C. Stephenson's older brother, a job running the typesetting equipment at the paper. Eager to help his brother escape their father and their depressing home outside of town, Arizona talked Cooper into hiring D. C.

D. C. Stephenson set about learning the business with the determination of a young man intent on leaving the farm for good. He wrote copy, set type, ran the presses, and delivered papers to homes and stores in and around Maysville. When he wasn't working, Stephenson relished Cooper's wild political rants and his animated predictions of a Socialist revolution. "The Socialists stand for the common man, the working man," he told Stephenson. "If you vote for a Democrat or a Republican, you're just a sucker for the rich man."

Talking to Cooper, it seemed to Stephenson that the Socialist Party was the place to be for any ambitious young man. In 1907, during Oklahoma's first gubernatorial election, the Socialist candidate had garnered almost twelve thousand votes,[19] the support of about 3 percent of the male voting population in the state; three years later, the Socialists earned more than twice that many. While they still lost, it was an impressive gain. In other parts of the country, Socialists were winning political offices: in 1910, Milwaukee elected a Socialist mayor and Wisconsin elected a Socialist congressman. Cooper's enthusiasm over the success of the party inspired Stephenson to join. He had learned firsthand that the most effective salesman is a passionate salesman.

Stephenson spent the next few years working under Cooper and honing his skills as a newspaperman. Cooper thought he could see something of the salesman in Stephenson as well. When it came time for the next gubernatorial race, Cooper convinced the Oklahoma Socialists to hire his young assistant as an organizer. Although just twenty-three years old, Stephenson had solid credentials. Anyone who spoke to him could see he was smart. He had a four-year apprenticeship in the newspaper business under his belt. He had grown up in poverty, another important qualification for any worthwhile Socialist. And perhaps most important, he was good-looking. His blond hair, piercing blue eyes, and winning smile would be valuable assets to have in his job of drawing a crowd. The party offered Stephenson twelve dollars a week to travel the state, drum up crowds, and deliver speeches in favor of Fred Holt, the Socialist candidate for governor. Stephenson could hardly believe his luck.[20]

On the campaign trail, Stephenson learned the ropes from pros like Socialist Oscar Ameringer, a pragmatist who once defined politics as "the gentle art of getting votes from the poor and campaign funds from the rich by promising to protect each from the other."[21] Veterans like Ameringer knew that politicians and their dry discourse wouldn't draw the crowds. Organizers needed showmen, not politicians. They needed musicians and singers, tents and parades, watermelons and lemonade to get the rugged farmers and their families to come out and hear the Socialist message, which they would sneak in between songs and plates of fried chicken.

Stephenson learned an age-old political truth during that campaign: make people feel like they belong, and they'll go along with whatever you say. By simply gathering poor farmers together and showing them a good time, the Socialists were delivering a message. Even before the first speech was delivered, they were saying that they understood those farmers and their families, that they liked being around them, and that they cared about them. Stephenson learned the power of inviting people to belong, especially people who may have never before been invited to join anything.

Despite the Socialists' picnic campaign, Fred Holt lost the Oklahoma gubernatorial race in 1914. Stephenson's political career was over for a time.

After the excitement of the crowds, the rallies, and the travel, Stephenson had difficulty settling down into a normal life. He floated across Oklahoma, getting newspaper jobs and losing them in short order. In 1915, he landed in the town of Hugo, where he drifted into a marriage with Nettie Hamilton. He left her while she was pregnant with their child. For months Hamilton tracked Stephenson across Oklahoma as he skipped from newspaper to newspaper in the towns of Sulphur, Ada, Cushing, and Miami. Hamilton gave birth to their child on May 16, 1916, and then resumed her chase. Finally, Stephenson left the state to escape her, fleeing to Iowa. Hamilton gave up at the state line, filing for divorce in February 1917.

Stephenson was working for a printer in Story City, Iowa, when the United States entered the war in April 1917. Like most Americans, Stephenson was itching to join the fight. Even as a newspaperman and somewhat of a political insider, by now familiar with the forces that were driving the populace into a patriotic frenzy, Stephenson was not cynical about the war. He held the same romantic notions that were making men line up across the country to get "over there." Stephenson enlisted at the Story City post office and was ordered to Fort Des Moines.

The young man who had memorized accounts of Waterloo and Austerlitz undoubtedly had dramatic visions of himself charging across the battlefields of Europe. The army bureaucracy, however, saw that Stephenson's natural ability was in sales. They made him an officer and a recruiter. He never left American soil.

2

FR. SORIN AND THE BIRTH OF
NOTRE DAME

MATTHEW WALSH WAS FIFTEEN YEARS OLD WHEN HE
arrived at Notre Dame in 1897. The school was itself an ado-
lescent at the time, growing rapidly and awkwardly although already
a rousing American Catholic success story. Notre Dame had been
founded only fifty-five years earlier in an overwhelmingly Protestant
state by a young French priest from an obscure order with no money
and numerous enemies—including his own bishop. How such an
institution could survive and grow into a nationally known symbol of
Catholic achievement is a story as unlikely as it is inspiring. It is
largely the story of Fr. Edward Sorin.

In the late eighteenth century, during the French Revolution's
Reign of Terror, the revolutionary government saw the Roman
Catholic Church as aligned with the oppressive monarchical regime
it was working to overthrow. Catholics were treated as enemies of the
state. Catholic schools, monasteries, and churches were closed.
French Catholics hid their faith or ceased practicing it entirely.
Hundreds of priests were guillotined; the more fortunate were exiled.

The chaos of the Revolution gave birth to the reign of Napoleon.
He shrewdly embraced the church, calculating correctly that the
long-suppressed Catholics would take him up as their champion.
Under the emperor's close, suspicious gaze, French Catholicism
began limping toward recovery. On February 6, 1814, just as this

21

recovery got under way, Edward Frederick Sorin was born in Ahuillé, in the province of Mayenne, France, the seventh child of a moderately prosperous Catholic family. The Sorins, sufficiently distant from Paris, had managed to maintain their estate and their Catholicism during the Revolution. They also were able to pass on to their son a certain Gallic haughtiness expected of people of their station. Sorin was a bright child from a large, pious family, so it was not unusual that he decided in his teens to become a priest. Nor was it surprising that his parents encouraged him to follow his calling. He was accepted to the seminary in Le Mans, France, and was ordained in 1838.

In 1840, Sorin joined a religious order that had been recently founded by Fr. Basil Moreau in Sainte-Croix, a small town near Le Mans. The literal translation of the town's name is "Holy Cross," and the order would become known in America as the Congregation of Holy Cross.

Fr. Moreau's order was one of many that were springing up across France to reopen Catholic schools and churches that had been closed during the Reign of Terror. Their task was nothing less than the reconstruction of the Catholic Church in France. France, however, wasn't the only place suffering from a lack of pastoral and educational ministries. The Catholic population in America's Northwest Territory was growing, and priests were needed to teach and minister to the people there. The missionary bishop of Vincennes, Indiana—Célestin de La Hailandière—traveled to France to solicit the help of the country's priests and brothers in ministering to his vast and growing diocese. As in France, the prospect of sending Catholic children to Protestant schools was considered a horror to be avoided in America—where even public schools were regarded as "Protestant." The bishop implored church leaders like Moreau to provide him with religious men to help him establish Catholic schools. He also spoke directly to priests about the challenges and the rewards of frontier life. He found a receptive audience in the twenty-five-year-old Fr. Sorin, who was intrigued by the adventures of French priests in America.

After much hesitation, and without clarifying who would pay for the expedition, Fr. Moreau agreed to send a small band of his religious men to assist Bishop La Hailandière in the New World. He offered to send six Holy Cross brothers and Fr. Sorin as their leader. On the eve of their departure, in a sign of things to come, the small group of missionaries found itself short of money on the pier in Le Havre, France. Fr. Sorin negotiated a place for himself and his men in steerage for fifteen hundred francs. They set sail on August 8, 1841.

Thirty-nine days later, their ship pulled into New York Harbor. After an eight-day journey up the Erie Canal to Buffalo by horse-drawn barge, Sorin and the brothers took a three-day steamboat trip across Lake Erie to Toledo and then a series of horse-drawn carts to Vincennes, Indiana, where they arrived on October 10, 1841. In all, the trip from France took nearly nine weeks.[1]

The America that greeted Fr. Sorin and the Holy Cross brothers in 1841 was not particularly welcoming of Catholics. In 1834, an Ursuline convent in Charlestown, Massachusetts, was burned to the ground by an anti-Catholic mob. A year later, Rebecca Reed, an escaped "inmate" from that same convent, published *Six Months in a Convent*, a book that told sordid tales of the sinister priests, perverse rituals, and sexual abuse Reed encountered while at the convent. It sold two hundred thousand copies in one month.[2] The book was the prototypical "convent tale," an anti-Catholic genre that grew into a small industry by the turn of the century. The success of Reed's book inspired many imitators in the years immediately prior to Sorin's arrival. The most significant was Maria Monk, whose sensationalistic *Awful Disclosures of Maria Monk*, published in 1836, recounted lurid details of the abuse she suffered at the hands of priests at the Hotel Dieu Convent in Montreal. Monk was later proven to be a fraud.

Despite these instances of anti-Catholicism in the United States, most native-born Protestants in the 1840s had not yet begun to see

the immigration of Catholics as a threat—they perceived
Catholicism as alien but not quite dangerous. Catholic immigrants
in the country were still a relatively small group, and most were
members of wealthy or middle-class families who were eager to assimi-
late. Even the Catholic Church in America positioned itself as an
almost democratic institution. Ireland's Potato Famine and the subsequent Irish diaspora would cause American anti-Catholicism to
metastasize four years later into something more ferocious, but in
1841, the year of Sorin's arrival, the Protestant majority did not yet
view Catholic immigration as out of control.

The Diocese of Vincennes upon Sorin's arrival was a good micro-
cosm of the country as a whole. It included all of Indiana and the
eastern half of Illinois, including Chicago. Of the area's roughly nine
hundred thousand residents,[3] relatively few were Catholic. Aside
from the French Catholics who had settled the area and a growing
number of German Catholics, most of the residents of Indiana were
Protestants. Their anti-Catholicism was mostly of the mildly suspicious variety, and it mirrored Sorin's own feelings about Protestants.
The Protestants in 1841 Vincennes did wonder, though, about the
Americanism of a people whose leaders spoke only French. Their suspicion manifested itself in ways no more hostile than the occasional
bigoted sermon from a Protestant pulpit.

The religious strife in 1841 Vincennes wasn't Catholic versus
Protestant; it was Catholic versus Catholic. Sorin began to battle
Bishop La Hailandière as soon as he and the brothers arrived. Sorin
and Moreau expected La Hailandière to support the small Holy Cross
mission financially without exercising any control over their work.
The bishop, for his part, balked at these terms. Since Sorin was from
the Congregation of Holy Cross, he did not, strictly speaking, report
to the bishop, although he worked within his diocese. Their relationship was analogous to that of a junior naval officer visiting the
captain of another ship. The bishop outranked Sorin, but Sorin did
not work for the bishop. Sorin's "captain" was Moreau, who was

thousands of miles away in France. Such ambiguous lines of authority have caused tensions between men far more flexible than Sorin and La Hailandière.

Sorin's constant hustling was unnerving to the bishop as well. On October 22, less than two weeks after his arrival in Vincennes, Sorin placed a newspaper advertisement touting a "school for young men,"[4] complete with courses in orthography, history—both ancient and modern—and bookkeeping. In a letter to Moreau, Sorin said that he had chosen not to mention in his advertisement that none of the school's teachers spoke English.

Tensions escalated between Sorin and La Hailandière as Sorin continued to press him for money. The bishop held the line, saying that he would not support Sorin financially without gaining some measure of control over his activities. Letters between Sorin and Moreau and between La Hailandière and Moreau traveled slowly back and forth across the Atlantic as the controversy festered.

Thanks mainly to Sorin's force of will and his considerable promotional skills, his "school for young men" grew into a successful operation in its first year. The settlers in the area—Protestant and Catholic alike—were eager beyond all expectations to educate their children. Sorin and his men soon learned passable English and were even able to recruit some local boys into the order: some Germans, some Irish, and some "genuine Americans." Sorin noted in his chronicles that the Irish "lacked stability." The Germans were less endowed than the Irish with the "qualities of the heart" but were "more persevering." As for the "genuine" Americans, Sorin had little hope for them. "The spirit of liberty as it is understood in the United States is too directly opposed to the spirit of obedience," wrote Sorin. He speculated that many years would pass before Americans were capable of taking religious vows.[5]

Without stopping to appreciate the early and surprising success of his primary school—and without consulting La Hailandière—Sorin made plans for a college and began constructing a building for it.

La Hailandière was furious when he learned of the project. He summoned Sorin and explained to him that he was already committed to supporting a Catholic college in Vincennes, one run by Eudists, and that there was barely enough demand to keep that school open. Sorin was convinced that the bishop was keeping him from fulfilling his destiny. The only thing that both men might have agreed on was that they could not continue to work side by side. The bishop offered Sorin a creative alternative.

There was some land, he told Sorin, in the northern part of the state that had quite a pedigree. Fr. Stephen Theodore Badin, the first priest ordained in the United States, was the land's original owner. Badin had fled France in 1791 when hostile revolutionaries closed the seminary he attended. Since Badin's training was nearly complete, the bishop of Baltimore ordained him in 1793. Badin spent the rest of his life ministering to the American Indians and pioneers on the frontier land from Kentucky to Michigan. He also became involved in real-estate speculation, selling land he bought in the frontier to settlers at a healthy profit. In the process, he was able to transfer valuable land to the church.

In 1835, Badin transferred 524 acres of land in South Bend, Indiana, to Bishop Simon Bruté of Vincennes, who may or may not have been his bishop at the time. Badin operated all across the frontier. It was not always clear to which diocese he belonged, and Badin, who enjoyed his independence, did nothing to resolve this ambiguity.

Badin attached two conditions to the transfer of the South Bend property. First, it had to be used for an orphanage or some other religious or charitable project. Second, Badin had to be reimbursed $750 for improvements he had made to the land at his own expense. Bishop La Hailandière offered the land to Sorin under somewhat more stringent requirements—within two years, Sorin had to establish both a college and a novitiate for Holy Cross brothers and priests. The land was 250 miles north of Vincennes, across an almost virgin wilderness. The sparsely populated area had even less of a need for a college than Vincennes, and there were even fewer Catholics there. The bishop probably expected that Sorin would be unable to fulfill either of the conditions and that the land would be returned to him in two years, along with a sufficiently humbled Fr. Sorin.

Despite the obvious challenges, the prospect of independence from the bishop made the deal too good for Sorin to turn down. Before leaving Vincennes, he displayed characteristic self-confidence by contacting an architect and designing with him a college building in the shape of a double hammer, 160 feet long and 3 stories tall. Sorin told the architect to come to South Bend the following spring and promised him that he and the brothers would manufacture all the lumber and bricks necessary for the project before his arrival.

Sorin was so eager to leave Vincennes that he chose not to wait for good weather. He departed with seven brothers on November 16, 1842. On cold and muddy roads, they traveled five miles on their first day.

South Bend is named for the southernmost turn in the St. Joseph River, which runs in a rough U shape from its origin around Battle Creek, Michigan, to where it enters Lake Michigan at St. Joseph, Michigan. Alexis Coquillard, the fur trader who named the town in 1823, still lived in South Bend when Sorin and his tired band arrived on November 26. Coquillard was slowly making the transition from frontier fur trader to successful small-town merchant as South Bend grew up around him. By the time of Sorin's arrival, about one thousand people lived in South Bend. Sorin estimated that among these lived only twenty Catholic families, including the Coquillards, who hosted Sorin and his hungry crew for a number of days while they recovered from their journey. As soon as the weather permitted, Coquillard took Sorin and the brothers to see the land that they had been offered.

The improvements for which Badin wanted $750 reimbursement were not immediately obvious. All but about 10 of the 524 acres were covered with water or heavy forest. There were a total of three buildings on the property—a storage shed, a trapper's clapboard home, and a "chapel" that had been erected ten years earlier. The two-story chapel was the biggest building on the property, at forty by twenty-four feet. Its first floor was designed to be a priest's residence, and the second story was the actual chapel, although it was "open to all the winds."[6] An exuberant Sorin saw only the property's great possibilities. In a letter to Moreau, Sorin recorded his first impressions:

> Everything was frozen, yet it all appeared so beautiful. The lake particularly, with its mantle of snow, resplendently white, was to us a symbol of the stainless purity of Our Lady. . . . Like little children, in spite of the cold, we ran from one end to the other perfectly enchanted by the beauty of our new home.[7]

What Sorin could not see, because of the blanket of snow, was that "the lake" was actually two lakes. Without suitable accommodations for the whole group, they returned to Coquillard's home for the night.

Sorin named the school Notre Dame du Lac, French for Our Lady of the Lake. He then set out to construct buildings for the campus, an activity that would occupy him for most of the rest of his life. He started by improving the decrepit chapel. He put the industrious brothers to work manufacturing 60,000 feet of lumber and 250,000 bricks from the marl they dredged from the lakes. When the architect from Vincennes failed to show up in the spring of 1843 to build the double hammer building, Sorin and the brothers took some of the bricks and constructed a small two-story building on their own at the very edge of St. Mary's Lake, to serve as the school's first permanent classroom and dormitory. The brothers constructed a solid building. Old College, as it is called now, still stands and serves as home to Notre Dame's first-year seminarians.

From the beginning, there was tension between Sorin's mission and the largely Protestant population of the area. "All the surroundings were strongly Protestant," wrote Sorin in his chronicles, "that is to say enemies more or less embittered against the Catholics."[8] The locals linked the arrival of the Holy Cross contingent to a papal conspiracy against their region. The religious men's stated plans for a college sounded far-fetched in light of the negligible Catholic population, the remoteness of the region, and the seeming lack of a demand for higher education in the area in any form. Only conspiracy theories seemed to completely explain the presence of Sorin and his men.

The religious intolerance in South Bend was not one-sided. When Indiana senator John Dougherty Defrees obtained a state charter for the fledgling university in 1844, giving them the power to grant degrees and desperately needed credibility, Sorin wrote that God had caused Defrees to "lay aside for once the prejudices of his sect" and described him as "an infidel then a Methodist."[9]

Notre Dame du Lac grew slowly but steadily. In the school's first shaky year, during the winter of 1842–43, Sorin enrolled two students: Alexis Coquillard's son Theodore and a young man named Clement Reckers. The following year, he enrolled five. In 1844, a total of twenty-five students were in residence at Notre Dame. As in Vincennes, settlers in South Bend had a surprisingly strong desire to educate their children.

The school was designed around a six-year European model, taking students through their last two years of high school and four years of college. Notre Dame provided a classical European curriculum—students took courses in Latin, Greek, composition, mathematics, and oratory, even as the teachers themselves continued to learn English. Sorin quickly saw that the population of South Bend alone could not support his grand vision for the school, so he began making trips to Chicago and Detroit to recruit students. His need for students even trumped his usual disdain for Protestants; students of all faiths were welcome at Notre Dame du Lac. Non-Catholic students had to observe Mass and participate in prayers before classes but were excused from catechism instruction. In an advertisement in the *South Bend Free Press*, Sorin promised local parents that "there will be no interference on the part of the faculty with the religious tenets of a non-Catholic student."[10]

While Sorin and La Hailandière continued to fight very personal battles over issues of jurisdiction, even the bishop had to concede that Sorin had met the stipulations he had attached to the property in South Bend. In 1845, La Hailandière transferred the title of the property to the Congregation of Holy Cross. Notably, he journeyed to France to give the title to Moreau instead of giving it to Sorin.

———

The early history of Notre Dame is a story of constant financial crisis punctuated by catastrophic fires. In December 1842, the college's chapel caught fire. The next year, another fire in the same building caused "great alarm," as Sorin wrote in his chronicles. Small chimneys that Sorin had designed into every room of Old College ignited a third fire in 1846. In 1849, a fire destroyed the school's kitchen, bakery, and workroom in two hours.[11] Even though he had lived in America for seven years, Sorin estimated the damages from the fire in francs. The early fires aggravated the school's financial woes, as Sorin didn't buy the school's first insurance policy until 1848.[12] After almost every fire, Sorin managed to obtain enough money through loans and donations to repair the affected building or build a replacement building grander than the one that had been damaged.

In 1844, Sorin opened a trade school at Notre Dame, which, among other things, supplied Notre Dame with some of the skilled tradesmen it needed to continue its growth. Here poor boys, many of whom were orphans, were taught carpentry, tailoring, masonry, and other trades that would make them productive members of society. Sorin also expanded his boarding school in 1844. While Notre Dame already enrolled young men in their last two years of high school, Sorin began admitting boys as young as six years old. These minims, as they came to be known, were housed and educated apart from the older students. Sorin called them his "little princes," and they are most famous in Notre Dame lore for the attention that he lavished upon them.

Tuition and fees from the grammar and high school students soon became the biggest and most reliable source of income for the University of Notre Dame. Still, the school struggled financially. In one of Sorin's less successful attempts at generating income, he formed the St. Joseph Company in 1850 and sent seven brothers west to prospect for gold. One of the brothers died in California, another left the order, and none of them found any gold with which to appease Fr. Sorin's numerous creditors.[13]

Throughout it all—the fires, the debt, the tensions with local Protestants, and the ongoing battles with La Hailandière in Vincennes—Sorin's school grew. In 1851, a new railroad line came through South Bend. Sorin immediately recognized the potential benefit to the university. "It would be difficult to set a money value on the benefit of this railroad to an establishment like Notre Dame du Lac," he wrote. "Before the end of this year, Notre Dame du Lac will be, by means of it, within two days of New York, twenty hours from Cincinnati, eight hours from Chicago, and a few hours from even its most distant missions."[14]

As Notre Dame's enrollment grew, its positive impact on the economy of the area became more and more conspicuous. The Catholic leaders of Notre Dame and the Protestant businessmen of South Bend began treating each other with the respect due potential customers. While the Protestants and Catholics of South Bend reached an uneasy truce, Catholics in other parts of the country were increasingly exposed to various manifestations of anti-Catholicism. One example of this was the American Party, better known as the Know-Nothings, which thrived in the 1850s on its anti-Catholic, anti-immigrant platform. The party had strengthened between the years of 1845 and 1849, when the Great Potato Famine caused the Irish to flee their homeland in great numbers. In the 1850s, almost one million Irish came to the United States—more than 13 percent of the total population of Ireland.[15] The Know-Nothing movement was the strongest where the Irish population was the biggest. In November 1854, the American Party took every senate seat in the state of Massachusetts.[16] Although the Know-Nothings didn't have much of a presence in Indiana, their existence in America signaled that native-born Protestants were becoming more apprehensive about the seemingly unlimited growth of the Catholic population.

Some Catholics in America were just as uneasy with the exploding Irish population. By virtue of their large numbers and their native organizational talent, Irish leaders were taking control of the church in America. By 1900, 75 percent of newly consecrated American bishops would be of Irish descent, a number that would stay relatively constant for sixty years.[17] Prior to the famine, the Catholic Church in America had presented itself as a reflection of the American experiment, complete with elected officials and constitutional laws. The Irish, though, came from a country where Catholicism had been nearly outlawed. The Irish bishops and cardinals in America viewed the culture with suspicion. John Hughes, the County Tyrone–born archbishop of New York for fourteen years, was one militant example. They advocated a church that was completely independent of secular influence, a church that wrapped Catholics in a cocoon of Catholic institutions from cradle to grave, providing hospitals, newspapers, social clubs, and, especially, schools. The emphasis on Catholic education directly benefited Notre Dame. By 1860, Notre Dame had 224 students and was growing every year.[18]

When the Civil War broke out in 1861, American institutions of higher education suffered. Notre Dame's chronicler estimated that half of the country's colleges closed. Notre Dame, however, profited from its remote location. The number of students enrolled at Notre Dame actually rose after the war started, according to the same chronicler, "owing to its distance from the theater of the war."[19]

Notre Dame's remoteness is also what led General William Tecumseh Sherman—a Protestant—to send his children to the university for the duration of the war. The youngest child, eight-year-old Willy, became one of Notre Dame's minims. By the time General Sherman marched through Atlanta, his wife, Ellen Ewing Sherman, was also living in South Bend. In 1865, shortly after the end of the war, General Sherman was the speaker at Notre Dame's commencement.

If Notre Dame was removed from the fight, her priests and nuns were not. The Congregation of Holy Cross sent eight priests to the front and more than forty sisters to the Union hospitals that desperately needed them. Sending the priests and especially the nurse sisters was a deliberate and successful attempt at extinguishing some of the anti-Catholic prejudices that had flared up before the war. In 1888, John Ireland, the archbishop of St. Paul, Minnesota, spoke at Sorin's fiftieth anniversary celebration. Ireland would spend an often frustrating lifetime trying to Americanize the Catholic Church. While Sorin had disagreed with much of Ireland's liberal program, Ireland recognized the good that Notre Dame's Civil War efforts had done for his goal. "Few things in the past half-century," he said at the celebration, "were done to break down more effectually anti-Catholic prejudice than sending our generous sisters to the battlefield and the military hospitals."[20]

The Notre Dame chaplain to gain the most lasting fame for his efforts in the Civil War was Fr. William Corby. At the Battle of Gettysburg in 1863, Fr. Corby stood atop a boulder in front of the Irish Brigade and granted the troops general absolution as shells and bullets screamed past him. The soldiers charged into battle immediately after receiving his blessing. A statue of Corby was constructed on the very rock from which he preached. It is one of only three individual monuments on the battlefield that does not depict a general.

The Civil War ended in 1865, as did an era in Notre Dame history. Sorin was named the head of the North American province of the Holy Cross order and reluctantly stepped down from the presidency in order to best attend to his new duties. Fr. Sorin was succeeded by the Irish-born Fr. Patrick Dillon. Sorin remained at Notre Dame, and as head of the province was Dillon's superior. Having run the school for all of its twenty-three years, Sorin had trouble completely handing over the reins to Dillon. One example of Sorin's continued involvement in running the university was his banning of St. Patrick's Day celebrations. Sorin's given reason for doing this was that he wanted to maintain an image of Americanism at the school. He was sensitive to the rise of the Know-Nothings and the increasingly common charges that American Catholics were disloyal. He also very much wanted the local population to send their sons to his school, regardless of their religion. A raucous celebration in honor of the Irish patron saint would not be good for business. Aside from those reasons, Sorin probably had as much disdain for Irish revelry as any of the local Protestants.

Perhaps as a consequence of Sorin's hands-on approach, Dillon's tenure as president was the shortest in the school's history, lasting only one year. The most notable milestone of Dillon's brief presidency was the building of Notre Dame's first domed building, which was completed in 1865. The six-story structure was made necessary by the school's steady growth. By 1865, its twenty-third year, the school had 512 students and was inching toward solvency. The school accepted, by its own admission, almost anyone who applied.

Fr. William Corby, the Civil War hero, succeeded Dillon as president in 1866. Corby, perhaps because of his experience under fire, was able to function slightly more independently under the provincial than Dillon ever could. In 1869, during Corby's presidency, Notre Dame opened its law school, the first Catholic law school in the country. Corby stepped down after a six-year term, a practice that became standard and was later made official by the order. Fr. Auguste Lemonnier—Fr. Sorin's nephew—succeeded Corby in 1872. Fr. Lemonnier was known for being considerably more lenient with the students than Sorin ever was. Like Fr. Dillon, Lemonnier also served a short term as president, dying in office in 1874. Perhaps thinking of his demanding uncle, his dying words were "Be good to the students." [21]

Fr. Patrick Colovin, an Irishman and Lemonnier's vice president, became president in 1874 and immediately began to struggle with Fr. Sorin. The provincial blamed every conflict at the school on his president's nationality. Fr. Colovin was proud of his heritage, a heritage he shared with a growing number of Notre Dame students and priests. He reversed Sorin's long-standing policy against celebrating St. Patrick's Day, and the holiday became a highlight of the school year. Colovin had, in fact, been ordained on St. Patrick's Day. The president and the provincial continued to battle each other until 1877, when Fr. Sorin forced Colovin to resign, citing a variety of transgressions that included excessive consumption of alcohol. Colovin was widely viewed by the students as a martyr for the Irish.

Fr. Corby replaced Colovin, becoming the only president to serve two nonconsecutive terms at the school. He would see Notre Dame through one of its darkest days.

On April 23, 1879, the university's main building, the six-story domed structure built in 1865, was destroyed by fire. The fire also consumed the adjacent St. Francis' Elderly Men's Home, the minim's gymnasium, the infirmary, and the music hall. Fr. Sorin was not on campus at the time—he was in Montreal, en route to France. Within a few hours of the fire, Fr. Corby and his staff had decided to cancel what little remained of the school year. Corby called the students to Sacred Heart Church, now the biggest building on campus. Corby promised them that the school would be rebuilt by the time they returned in September.

Once the damage had been assessed, everyone's thoughts turned to Fr. Sorin. He was sixty-five years old, and a major part of his life-work had just been destroyed. Corby sent Professor James Edwards, the school librarian, to Montreal to intercept Sorin before he left for Europe and to notify him of the fire.

The fire happened on a Wednesday; Sorin was able to make it back to Notre Dame on Sunday. Corby, seasoned leader that he was, had taken decisive action in Sorin's absence. He held two early commencement exercises for the graduating seniors and initiated fund-raising drives for the rebuilding effort. The school's insurance policy on the lost buildings was for forty-five thousand dollars, an estimated one-fourth of the rebuilding cost.[22]

No one knew quite what to expect when Sorin arrived. The school he had devoted his life to was still smoldering at his feet. But the sight did not crush his spirit. Instead, he seemed to gain strength as he walked among the embers. When he finally made his way into Sacred Heart Church to celebrate Mass, he was visibly energized. At that Mass, he delivered a homily that was a watershed in Notre Dame history, a statement of faith, determination, and confidence against the odds that was greater than any halftime pep talk ever given by a Notre Dame football coach. The fire was his fault, Sorin said, a sign from God. His vision for the university had been too small. The fire gave them a chance to build something worthier. His last words were "If it were all gone, I should not give up!"[23]

What rose in place of the destroyed building was the grand Golden Dome that stands today, the most recognizable symbol of the university. The building was the result of what Notre Dame historian Thomas Schlereth described as a "summer construction marathon"[24] and an equally Herculean fund-raising drive. As promised, the building was opened and classes began on September 8, 1879. It was in many ways Sorin's finest hour.

The burning of Notre Dame's main building symbolized the precarious position of Catholic immigrants in Protestant America. Sorin's determination to rebuild symbolized their refusal to fail. The great fire and the rebuilding effort did not exhaust Sorin, a man who had thrived on challenges all his life. In 1882, when he was sixty-eight years old, Sorin made his fortieth transatlantic passage to France. Upon his return to the United States, he took a train from New York to South Bend, arriving at the quiet train station at 2:00 in the morning. Due to a miscommunication, no one met Sorin at the station. Undaunted, the old man walked the two miles back to campus alone. When he arrived, the sun was just beginning to rise. Sorin went to Sacred Heart and celebrated Mass.[25]

When Fr. Corby stepped down as president for the second time, in 1881, wearied from battling Sorin for every measure of control, one of Sorin's own recruits was installed in office. Fr. Thomas Walsh was born near Montreal in 1853, the fourth of nine children of Irish parents. At fifteen years old, he enrolled at the College de St. Laurent, a Catholic boarding school near his home that was run by the Congregation of Holy Cross. When Fr. Sorin visited the school in 1872 in his capacity as superior general of the Holy Cross order, he recognized the potential in young Thomas Walsh and stole him away, bringing him to Indiana before he had even been ordained. After four years of study, three of which were in France, Walsh returned to Notre Dame for good in 1876.

Thomas Walsh moved rapidly through the ranks at Notre Dame. The year of his arrival was the last year of Fr. Colovin's tumultuous presidency. When Colovin was forced to resign in 1877, Fr. Corby replaced him and asked the twenty-four-year-old Walsh to be his vice president, although the young man was not yet ordained—he would become a priest later that same year. When Corby stepped down four years later, Walsh was the natural choice for his successor.

Despite his Irish ancestry, Walsh was able to build a good working relationship with the school's demanding founder. As a result, he served twelve years as president. He was the first president to serve more than six consecutive years in office since Sorin himself.

Under the steady leadership of Fr. Walsh, the school saw many improvements. Notre Dame is one of several American colleges that claim to be the first to have electric lights—they came to Notre Dame in 1885. Walsh also commissioned a series of murals to be painted inside the new Main Building by Luigi Gregori, a well-known Vatican painter. The murals depicted Columbus's discovery of the New World. This Catholic mission of discovery was an obvious choice of subjects—what better way to demonstrate the legitimacy of the Catholic claim to a piece of the American dream? Columbus's patroness is identified in her portrait as "Isabella the Catholic." For the face of Columbus, Gregori used Fr. Thomas Walsh as his model in all of the murals except one. For the bearded Columbus on his deathbed, Gregori painted Sorin.

As other finishing touches were being put on the new building, Fr. Sorin fought one of his last battles with those around him who dared think too small. Sorin insisted that the new dome be covered in real gold. Many in the administration thought that real gold was too extravagant and argued for gold paint instead. By congregation rules, all expenses had to be approved by a council of administration, which normally rubber-stamped its approval of Sorin's initiatives. The council that reviewed Sorin's plan for gilding the dome, however, found the endeavor so wasteful that it took the ill-advised step of disapproving Sorin's request.[26]

Sorin, as superior general of the order, had himself named chairman of the council. He then left the campus every Tuesday during the council's weekly meetings. Without the chairman's presence, the council could not conduct any business. After weeks of this, enough council members finally saw the futility of resisting Sorin's will. Chairman Sorin returned to campus, and the council voted in favor of his gold. The dome is 139 feet in circumference. The height of the building, to the top of the Mary statue that crowns the dome, is 197 feet. The total cost of the gilding in 1886 was $860.[27]

Another milestone of Thomas Walsh's administration was Notre Dame's first intercollegiate football game, which took place on November 23, 1887. The University of Michigan football team came to Notre Dame and defeated the school 8–0. At a dinner for both teams afterward, Fr. Walsh thanked the visitors and suggested a series of games between the two schools in the future. The sport rapidly grew in popularity at Notre Dame, although the team would not win its first game until December 6 the following year, when the school beat Harvard Prep School of Chicago by a score of 20–0.

Near the end of the school year in 1893, Fr. Walsh fell ill with a degenerative disease of the kidneys. There was little that doctors could do for him as the disease ravaged his body. It was thought that the waters of Bethsaida Springs in Wisconsin might offer him some relief—Walsh was on his way there when he met the young Matthew Walsh at St. Columbkille's in Chicago. Shortly after that visit, on July 17, 1893, in Wisconsin, Fr. Thomas Walsh died. He requested on his deathbed that Fr. Andrew Morrissey succeed him as president.

Less than a month later, on October 31, 1893, Fr. Sorin died quietly in his bed at the age of seventy-nine. He had been running the University of Notre Dame since he stumbled upon that frozen land in November of 1842. In a remarkable lifetime, he took three dilapidated cabins in a wilderness and turned them into a great Catholic university. No one but Sorin could have done it.

———

For most of its first fifty years, Notre Dame was the only Catholic boarding school between Cleveland and Chicago.[28] During that same period, railroads began connecting South Bend to those cities and others, transforming the onetime frontier backwater into the second

largest city in the state. In the background, the leadership of the
Catholic Church in America, increasingly dominated by the isola-
tionist Irish, was striving to create a self-sufficient Catholic society.
Catholic schools were the centerpiece of this program, and a
Catholic college education was its highest realization. Perhaps most
fortuitously, Notre Dame came of age during a period in which the
Catholic populations in large midwestern cities were exploding and
Catholic immigrants in the Midwest were working their way into the
middle class. The most successful were able to send their sons to college, and for reasons both geographic and religious, Notre Dame
became their school of choice.

The golden age of immigration coincided with American industrialization—the tireless immigrant workforce and America's
booming manufacturers were looking for each other. In Indiana,
companies like U. S. Steel in Gary and Studebaker in South Bend
lured immigrant workers with the promise of a new life and seventeen cents per hour. While immigrants were being drawn to the
industrial regions of Indiana, the state as a whole did not see the
level of immigration that other states experienced. In 1920, only
150,000 of Indiana's roughly 3 million residents were foreign born.[29]
At 5 percent of the population, this was far below the national figure
of 13 percent. The foreign-born population in Indiana actually
dropped throughout the golden age of immigration, from almost 9
percent in 1860 to about 7 percent in 1890. Indiana's midwestern
neighbors were much closer to the national average: the population
of Illinois was 19 percent foreign born in 1920; in Ohio it was 12 percent; and in Michigan it was 20 percent.[30]

Only southern states had smaller foreign-born populations than
Indiana in 1920. Those states, however, had huge African American
populations. Mississippi in 1920, for example, was 52 percent African
American; Georgia was 42 percent. In 1920, Indiana had even fewer
blacks than immigrants—around 3 percent of its population was

African American. By any measure, Indiana was one of the most homogeneous states in the country.[31]

In 1920, the county with the largest foreign-born population in Indiana, with 29 percent, was Lake County, home of Gary and U. S. Steel, the largest steel mill in the world. St. Joseph County, the home of South Bend, was second in foreign-born population. In 1920, 17,174 residents of St. Joseph County had been born in another country, out of a total population of 103,304—about 17 percent. Of that 17 percent, 76 percent lived in the city of South Bend.[32]

Where did they come from? The largest immigrant group in South Bend in 1920 came from Poland—South Bend had 4,229 Polish residents at that time.[33] Political turmoil was certainly a factor in the Polish exodus, but as with most immigrants, the main motives of those fleeing Poland were economic. After the Poles, the next-biggest group in South Bend was the Hungarians. The Hungarian inrush grew steadily in the decades prior to World War I: in 1900, 733 South Bend residents had been born in Hungary; by 1910, the number had ballooned to 3,829.[34] In 1920, the Hungarian population in South Bend was 3,229, and the Hungarians and the Poles together made up 57 percent of South Bend's foreign-born population. Like the Poles, the Hungarians had fled their country because of political turmoil and a lack of economic opportunities.

The third-largest immigrant group represented in South Bend in 1920 was the Germans, all 1,741 of them. In the two censuses taken in South Bend prior to 1920, the Germans were by far the biggest foreign-born group in the city. In fact, in 1910, 5,347 South Bend residents had been born in Germany, a number never matched by any other foreign-born group in the city. By 1920, even though the number of German immigrants had dropped below that of the Poles and the Hungarians, the German influence in South Bend was still strong. A German immigrant family—the Studebakers—founded South Bend's largest and most famous company.[35]

Despite the growing popularity of Notre Dame's nickname in 1920, the Irish were never a very well-represented group in the area. While Irish immigrants were pouring into New York, San Francisco, and especially Boston, only 155 South Bend residents in 1920 had been born in Ireland.[36] There were more Russians, Swedes, Belgians, and Italians than Irish in South Bend. Notre Dame's nickname was more a reflection of their students and their fan base than of the local population. It was also symbolic of the Protestant notion that the words *Irish* and *Catholic* were interchangeable.

Geography, the golden age of immigration, the militancy of the Irish church leaders, and a thousand other factors had aligned perfectly to transform Fr. Sorin's little school into a nationally respected university. Many of these same factors would transform a dormant southern fraternal order into a national political force whose secret members included governors, senators, and a president. Like Catholic higher education, the Ku Klux Klan would find its greatest success in the fertile soil of Indiana.

3

THE REINCARNATION
OF THE KU KLUX KLAN

I HAD TO WAIT UNTIL THE KIDS WERE IN BED TO START THE movie. They wouldn't stand for me monopolizing the TV with a three-hour silent epic, whatever its historical significance. I looked at the clock. If I started the movie immediately, I could be in bed by midnight. I peeled the plastic off the videocassette that I had purchased for $4.95 plus shipping. It was one of several Klan-related purchases I had made at Amazon.com that were putting me in an increasingly weird corner of their marketing database. Now when I log in, the Web site suggests that I might enjoy *The Turner Diaries* or *Mein Kampf*.

I was hoping the movie—D. W. Griffith's racist masterpiece, *The Birth of a Nation*—might answer a question I had been considering for a while: How did a dormant southern vigilante group give rise to the Klan of the 1900s, which was so successful in my home state of Indiana? The movie depicts the Reconstruction-era Klan of the 1860s, but the film came out in 1915, at the dawn of the new Klan. *The Birth of a Nation* was a direct inspiration for those men who were trying to resurrect the KKK, and it also became their greatest early recruiting tool. At a time when the motion-picture industry was still in its infancy, twenty-five million people saw the film in its first two years.[1] For a great many of them, it was the first movie they had ever seen. I was curious about its power: Would the same film inspire me if I were a Hoosier in 1915 seeing a movie for the first time? Would I be awed in some dark, smoky theater as I watched the story of the Invisible Empire unfold on the screen while an unseen orchestra performed the score? Would I want to shell out ten dollars for a white robe of my own? In my family room in Valparaiso, Indiana, almost ninety years later, I was trying to re-create that experience.

I read the box as the movie began. The cassette was produced by Madacy Entertainment of Quebec as part of their "Hollywood Classics" series, which included *Three Stooges* films and *Our Gang* comedies. *The Birth of a Nation* was filmed in Southern California, so the "Hollywood" part was reasonably accurate. Almost everything else on the box was wrong. It was not the first feature-length silent film; it wasn't even Griffith's first. It was not based on *The Leopard's Spots* by Thomas Dixon—not completely, anyway. It is more accurate to say that the film was based on Dixon's *The Clansman*.

Another inaccuracy grated on my nerves as the movie began—the score seemed off. One of *Birth of a Nation's* many innovations was a complete orchestral accompaniment. I had read several accounts and critiques of the film that described the music for specific scenes in detail. Strains of "Dixie" were supposed to accompany one of the early scenes. Griffith's idea of "jungle" music was supposed to accompany another. The music on my videocassette didn't seem to bear any relationship to the action on the screen. It appeared to be the musical equivalent of clip art.

I settled in to watch, trying to ignore my frustration. If not the first feature-length silent film in the world, it was without question the first feature-length silent film I had ever seen. Overall, I was surprised by how few words appeared on the screen. I had imagined that there would be lines of dialogue on the screen after every scene. For the most part, I was left to figure out on my own exactly what was being said, based on the actions and reactions of the characters. Acting in silent films, it seemed to me, was really an advanced form of pantomime.

I had studied the history of the movie and its famous creator before watching it. David Wark Griffith left his position as a movie director at Biograph Studios in New York in 1913. The motion-picture medium was still very new—*The Jazz Singer,* the first film to use sound, would not be made for fourteen years—but Griffith sensed that film had a potential that went far beyond the one-reel movies and nickelodeon reels he made at Biograph. Others believed in him; when he left Biograph for Southern California, almost all of the studio's stars left with him, including Lillian Gish, the most famous actress of her day. His stated aim: to make "the big picture."[2]

For his first effort, Griffith chose Thomas Dixon's novel *The Clansman* and purchased the movie rights for twenty-five hundred dollars from the author. The novel had been a best seller when it was published in 1905, and its dramatic wartime setting fit the bill for Griffith's "big picture." The book depicted wartime and postwar events from a distinctly Southern point of view, but the bias didn't bother Griffith. He himself was a southerner from Kentucky. His father had been a colonel in the Confederate army, a minor wartime legend known as "Roaring Jake." Griffith had grown up steeped in the myths, and the prejudices, of the old South.

These prejudices are most clearly seen in Griffith's depiction of blacks in the film. They fall into two categories in the movie: sinister predators and simpleminded buffoons. Blacks who appear in the back-ground, such as actors playing black Union soldiers, are in many cases portrayed by African Americans. The more significant black roles are played by white actors in blackface. It is Griffith's racist presentation of blacks that is perhaps most jarring to the modern viewer.

The story is at its heart a forbidden love story of the most basic kind. The Camerons live in the South, the Stonemans in the North. Before the war, the two families are friends. Austin Stoneman, the patriarch of the Northern family, is a Republican congressman, modeled on real-life abolitionist Thaddeus Stevens. The Southern patriarch is Dr. Cameron, a slaveholding plantation owner. When the Civil War begins, the two men and their families are pitted against each other. Naturally, though, true love transcends the conflict. Elsie Stoneman, played by Lillian Gish, and Ben Cameron, played by Henry Walthall, fall for each other. Most of the movie's plot revolves around these two star-crossed lovers trying to overcome history and unite.

It is the historical backdrop that makes the film more than a love story. In fact, the first seventy minutes are devoted to the Civil War, or to even earlier events in history. One of the first scenes depicts the slave trade in Africa, "the seeds of disunion," as it is described on screen. The Civil War scenes that follow have a kind of newsreel realism, with billowing smoke frequently obscuring the camera's view and crazed horses bucking their equally terrified riders. The soldiers charging into battle seem genuinely unaware that they are being filmed—and genuinely intent on killing their adversaries. While watching the movie, it occurred to me that in 1915, many people who had witnessed these events firsthand—the Petersburg Campaign and Sherman's March to the Sea—were still alive.

The scene in which Abraham Lincoln is killed, five days after the surrender at Appomattox, also offers startling realism. The predatory John Wilkes Booth lurks in the background while Lincoln's oafish bodyguard moves to get a better view of the play. After Booth shoots Lincoln, the president flops awkwardly forward, sparing viewers the drawn-out, melodramatic death that silent films are known for. When Booth jumps to the stage, it really looks like he breaks his leg.

In the movie, Lincoln's death is portrayed as tragic primarily because it allows the radical Republicans to take charge of the federal government and reverse Lincoln's policy of leniency toward the South. This is a somewhat accurate interpretation of historical events. What Griffith leaves out, though, is what happened in the South before this reversal. Even before the war ended, Lincoln had allowed the Southern states to reestablish their governments as long as at least 10 percent of the voting population took an oath of allegiance. By

1865, all the Confederate states but Texas had reestablished civil governments. Though newly elected, these state legislatures were populated by many of the same men who had voted to secede from the Union. They began to immediately pass laws, known as "Black Codes," that virtually re-enslaved blacks. The most notorious were Mississippi's. In Mississippi, blacks could not own or lease land. They could not own businesses. Unemployed blacks could be arrested as vagrants and hired out to any white man who paid their fine. Whites who dealt with blacks on equal terms could also be prosecuted. The outraged North watched as the South tried to undo the results of its hard-fought victory.

The North tried to implement a policy of ironhanded rule of the South with the Wade-Davis Bill, but Lincoln maintained his lenient policy by pocket vetoing the bill. As Griffith's film depicts, Lincoln's death brought the crisis to a head. Many in the North believed that Lincoln's murder was the result of a widespread Confederate conspiracy, adding to the belief that the defeated South needed to be ruled with an iron hand, not kid gloves. Perhaps most disastrously, Lincoln's assassination resulted in the ascendance of Andrew Johnson to the presidency. Johnson was a Southerner (from Tennessee) and a spectacularly unskilled politician. At first he seemed to be working with the radical Republicans, but soon he was enforcing a policy of restoration for the South that was as lenient as Lincoln's had been. The North and the radicals were fed up. In the November 1866 congressional elections, a short time into Johnson's term, a two-thirds radical Republican majority was elected into both houses. The radicals quickly repudiated Johnson's policy of restoration for the South and set their own policy in motion. History would call the new policy Radical Reconstruction.

The new policy began in March 1867 when the new Congress convened. Ten Southern states saw their governments abolished—every Confederate state except Tennessee, which had spared itself by ratifying the Fourteenth Amendment. The Republican Congress then divided the South into five military districts, arguing that by their actions the Southerners had committed "state suicide." Congress compelled the Southern states to hold new constitutional conventions that would include representatives from the state's entire population, black and white. The Southern states would write new state constitutions and elect new state governments. States would not be readmitted into the Union until they ratified the Fourteenth Amendment, which defined U.S. citizenship for the first time and forbade states from infringing on people's constitutional rights.

The Republicans soon found that the Fourteenth Amendment was not specific enough to protect the rights of recently freed slaves. In 1870, the Fifteenth Amendment was ratified, guaranteeing people's right to vote regardless of "race, color, or previous condition of servitude." Federal troops were sent to the South to enforce the Fifteenth Amendment during elections. In states with large black populations, the results of the elections were dramatic. In all, Reconstruction would see the election of two black senators and twenty-two black representatives. South Carolina, the setting for *The Birth of a Nation*, was the only Southern state to achieve a black majority in its House—75 of 124 representatives. Southerners saw the election of black officials as another punitive measure imposed on them by the North and pointed out the hypocrisy of the Northerners, who for all their moralizing didn't see fit to elect black officials in their own states.

It is this military regime that forms the backdrop of the second part of *The Birth of a Nation*. In the film, almost all of the Union troops who have been sent to the South to enforce blacks' right to vote are black. Their presence is portrayed as a slap in the face to the defeated South. Black soldiers are seen pushing white people off sidewalks and, most significantly, leering at the virginal white daughters of the South. Union government leaders are also frequently black in the movie.

As the second part of the movie begins, Austin Stoneman, the Northern congressman from Washington, D.C., sends his mulatto protégé, Silas Lynch, to South Carolina, where elections are about to take place. Thanks to the newly enfranchised black population, Lynch is elected lieutenant governor of the state. Austin Stoneman and his beautiful daughter, Elsie, also go to the Palmetto State to assist in the reconstruction of the South. They stay with their old friends the Camerons, whose oldest son, Benjamin, is in love with Elsie.

In Griffith's film, black soldiers rule the streets of the South. Black legislators drink whiskey and dance in the halls of Congress. Black laborers in the fields abandon their work. In Griffith's portrayal, all this uncontrolled black power leads inevitably to tragedy.

It is at this point in the movie—nearly two hours into it—that the Klan is born: the birth of a nation. To curtail the power of the blacks, Ben Cameron forms a vigilante band of Southern men to restore the old social order. Taking inspiration from a group of children playing in bedsheets, he has his men disguise themselves in white robes. They do not have to wait long for their first mission.

A black Union soldier, Gus, stalks the youngest Cameron daughter through the woods. He asks her to marry him—the black-ruled legislature has just legalized interracial marriage. She runs from Gus, but he chases her to the edge of a cliff. Rather than face Gus's depredations, she flings herself over the edge. I could almost hear the 1915 audiences gasp as her body hit the ground.

Ben Cameron rallies his band of robed men to capture Gus and avenge his sister's death. It was the most peculiar scene in the film for me, a scene that must be completely lost on modern viewers: a terrified Gus is on his knees, surrounded by robed Klansmen who are about to kill him—and the Klansmen are supposed to be the good guys. They dump Gus's body on Silas Lynch's porch with a piece of paper that reads "KKK" pinned to his chest.

In fact, the Klan did not begin its life as a vigilante group. It also did not originate in that Confederate powder keg of South Carolina, as depicted in *The Birth of a Nation*. The actual birth of the Klan was much less dramatic than the one portrayed by Dixon and Griffith. Six profoundly bored young men created the Klan in 1866 as a social club, a much-needed postwar diversion in the sleepy town of Pulaski, Tennessee. The charter members were James Crowe, Richard Reed, Calvin Jones, John Lester, Frank McCord, and John Kennedy. All had Scotch-Irish roots—Celtic rituals and terminology were key inspirations for the early Klan. All six men were in their twenties, and all were Confederate army veterans.[3]

At the time, Tennessee was not as uniformly Confederate as the Klan's six founders. It had been deeply divided throughout the war. Lincoln's election had precipitated the secession of the most belli-cose Southern states in late 1860 and early 1861: South Carolina being the first, followed by Mississippi, Florida, Alabama, Georgia, Louisiana, and Texas. Tennessee was one of several Southern states whose voters and legislatures initially refused to even call for a seces-sion convention. These states hoped to remain neutral or for a reso-lution to be reached between the two sides. Their hopes were dashed, however, on April 12, 1861, when the Confederate states opened fire on the federally held Fort Sumter. The Union surrendered the fort on April 14, 1861. With war now clearly under way, the governor of Tennessee, along with the leaders of most of the other Southern states that had initially rejected secession, reluctantly threw in his lot with the Confederacy. Tennessee's secession was ratified by a popular referendum on June 8, 1861, by a margin of more than two to one. Parts of Tennessee, especially in the mountainous east, remained strongly devoted to the Union. The Appalachian dirt farmers there saw slavery as a rich man's cause and were not at all eager to lay down their lives for it.

The six soldiers who would ultimately found the Klan fought just as enthusiastically for the Confederacy. Kennedy, a captain, was wounded in battle three times and imprisoned at Camp Douglas. James Crowe was wounded at the First Battle of Bull Run. All the rest served in the Tennessee Infantry. As it was for most Civil War soldiers, on both sides, their military service was marked by nearly constant combat of the bloodiest kind. When the war ended, the six men were no doubt relieved to be going home in one piece. Their relief was tempered, however, not only by the sting of defeat but by a sudden and severe state of boredom.

Their hometown of Pulaski had never been an exciting place to live—residents called it the "dimple of the universe."[4] For these six veterans, though, the boredom was unbearable after the violence and chaos of Manassas and Murfreesboro.

So, late in the spring of 1866, the six of them gathered in the law offices of Calvin Jones's father and decided to form a club. Three men were tasked with naming the group.

They settled on the Greek word *kuklos*—meaning "circle" or "cycle." They then bastardized *kuklos* into "Ku Klux." "Klan" was added because it was phonetically pleasing and as an homage to the founders' Scottish roots. The resulting name was memorable, evocative, and mysterious—its role in the Klan's growth and popularity throughout history should not be underestimated.

In the beginning, the club's activities were no more sinister than fraternity-style hijinks. James Crowe stated that the group's charter was "to have fun, make mischief, and play pranks on the public."[5] The six took to riding horses through the dusty roads of Pulaski draped in white bedsheets, amusing themselves and the similarly bored local citizens. They decorated their robes with occult symbols like stars, moons, and crosses to enhance their magical image. The appearance of the masked riders soon became an anticipated thrill at Pulaski barbecues and picnics.

The early Klan's overall lack of solemnity can be seen in its oft-described initiation ritual. Prospective members would be plucked off the street by robed horsemen, blindfolded, and taken to a ruined mansion in the countryside outside Pulaski. The initiate would have a "crown"—a hat with donkey ears on it—placed on his head. After everyone present recited several poems and chants, the new member would be placed in front of a mirror, and the blindfold would be removed. He would see that he had made an ass of himself, to the amusement of all.[6]

Perhaps inevitably, the newly formed Ku Klux Klan began to turn its mischievous eye toward the freed slaves in the area. Pulaski—located near the Tennessee-Alabama border in the middle of the state—and its surrounding areas had been a large slaveholding region before the war, and rabidly Confederate during. Fully half of Pulaski's residents in 1866 were recently freed slaves.[7] For decades, whites across the South had terrified themselves with rumors and predictions of bloody slave rebellions. The sudden freedom of the slaves made the realization of this collective nightmare seem imminent. In May of 1866, nearby Memphis was rocked by a race riot that resulted in the deaths of forty-six blacks and two whites. The violence confirmed the popular belief of whites in the South that peaceful coexistence with blacks was impossible.

The Klan began targeting local blacks, at first by playing mean-spirited pranks on them. In one well-known stunt often performed by the early Klan, which was rapidly expanding beyond the Pulaski area, a robed, masked horseman would appear at the door of a black farmhouse and demand a drink of water. Using a hidden tube and wineskin, the Klansman would consume an impossible amount of water, always demanding more. He would then proclaim that he had not had a drink since he died at Shiloh, the Civil War battle in southern Tennessee in which more than twenty-three thousand men were killed or wounded. This persona, the avenging ghost of the Confederate dead, would become a central part of the Klan's identity.

The elaborate pranks developed quickly into active terrorizing of the area's blacks. The Klan began targeting teachers at black schools and workers of the federal Freedmen's Bureau, the government agency that was charged with helping blacks adjust to a life after slavery. Whites in the South were determined to keep blacks "in their place," no matter what the outcome of the war had been and no matter what the federal government mandated. The Klan thrived in the South because whites there believed that only it could save them from the tyranny of the vengeful North and its black pawns.

In this respect, Griffith's depiction of Southern attitudes in *The Birth of a Nation* is entirely accurate. After Gus is killed, the mulatto lieutenant governor Silas Lynch arrests Dr. Cameron. When Elsie Stoneman goes to plead for help, Lynch, who has always lusted after her, accosts her with a marriage proposal. Ben Cameron rallies the Klan troops to ride to her rescue. This time, to alert the Klansmen of the area that their help is needed, he uses a fiery cross as his signal. The cross is tiny compared to the ones now popularly associated with the Klan. Cameron designates a Klan horseman to alert the other Klansmen; the horseman carries the cross, made of two burning twigs, in his free hand as he rides though the countryside.

The burning cross had never been associated with the KKK prior to Thomas Dixon's novel. There is no historical record of the Klan of the Reconstruction era ever using anything like it. Dixon included the cross in his novel as a tribute to his Scottish heritage. Scots used fiery crosses as a rallying signal on their way to battle. In Dixon's *The Clansman*, Ben Cameron explains, "In olden times when the Chieftain of our people summoned the clan on an errand of life and death, the fiery cross, extinguished in sacrificial blood, was sent by swift courier from village to village."[8]

In the end, the Klan rescues Elsie. Final scenes of legions of Klansmen on horseback confirm that the Klan has restored order and justice to the South.

The Birth of a Nation cost Griffith $110,000 to make, an unheard of sum for the day.[9] The film's final length was just as absurd: twelve reels. Two years earlier, Griffith had completed the first American four-reel film, *Judith of Bethulia*. The final version of *Birth of a Nation* ran for more than three hours. It premiered on February 8, 1915, at Clune's Auditorium in Los Angeles, with the title *The Clansman*.

Bill Clune had invested fifteen thousand dollars in the film in exchange for its premiere.

After the premiere, Griffith changed the film's name to *The Birth of a Nation* at the suggestion of author Thomas Dixon. The film generated both praise and controversy. It featured a number of cinematic innovations; a full orchestral accompaniment, night photography, a brief color sequence, natural backdrops, tracking shots, and total screen close-ups were all used for the first time in Griffith's film. When evaluating Griffith's technical achievements, one must bear in mind his limited toolbox. He filmed the entire epic with one camera and two lenses over the course of one summer.[10]

Reviewers and audiences were overwhelmingly awed by Griffith's achievement, but black leaders did not see a technical masterpiece in the film—they saw an attempt to resurrect old hatreds and reopen only recently healed wounds. The young National Association for the Advancement of Colored People (NAACP), represented by W. E. B. Du Bois, swung into action to fight the film. Black leaders wrote editorials condemning the film. Other opponents began to disrupt showings in larger cities. Their activism eventually resulted in the film being banned in eight states.

To counter the protests, Griffith and Dixon arranged for the movie to be the first film ever screened at the White House. They had a friend in President Woodrow Wilson—he had attended Johns Hopkins with Dixon. He was also a racist southerner from Virginia who had ordered that the federal workforce be segregated. Wilson watched the film with his family and loved it. It was, he said famously, "like writing history with lightning."[11] With the presidential endorsement, the film became even more popular and even harder for opponents of racism to fight in the court of public opinion.

The NAACP won some minor victories. President Wilson eventually issued a weak disavowal of the film.[12] On the whole, though, the public saw *The Birth of a Nation* as a work of unmitigated genius. Most people, like the president, took it for granted that the movie depicted Reconstruction accurately. The film was even shown to general acclaim in Washington Hall at the University of Notre Dame.[13]

The film achieved national distribution in its first year and was scheduled to premiere in Atlanta on December 6, 1915. It was nervously anticipated by a defrocked minister named Colonel William Simmons. Simmons had resurrected the Ku Klux Klan on Thanksgiving Day 1915, when he and fifteen charter members burned a cross atop Stone Mountain, just outside the city. His goal was to create and be the head of "the world's greatest secret, social, patriotic, fraternal beneficiary order."[14] The Atlanta premiere of *The Birth of a Nation* was a critical part of his plan.

Since being suspended by the Methodist Bishops' Conference in 1912 for "inefficiency," Simmons had become a serial joiner of the fraternal organizations and societies that were growing in popularity across the country.[15] He was a Mason, a Knight of Pythias, a Woodman of the World, and an Odd Fellow, in more ways than one. He soon became a successful recruiter for the clubs. In 1914, he was named district manager for the Woodmen of the World, one of dozens of indistinguishable groups that existed mainly to collect dues and sell uniforms, manuals, and insurance to their members.

Simmons's success as a district manager for the Woodmen—he was making ten thousand dollars a year—convinced him that he should form a fraternal organization of his own.[16] He said later that a mystical vision of ghost riders in the sky inspired him to model his new group on the Ku Klux Klan of the Reconstruction era. In reality, the success of Griffith's film was just as big a factor. Simmons embraced the film's language of white supremacy and "pure Americanism" because his keen business sense told him that it would sell the most memberships. This is not to say that Simmons was not a bigot; his later writings and speeches show that he was. If Simmons had a white supremacist agenda, though, it was secondary to his business goals. Linking his new group's philosophy to the most successful motion picture in history was simply a good marketing decision.

After his Thanksgiving Day cross burning on Stone Mountain, Simmons began running ads for his new group in Atlanta newspapers alongside ads for the movie. On the day of the premiere, Simmons had his charter members dress in bedsheets and gallop on horseback past the lines of moviegoers waiting in front of the Atlanta theater. Simmons's goal was to attract new members, and the gimmick worked. He soon initiated ninety-two new members into his group.[17]

Those initiates, like those of the Reconstruction-era Klan, went through an elaborately hokey initiation ritual. The ritual that Simmons designed, however, contained explicit references to race, religion, and ethnicity. "Are you a native-born, white, gentile American citizen?" new members were asked during the ceremony. "Do you believe in and will you faithfully strive for the eternal maintenance of white supremacy?"[18]

Simmons had national ambitions for his group, and he sensed that the rising tide of nativism in the country might carry him further than the primarily southern battle cry of white supremacy. "Do you believe in the tenets of the Christian religion?" was one of the "qualifying interrogatories." Another was "Do you esteem the United States of America and its institutions above any other government—civil, political, or ecclesiastical—in the whole world?" According to the revived Klan's new code, "only native-born American citizens who believe in the tenets of the Christian religion and owe no allegiance of any degree or nature to any foreign government, nation, political institution, sect, people, or person are eligible."[19] The foreign person referred to was, of course, the pope; the foreign government, the Vatican. Simmons had codified American anti-Catholicism.

Simmons was a superior salesman but a poor manager. The Klan teetered on the edge of bankruptcy even as its membership swelled across the South, as Simmons spent freely and made poor investments with the group's profits. *The Birth of a Nation* continued to be his best recruiting tool. Many likely joined the Klan because of the movie, or because they liked the robes, or because of the clever titles, such as Klaliff, Klexter, and Klokard. If that had been the sum total of the Klan's appeal, though, it would have never been anything more than another obscure fraternal order, another Woodmen of the World. Simmons's group would ascend to unforeseen heights because of that marketing decision he had made in 1915, to capitalize on the anxiety disguised as patriotism that he had sensed growing steadily across the country.

Events too—such as World War I and the passing of the National Prohibition Act in October 1919—would contribute to the Klan's rise by reinforcing nativist sentiment in America. The Klan began promoting itself as the enforcer of Prohibition, a law that was widely viewed as a strike against hard-drinking immigrants.

The Klan also exploited the labor unrest that was becoming increasingly violent in the early twentieth century. More than three thousand strikes took place in the United States in 1919 alone. Opponents of organized labor like the Klan accused strikers of being the pawns of Communists and foreign agitators. In January 1920, the Justice Department, led by Attorney General A. Mitchell Palmer and J. Edgar Hoover, arrested more than four thousand suspected Communists in twenty-three states, confirming the Klan's claims about the magnitude of the "Red Menace." Later that year, twelve people were killed during a coal miners' strike in West Virginia, in what came to be know as the Matewan Massacre. It was impossible not to notice that similar labor unrest had led to the Bolshevik revolution in 1917 and blood in the streets of Europe. The Klan simultaneously took advantage of people's fear and validated it. It was a fear not just of labor strife but of sinister foreign conspirators. In the eyes of many, only the Ku Klux Klan promised an appropriately militant response.

Social changes as well drove men into the arms of the Klan, with its promise to defend old-fashioned Protestant values. To many Americans, the changes brought by technology and industrialization were changes for the worse. Religious beliefs were being challenged in schools with the teaching of evolution, sparking a battle that would come to a head with the Scopes trial in 1925. In the eyes of Klansmen and other Protestant Americans, the torrent of Catholic and Jewish immigrants into the country was eroding the nation's fundamental Protestantism, as the immigrants brought with them not only their religions but also their own languages and cultures.

As the Klan grew, Simmons remained ingeniously vague in his description of the organization's mission. He certainly did not abandon the original Klan's mission of keeping blacks "in their place." In the South, this remained a central part of the group's appeal. Outside of the South, though, Simmons told prospective members that the United States of America was under attack, and the attackers—Italian priests, Bolsheviks, Jews, the hard-drinking Irish—were not real Americans. These invaders, he told the American public, were determined to destroy the American way of life. It was a claim that many ordinary people believed. Simmons sold them the Klan by promising to defend them.

In 1920, Simmons made another crucial decision that set the Klan on a course to becoming a national power: he hired a marketing firm. The group he hired had a grandiose name—the Southern Publicity Association—but in reality, it consisted of just two people, Edward Clarke and Elizabeth Tyler. The deal they signed with Simmons allowed their firm to keep 80 percent of all the initiation fees collected from new Klansmen in return for developing and implementing a modern marketing strategy for the group.

The firm took immediate steps to professionalize the Klan's sales force. Their goal was to put an army of skilled men into the field with the ability to make a good living by selling Klan memberships. The "Kleagles," as they were called, kept four dollars from every ten-dollar membership they sold. In return, Clarke and Tyler required weekly reports, sales forecasts, and marketing plans from their salesmen. Most of all, they demanded results—and those results were impressive.

Clarke and Tyler's army of Kleagles grew the Klan membership from three thousand in 1920 to more than one hundred thousand by the end of 1921.[20] The professional marketers saw the Midwest as the area with the greatest potential for growth, and while the Klan was making minor inroads there, Clarke and Tyler felt it needed a more focused effort. They sent Joe Huffington, one of their best Kleagles, to Evansville, Indiana, to find a good salesman—his trip would turn out to be wildly successful.

———

D. W. Griffith's *Birth of a Nation* amazed audiences across America and helped spark the revival of the Ku Klux Klan, but my attempt at re-creating what it must have felt like to watch the film as a Hoosier in 1915 had failed. I could not re-create that feeling in my suburban family room, some ninety years later. I had seen too many movies to be struck just by the spectacle of moving pictures on a screen. My memory was too full of images and stories about the Klan to ever see them as heroes. The racist portrayals of blacks in the film were too shocking for me to simply accept as part of a story line.

The film was beloved in its day, and it had a profound effect on those who saw it. Some denounced it for its blatant racism, while most—including a great many Hoosiers—found something frightening and true in it. They flocked to the Klan, giving Indiana the largest Klan membership in the country. I knew that *The Birth of a Nation*—one of the Klan's most successful recruiting tools—had worked better in Indiana than anywhere else. But why it had worked so well here was something I had yet to discover.

It was midnight when the movie ended. I looked out my window at the flat, frozen Indiana plain as the movie noisily rewound in my old VCR. Snow had fallen during the movie—it appeared blue in the moonlight and made our new neighborhood closely resemble the farmland that it had recently been. I headed off to bed, pondering the Klan, Indiana, and my lingering questions.

4

NOTRE DAME AND THE INDIANA KLAN

Y OU MIGHT BE WALKING ALONG AMONG THE TENTS SOME
morning," the old major postulated, "and glancing in, you might
see a number of soldiers squatting down and playing cards. What
would you do?"[1]

Matthew Walsh wrote the question down neatly in his notes, even
though it irked him; the major had a way of dwelling on those sins
that were of most concern to his Protestant comrades-in-arms. It was
February 1918, and Walsh was at the Army Chaplains' School in
Fort Monroe, Virginia. His class included seventy-one other clergymen, both Catholic and Protestant. For the most part, Walsh had
been surprised at how well they all got along. He had been raised
to believe that Protestant clergy spent their days railing against
Catholics. In truth, they seemed just as friendly, nervous, and be-
fuddled by the army as the priests. Still, it irritated Walsh that the
school's minimal religious curriculum was distinctly Protestant; it
was one of the episodes that he recalled when recounting his war
years with historian Arthur Hope.

"I'd break up the game by entering the tent and talking about their
mothers," volunteered one eager Lutheran minister. "The thought
of mother generally brings them around."

"Quite effective, yes," said the major. "What would you do,
Chaplain Brown?"

Chaplain Brown, a Southern Baptist from Atlanta, paused. "I'd go in and sit quietly for a moment, and then I'd start singing. The singing might take their minds away from the gambling," he said.

"Very good, very good," said the major. "How about you, Fr. Lenan?" he asked the Irish priest sitting next to Walsh. "What would you do if you found soldiers playing cards?" Walsh liked Lenan. A priest from Boston, he was the kind of brash Irish fellow whom Walsh often got along with.

Lenan stroked his chin and furrowed his brow in exaggerated concentration. Finally, he said, "I'd ask them to deal me in."

All of the chaplain students, Protestant and Catholic alike, roared with laughter. The major returned to his notes in a huff and moved on to the next morally perilous situation that the chaplains might encounter.

The army presumed that the clergymen at Chaplains' School were sufficiently educated in spiritual matters, so they spent their days learning the peculiarities of military life. Walsh and the others took classes in military drill, military law, army regulations, and insignia of rank. There was a one-hour class every day on "equitation and care of the horse," a class that the citified Walsh dreaded more than any other. Time was also set aside for "actual participation in social entertainments" every Thursday, from 8:00 PM to 10:30 PM.[2]

What religious instruction the Chaplains' School did provide strongly emphasized the chaplain's duty to minister to all soldiers, regardless of denomination. The official army training manual for chaplains, *The Chaplain: His Place and Duties*, informed Walsh and the others that "it is usual to conduct at least two services for the command each Sunday, no matter what the chaplain's denominational allegiances may be."[3] The chaplain should hold services in his own faith first, the manual went on to say, and then offer a general service for everyone later in the day.

The instruction that Walsh received from the Catholic hierarchy was less ecumenical. Walsh carried with him *Practical Hints for Catholic*

Chaplains, published by the Catholic Ordinariate of New York City. In addition to offering truisms like "The chaplain must be tactful and watchful" and "Be punctual in all things," the booklet warned chaplains to avoid the interdenominational embrace that the army seemed to be encouraging. The book told them of the inevitable invitation they would receive to deliver services alongside a Protestant chaplain and explained that this was unacceptable: "Interdenominational service, i.e., where two or three ministers of gospel officiate at the same service together, is forbidden to Catholic chaplains and should be tactfully but absolutely avoided."[4]

Walsh knew the rules. He also knew that he would without a doubt have Protestant men in his unit; he would not be like Fr. Corby standing in front of the Irish Brigade in 1863. Walsh's religious training had in some ways been an ideal preparation for the regimentation of army life, but it had not taught him to be particularly flexible, especially when it came to other religions. He would have to find a way to minister to all the soldiers he encountered. Walsh thought that maybe this was his real mission at Fort Monroe. He resolved to be respectful of all religions, and he hoped that his Protestant classmates would do the same. After the war, they could all go back to the comfort of rigid interpretations and inflexible dictums.

After six weeks of instruction, the army declared the chaplains ready for wartime service. Walsh received orders to report to the 135th Machine Gun Battalion.[5]

En route to Europe on an ancient steamship, his orders changed— he would report instead to the Thirtieth Infantry of the Third Division. The numbers meant nothing to Walsh; one unit was as good as another. During the journey, Walsh thought that the soldiers on the ship might want him to hear their confessions, or at least listen to their fears about the war. He imagined that men who had fallen away from the church might come to him, wanting to experience the sacraments once more before going into combat. He was disappointed. The mood on the boat was lighthearted, not reflective.

The most prevalent fear seemed to be that the fighting would end before they arrived.

Once in France, Walsh learned that his new unit was nowhere to be found. He spent a day asking around, but the scene was hectic, and everyone he spoke to was either too busy to help or as lost as he was. Following a rumor about the whereabouts of the Thirtieth, he ventured into the countryside, walking and occasionally hitching a ride with another unit. He began composing letters in his mind for his mother and Fr. Cavanaugh about all the quaint towns and picturesque landscapes he passed through. Every time he encountered American troops, he asked them if they knew where he might find the Thirtieth Infantry. They would ask around, trade reports from the front, and invariably come up with nothing. Walsh would continue his search in the next village down the road.

Walsh could easily distinguish between those troops who had been to the front and those who were new, like him. In addition to having dirtier uniforms, the veteran troops were quieter in their ranks, less apt to talk and joke. In one French town, a British officer remarked to Walsh that the Yanks had a habit of charging fearlessly en masse out of their trenches, only to be mowed down in rows. The Europeans, he explained, had learned to be considerably less valiant during four years of trench warfare.

Just when Walsh was beginning to think that he might spend the entire war sightseeing across France without ever joining his unit, he found his group marching through Château-Thierry, a rural French town along the Marne River, on July 15, 1918. Ecstatic at his luck, Walsh ran down the road to catch up with them, tightening the straps on his pack as he went. He fell in, out of breath. He asked the soldier next to him where they had been.

"We were in the Vosges section," he told Walsh. "Near Switzerland. Beautiful, quiet—in the mountains."

"Where are we going now?" Walsh asked him.

"I think we're there," said the private. "Isn't that the goddamn Marne?" he asked, pointing at the river.

Walsh realized that the straps of his pack were hiding his chaplain's insignia. "Yes . . . yes, I think it is," he said.

"The goddamn Marne," the private repeated.

Crossing the Marne had been a goal for the Germans since the war began. The Marne is a river in northern France that runs east to west into Paris. For most of the war, the opposing armies faced each other along a line that roughly followed the river. The First Battle of the Marne had been fought before the arrival of the Americans, in 1914. The French soldiers, some of whom had arrived at the battle in Parisian taxicabs, had barely turned back a bloody German attack. For most of the war, the armies had been lining themselves up for a rematch along the river. The private evidently didn't relish the thought of taking part.

Walsh was about to ask where he might find the unit's commanding officer when the first shell hit. There was a brief screech followed by an incomprehensibly loud explosion. Walsh watched the unit's formation dissolve as the men sprinted for cover. Not everyone made it. The men hit directly by the shell were transformed from living, marching soldiers into entrails dangling from tree branches. Other men were pierced by the shrapnel that chased them in all directions. Walsh managed to follow a small group into a dugout. Just as they entered, another shell hit, precisely where he had been standing. Walsh heard shrapnel whizzing by his head as he threw himself onto the ground.

The next shells came in rapid succession as the German artillerymen homed in on their position. Walsh heard shells slamming into the road outside the dugout. If one landed on the dugout, the thin roof would offer no protection.

The shelling lasted for three days. That first day, Walsh didn't sleep and barely looked out of the dugout. Day and night blended together. He couldn't learn the names of the other men because the noise was too loud, and nobody felt like talking anyway. He noticed that one of the men had a nasty gash in his leg—from shrapnel, Walsh assumed. The soldier did not seem overly concerned about it. On the second day, a wide-eyed messenger appeared at the entrance of their dugout and told them to move farther up the river, as the Germans were crossing just south of their position. It was a terrifying journey for Walsh. They ran up the road to the next trench and jumped in. The men in the trench were firing their rifles and their machine gun with a feverish intensity. Walsh could see German troops on the other side of the Marne.

The gas came on the third day. The shells carrying it burst over their heads and enveloped them in a greenish haze. Walsh learned from the others that the gas was actually a liquid that turned into a fine mist when the shells that carried it exploded. One tiny drop on the skin raised a painful wet blister. If you breathed it in, you would become incapacitated, and you might even die. Walsh received a crash course in how to wear a gas mask. Sometimes, when the gas was extremely heavy, he could smell it even through the rubber seal on the mask. The Germans were inching closer to them now, and the soldiers in Walsh's trench taught him how to feed the ammunition into their machine gun. He was grateful to be able to do something useful.

They received word that the Germans had crossed the Marne north of their position as well. Walsh pictured hordes of Germans on either side of them, pouring across the Marne with their pointy helmets and handlebar mustaches. He was certain that he would die. He began to wonder abstractly if it would be better to be hit directly by an air bomb or be killed by a piece of flying shrapnel.

The men in Walsh's trench refused to budge. So did the rest of Walsh's division. After bombarding the Allied forces for a week along the Marne, the Germans gave up. They had thrown fifty-two divisions at the legendary river in one last attempt to break through before the Americans got their footing in Europe. North and south of Walsh's unit, the Germans had actually crossed the Marne, but the steadfast defense of the Americans in the middle made it impossible for them to gain a foothold on the opposite shore.

After the failed German assault, the Allied forces, led by French general Ferdinand Foch, pushed the enemy back more than four miles during a plodding monthlong counterattack. The battle earned Foch a promotion and the Third Division a nickname that it would take into World War II and Korea: "the Rock of the Marne."

The Germans retreated, and the Allies gained the initiative for good. The battle would become known as the Second Battle of the Marne.

Two weeks after the battle, Walsh finally found the time to write home. He was sitting on top of his dugout, in the same clothes he had been wearing since joining the unit, as a small Dutch plane circled over him. Despite the exhaustion and anxiety that he still felt, he forced himself to describe for his mother the charming scenery, dandy officers, and a unit that was 80 percent Catholic. It was more or less a replica of the letter he had composed in his head before the shelling began. He wrote a more graphic letter to Fr. Cavanaugh but asked him to keep the details about combat to himself. The last two weeks, he told Fr. Cavanaugh, had "knocked all the joy out of life and made me more serious than I have been in a long while."[6]

Walsh's unit remained in the thick of things. One evening, the unit's captain was notified that all of his intelligence officers had been killed. As was customary, he asked the unit's college graduates to step forward and become replacements. None stepped forward—all of the unit's college graduates were dead.[7]

The situation puzzled Walsh, because he knew that Dan McGlynn, one of the privates in their unit, was a Notre Dame man. That evening, Walsh told the captain privately that McGlynn was an athletic young man from a good family in East St. Louis and would make a fine intelligence officer.

Later that night, McGlynn found Walsh. He explained that he couldn't be an intelligence officer because he didn't meet the requirements—he hadn't yet received his degree from Notre Dame. He had been due to graduate at the end of the 1917–18 school year.

Walsh laughed and laid his hand on McGlynn's shoulder. "By virtue of the power vested in me as vice president of the university," he said, "I confer on you the degree of bachelor of laws." McGlynn walked away happy, promoted to college graduate and intelligence officer in the same day, in the trenches of France.

Shortly after McGlynn's promotion, Walsh was transferred to Paris. There were ten military hospitals in the city, all overflowing with wounded and dying men and desperately in need of chaplains. Although the transfer took him away from the front, Walsh's wartime adventures were not over. He reported to Paris on August 25, 1918.

Walsh soon discovered that it would be impossible for him to attend to even the barest spiritual needs of the American Catholics in all ten hospitals. Distressed, he estimated that every day, thirty to thirty-five American Catholic soldiers in the city died without receiving last rites. Even while struggling with this burden, Walsh voluntarily expanded his responsibilities.

There were fourteen hundred American soldiers serving time in a Paris military prison—which they had nicknamed "the Bastille"—for a range of wartime offenses, including larceny, desertion, and cowardice. The inmates of the Bastille had no chaplain, so Walsh took on the job.

Approaching the prison gate for the first time, Walsh could see that the Marines standing guard outside were nervous. As he got closer, he could hear a roar coming from inside the prison. It was hollow and mindless—the sound of a mob. Years later, Walsh would recount the story in detail to his friend Arthur Hope.[8]

The guards at the front gate quickly explained the situation to Walsh. Two brothers had attempted to go over the wall. One of the brothers had fallen during the escape attempt and was now lying dead inside the prison yard. The highly agitated prisoners were massing around the body. The guards, armed only with clubs, feared that they were on the brink of a full-blown revolt. After trying to dissuade Walsh from entering, they opened the gate and let him in.

An officer grabbed Walsh as he stepped inside. "I've got to see you!" he said, panicked. "I'm the only one here with a gun! What can I do if those fellows break out?" Walsh realized that the man was the commander of the prison.

"I'm your new chaplain," Walsh replied, unable to think of anything better to say. This announcement seemed to make the warden even more anxious.

"I was in the seminary once!" he said, grabbing Walsh's arms. He stepped closer to the priest. "Will you hear my confession?"

Before Walsh could respond, the man was on his knees, confessing his numerous sins. Walsh tried to listen, but he could see the other guards observing them, visibly abandoning hope as they watched their commander lose his mind. The mob's yell from the unseen prison yard was increasing in volume and pitch. It was a sound Walsh recognized from the battlefield, the sound of men rallying before a charge.

A prisoner in the yard suddenly shouted, "Everybody out!" Walsh left the muttering officer to go to the wall with the other guards. He stood next to a burly sergeant who had been watching his interaction with the commander. The sergeant turned to Walsh and said, "Come with me." The other guards standing near them seemed to be busy plotting their escape. Walsh nodded, eager to stay close to the only man present who appeared to know what he was doing. They stepped out onto a mezzanine in plain view of the prisoners. There were hundreds of them, all in dirty army uniforms. Seen from above, the mob looked like one huge living organism vibrating with nervous energy. The nucleus was the body, lifeless and twisted at unnatural angles. The mob was in constant motion but maintained a respectful halo of space around the corpse.

"Atten-hut!" the sergeant yelled. In a great testament to the efficacy of military training, a fair number of the rioting prisoners came to attention and faced the sergeant and the priest.

"This here is a Catholic priest!" shouted the sergeant. "All you fellows who are Catholic, right face!" Again, a large number of the men obeyed the order. "Now, all you Catholics who want to go to confession, come up these stairs, one by one." Another sergeant ran down the steps and unlocked the gate at the bottom of the stairs. At first, no one moved. Walsh wondered how long he and the prisoners would stare at each other before the riot began anew. Then one man broke away from the group. He ran toward the steps, where he awaited permission to see the priest. Before he had ascended the steps, several dozen more men had broken away from the group and were lined up neatly at the gate.

The sergeant took Walsh to a cell that was filled with files and a dirty desk. He showed Walsh to the desk chair and then took his place at the door. Before Walsh had even sat down in the chair, the first prisoner was admitted.

The penitent was small and shockingly young. His uniform was dirty and torn; Walsh couldn't read the name on the chest of it. As the priest tried to comprehend exactly what was happening, the prisoner reverted to tradition. He knelt at Walsh's feet. "Bless me, Father," he said in a voice hoarse from yelling, "for I have sinned."

About three hundred other prisoners followed. Each had detailed, and at times gut-wrenching, sins to confess. There were the sins of the battlefield, the killings with guns, bayonets, and bare hands. There were the depredations away from the front, the stealing and looting. There were the sins of the flesh, in brothels, bars, and even Parisian doorways. It took Walsh until late in the evening to hear them all, but by the time the last man had confessed, the prison yard was empty and the danger of a riot had passed.

Walsh continued his ministry in the Parisian hospitals as the war lurched to a close. A month after Walsh was transferred, on September 26, 1918, the men of Walsh's old division, the Third, participated in an offensive in the Argonne Forest, in eastern France, along the Meuse River. The American general John "Black Jack" Pershing held the Third in reserve during the initial assault—they were considered veteran troops after just seven months in Europe, and Pershing wanted his more battle-hardened men to take over after the initial charge.

The assault through the fallen trees and brush of the Argonne went slower than expected. On October 4, Walsh's former division was called into action. The American soldiers steadily pushed the Germans back. By October 10, the Argonne was cleared. While the other divisions rested, the Third Division was sent into the hills to ferret out whatever German resistance remained.

For three dangerous weeks, the Third Division fought the Germans, one hill at a time. The last of them surrendered to the Third on November 1, 1918.

The German high command saw what the Americans could do. Ten days after the Germans surrendered to the Third Division in the Argonne, the entire German army surrendered. The war was over.

Walsh remained in France after the armistice, ministering to the American Catholic soldiers who still filled the Paris hospitals. On March 12, 1919, he received his travel orders to return home. On April 16, an army doctor gave him a certificate declaring that he was "free from any contagious or venereal disease, or vermin."[9] With that unglamorous finale, he was allowed to board the SS *Buford* and return home.

After some final administrative odds and ends were taken care of, Matthew Walsh was honorably discharged from the army on May 6, 1919, at Camp Jackson, South Carolina. On the back of his discharge certificate, where he was to list his battles, skirmishes, and engagements, Walsh wrote only "Marne." A quartermaster stamped the certificate to confirm that Walsh had been paid his sixty-dollar bonus.[10]

Walsh's time in Europe, like America's, was short but transforming. The United States had entered the war late, but their presence broke a long stalemate and helped turn the tide against the Germans. After only nineteen months at war, the United States was an unqualified world power. As for Walsh, prior to the war he had spent most of his life in the care of the Congregation of Holy Cross. From that sheltered existence, he had gone into the heart of the most vicious combat the world had ever seen. In all, 451 soldiers of the Third Division earned the Distinguished Service Cross—including Fr. Matthew Walsh.[11]

The United States had mobilized a total of 4,355,000 men for the war. Of that number, 234,000 were wounded, 4,526 were missing, and 126,000 were killed—a number that included 46 men from the University of Notre Dame.[12]

———

D. C. Stephenson's visions of battlefield glory, in contrast, went unfulfilled. When the war ended, he was given his honorable discharge on February 4, 1919, at peaceful Camp Devens, Massachusetts.[13]

He returned to Iowa and picked up a job selling typesetting equipment to newspapers across the Midwest. It was a natural fit for him, with his newspaper experience and innate sales talent, which his time as an army recruiter had honed. He had loved life on the road with the Socialists before the war, and he took to his new traveling career with gusto.

He soon discovered that life was even better than it had been with the Socialists. Stephenson could now eat at the best restaurants and wear the flashy suits he thought he deserved. On a sales call in Akron, Ohio, Stephenson met a local beauty named Violet Carroll. He pursued her with professional doggedness, bombarding her with flowers, letters, and urgent timetables. He had an opportunity in Indiana, he told her, but he needed to move quickly—would she come with him or not? He wouldn't be denied. After a whirlwind courtship, they married on January 7, 1920. Immediately after, they boarded a train to Evansville, Indiana.

Located in the southern part of the state along the Ohio River, the city's most important natural resource, Evansville was a river town filled with hustling salesmen like Stephenson, each of them determined to get his own piece of the postwar boom. With three daily newspapers, the city was a strong potential market for a man in Stephenson's business. He and Violet moved into the Vendome, a luxurious new downtown hotel owned by the nephew of the mayor, Benjamin Bosse.

Some salesmen find success by disguising the fact that they are salesmen, posing as consultants or experts and sneaking the sale in along with their advice. Stephenson was of the opposite school. He wore expensive suits and glistening shoes, had carefully combed hair, and was immediately recognizable as a salesman from across the room. While he did have solid credentials as a newspaperman, his real expertise was in smooth talking, glad-handing, and backslapping. The newspaper owners bought equipment from Stephenson because they believed what he said and they liked being around him. He became an unofficial leader of the sales community in Evansville—men gathered around him to talk about Napoleon, politics, and the war. "Major" Stephenson's war stories were all lies, a common enough offense in the lounge of the Vendome.

Stephenson's reputation as a skilled salesman eventually earned him a job selling stock for a local coal brokerage firm. The hills just north of Evansville were home to a number of coal mines, and the Ohio River was a key conduit for the nation's chief energy supply. Stephenson continued to sell typesetting equipment and began selling stock in the coal company on the side. He was successful in both endeavors.

As his reputation grew in Evansville, Stephenson attracted the attention of other organizations as well. A group of young veterans approached him about selling memberships to a social club they were organizing. It was to be a patriotic organization modeled on the fraternal orders that were popular at the time. In the pattern of those fraternal groups, this group would sell its memberships at a profit, and the leadership would pocket a portion of the money. Stephenson recognized a good opportunity when he saw it. The nation was enjoying a postwar glow. The "Red Scare" was whipping Americans into a frenzy. Selling memberships to a patriotic organization seemed like a sure thing.

Whether he was selling typesetting machinery, stock in a coal company, or memberships in a veterans' group, Stephenson found success. His reputation and his bank balance grew.

When another fraternal-order recruiter arrived in Evansville in 1920 seeking a hard-hitting salesman, one name kept coming up: D. C. Stephenson. Joe Huffington, the Klan recruiter from Texas, had been sent by the Southern Publicity Association team of Edward Clarke and Elizabeth Tyler to find a salesman who could sell memberships in their flag-waving organization. It seemed to Huffington that this Stephenson he was hearing so much about was just the man for the job.

"Where can I find D. C. Stephenson?" Huffington asked a sweaty lumber broker at a lunch counter in downtown Evansville.

"The Vendome, the fancy hotel down the street," said the broker. "If I was hiring a salesman, that's who I'd hire." The broker, like most of the Evansville natives Huffington met, had a surprisingly strong southern accent. Huffington knew that only the Ohio River separated them from Kentucky, but still it surprised him to hear such a drawl in Indiana. He took it as a good sign: the city where the Klan would begin its northern campaign had a southern heart.

"How will I recognize him?" asked Huffington.

The lumber broker laughed. "You'll know him when you see him."

Huffington waited until the next morning to go to the Vendome. He thought that if he went early in the workday he might catch Stephenson alone, rather than in front of a crowd of his cronies, where he would be tempted to put on a show.

The lounge of the Vendome was cool and quiet. Electric ceiling fans circulated the air in advance of the muggy Ohio Valley afternoon. A black bellhop tipped his hat as Huffington walked through the lobby, his shoes clicking against the waxed floor.

He threw his cigarette butt into a clean, empty ashtray. A young clerk moved silently and efficiently behind the registration desk. Stephenson must be a good salesman, Huffington thought, to be able to afford this place. He recalled his own dingy room at the boardinghouse.

The lounge was nearly empty, but even in a crowd Stephenson would have been easy to spot—the lumber broker was right. Stephenson sat smoking a cigar and reading the paper in a wingback chair next to an enormous potted plant. His blond hair was perfectly combed, and he wore an expensive white suit tailored to display his slight paunch in a way that advertised success in 1920. Lovingly shined shoes glowed at the ends of his crossed legs. His hat was in the chair next to him, suggesting that he did not want to be bothered. Huffington was suddenly aware of his own inexpensive, wrinkled clothing. He approached Evansville's legendary salesman.

"Are you D. C. Stephenson?" he asked.

Stephenson looked over the top of his paper at Huffington. He took the cigar out of his mouth without saying a word.

"We'd like you to sell memberships in the world's greatest secret, social, patriotic, fraternal beneficiary order," said Huffington. "The Ku Klux Klan."

Stephenson's guffaw echoed across the quiet lobby. "The Klan?" he asked loudly. Huffington saw the bellhop glance in their direction. "Aren't you the boys that take Negroes out, cut their noses off, and throw them in the fire?"[14]

"We're not like that anymore," Huffington started to explain.

"Are you the head salesman?" asked Stephenson. "Are you the best they've got?"

"This is the new Klan," Huffington said, trying to get into the rhythm of the sales pitch he had rehearsed in front of his mirror that morning.

"Not interested," said Stephenson, cutting Huffington off. He raised the newspaper back between them with a snap.

"Listen," said Huffington, "I came all the way from Texas to talk to you." Huffington had appealed to Stephenson's ego just enough. He lowered the paper halfway, revealing the skeptical smirk on his face. But he let Huffington talk.

"This is the new Klan," said Huffington. "We're not out to lynch Negroes. We're out to unite the native-born gentile citizens of the United States of America. We want to shield the sanctity of the home and the chastity of womanhood. We're out to protect the distinctive institutions, rights, privileges, principles, traditions, and ideals of pure Americanism."

Huffington was almost out of breath. Though not impressed with the way the sales pitch was delivered, Stephenson was impressed with the man's passion.

"Who can join?" asked Stephenson.

"Any white, male, native-born gentile citizen of the United States of America who owes no allegiance of any nature or degree to any foreign government, nation, institution, sect, or ruler," Huffington replied.

"That's a lot of people," said Stephenson with a smile. His newspaper was now forgotten in his lap. He replayed Huffington's sales pitch in his head, already rewriting it, working it into something more convincing for his friends and neighbors in Evansville.

Huffington wanted to close the deal. "Are you in? Can you sell these memberships?"

Stephenson's eyes narrowed. "What's my cut?" he asked.

"The klecktoken—that's what we call our membership fee—is ten dollars. One dollar of this goes to the King Kleagle—the head recruiter for the state. Fifty cents goes to the local Grand Goblin. Four and a half dollars goes to headquarters in Atlanta. The rest goes to the Kleagle—to you."[15]

"Four dollars?"

"For every membership."

Stephenson's attention drifted as he did some mental calculations. The potential market was hard to resist. Indiana was almost all white—you didn't have to be a census taker to see that. He had heard that there were pockets of immigrants up north, but on the whole, the state was pretty close to the Klan's dream of an all-Protestant, white-ruled society. In addition, the state was crazy about fraternal organizations. Hoosiers were members of well-known groups like the Masons, the Odd Fellows, and the Elks and obscure orders like the Knights of Pythias, the Tribe of Ben Hur, the Independent Order of Foresters, the Knights of the Maccabees, the Knights of the Modern Maccabees, and the Order of Owls. All of these groups and more were thriving, and none had the name recognition of the Klan, or the marketing force, or D. W. Griffith's movie. Stephenson's cigar went out as he contemplated the possibilities. Joe Huffington followed a piece of sales wisdom he had received long ago. When you're sure you've won the deal, stop talking.

Matthew Walsh returned to Notre Dame in 1919 to find that he had not left death behind in the trenches and hospitals of France. The influenza pandemic struck the university hard, affecting hundreds of students and killing nine.[16] The war had also drastically reduced the number of students enrolled at Notre Dame, putting the school's finances back in their familiar dire straits.

Fr. Cavanaugh had been left to battle these crises without the help of his able vice president. Fr. Morrissey, the venerable provincial, had been frequently ill during that time, adding to Cavanaugh's workload. The famously jocular priest became morose under the strain. Writing to a friend at the time, Cavanaugh said that the campus had seen the "death of all human joy."[17] He was greatly relieved when in 1919 the Holy Cross order ruled that the number of years a president could serve would be limited to six. Having already served more than fourteen years as president, Cavanaugh gratefully resigned.

His successor was Fr. James Burns, the former director of the Holy Cross house of studies in Washington, D.C. Matthew Walsh, Burns's former student, agreed to continue as vice president. Like Walsh, Burns was the child of Irish parents and had arrived at Notre Dame at the age of fifteen. He enrolled in the trade school to become a printer but soon transferred to the college and the seminary and was ordained in 1893. Burns, a protégé of Fr. John Zahm, believed that Notre Dame was destined to become more than a glorified boarding school. He was the first Notre Dame president to hold a PhD, a doctorate in education from Catholic University that he received in 1906.

Although Notre Dame would continue for some years to admit virtually anyone who applied, the school under Burns's leadership steadily marched toward his goal of academic excellence. He phased out the prep school, believing that the presence of high schoolers was not conducive to higher learning. The last high school class graduated from Notre Dame in 1922. During his tenure, Burns also formally divided the university into four schools—Arts and Letters, Science, Engineering, and Law—and nearly doubled the number of lay professors at Notre Dame.

While Notre Dame was beginning to make a name for itself as a reputable academic institution under the guidance of Fr. Burns, it was also making a name for itself as a college football power under the tutelage of Coach Knute Rockne. Rockne had been promoted from assistant coach to head coach of the Notre Dame football team in 1918, when Coach Jesse Harper resigned to take over a wealthy relative's ranch in Kansas. Rockne's family had immigrated to Chicago from Norway in 1893, when he was five years old. He enrolled in Notre Dame in 1910 and graduated four years later with a degree in pharmacy. While teaching chemistry at Notre Dame's prep school, Rockne also served as head coach of the track team and as Harper's assistant.

The Notre Dame football program became a nationally known enterprise under Coach Harper, a feat for which he seldom receives credit. In his five years as head coach, Harper went 34–5–1. He understood the importance of publicity and began the practice of strategically scheduling games across the country in order to maximize the press coverage of the team. Under Harper, the well-publicized Notre Dame team moved toward its eventual status as the official football team of all American Catholics. As one sign of Harper's prestige at Notre Dame, he was for his entire career the highest-paid employee of the university. Harper's considerable achievements, however, would soon be eclipsed by those of his assistant.

Rockne's career record of 105–12–5, a winning percentage of .881, remains the best in the history of college football. He developed an offense built around speed and passing that made the college game explode in popularity. He made Notre Dame famous, and in the process he made Notre Dame a fortune at a time when the university desperately needed the money. In 1919, Rockne's team won all nine of its games in front of a total paid attendance of 56,500. Ten years later, Rockne's Fighting Irish would play a single game against the University of Southern California at Chicago's Soldier Field in front of 112,000 rabid fans.

While Rockne was an undeniably great football coach, he was also at times a prima donna given to self-promotion. He had an especially strained relationship with Matthew Walsh, who was president of the university during most of his tenure as coach. He frequently leaked rumors to the press that he was leaving Notre Dame for another school, one more appreciative of his talents. At one point, he even signed a three-year contract to coach football at Columbia while he was still under contract with his alma mater. Rockne eventually admitted that he had made an honest mistake, but Walsh forced the coach to sign a secret memorandum admitting that he was fully culpable for the incident. Walsh promised Rockne that any future transgressions would result in the release of the memo; it was an ingenious way to keep the publicity-minded coach in check.[18]

In his earliest days as head coach, Rockne benefited from the talents of one of the finest athletes to ever play the game. George Gipp, like his coach, often rewrote the rules for himself and was not sympathetic to the men who were nominally in charge of him. As with Rockne, Gipp's extraordinary talent balanced his occasionally difficult behavior.

Gipp arrived at Notre Dame in 1916, when Rockne was still an assistant coach. He was from Laurium, Michigan, a tough mining town on the Upper Peninsula. The Gipps were a large Baptist family, but a local Catholic priest recognized George Gipp's athletic gifts and convinced him to apply to Notre Dame. The school offered Gipp an athletic scholarship—in baseball.

In an episode tailor-made for the movie that would come later, Assistant Coach Rockne discovered Gipp as he and some friends were kicking footballs across the quad. Rockne convinced him to try out for the football team.

Rockne had a good eye for talent. In his first game, Gipp drop-kicked a sixty-two-yard field goal after Coach Harper ordered him to punt. In a game against Army in 1920, he rang up 480 yards passing, running, and returning kicks. In that same season, he averaged 185 all-purpose yards per game. Several of Gipp's records still stand at Notre Dame, more than eighty years later. He holds the record for rushing yards per attempt in a season (8.1 yards per carry, 1920); total offensive yards per attempt in a season (9.37 yards, 1920); and kickoff returns in a game (8 for 157 yards against Army in 1920). In addition, Gipp's record for career rushing—2,341 yards—stood for more than fifty years, until it was broken by Jerome Heavens in 1978.[19]

Gipp's academic achievements were less remarkable. He showed no interest in pursuing his studies, and the university showed little interest in holding him to the line. Gipp bristled at the discipline imposed on Notre Dame students, especially those rules that kept him from the pool rooms and dance halls of South Bend. Off the field, Rockne had absolutely no control over Gipp, who was, after all, only seven years his junior.

Shortly after being elected team captain in 1920, Gipp was suspended from the university for entering South Bend's verboten Tokio Dance Hall. Eighty-six prominent South Bend businessmen petitioned Fr. Burns to grant Gipp clemency.[20] Burns, who was loath to jeopardize the revenue and fame that football was bringing to the school, allowed Gipp to return. The school's president was rewarded for his understanding, as George Gipp had his best season that year and was selected as Notre Dame's first all-American. He was the most famous football player in the country, and Notre Dame was becoming the most famous football program.

As is true of Notre Dame football players today, Gipp spent many hours outside in severe weather. In the era before pads and helmets, he also took a severe physical beating in each game. At the end of 1920, his all-American season, Gipp became seriously ill. He played his last game against Northwestern University in Chicago on November 20, 1920, and appeared weak even to the twenty thousand spectators who chanted his name. It was the largest crowd to ever see a Notre Dame game up to that point. After the game, Gipp returned to his room in Sorin Hall but was soon moved to St. Joseph's Hospital in South Bend. He suffered from both pneumonia and a severe streptococcal infection. A stream of doctors tried to save the famous athlete, but in the days before antibiotics there was little they could do. He died on December 15, 1920.

A conversation between Rockne and Gipp on his deathbed would become one of the great sports legends of all time. Rockne's version of the story became so famous that it can be hard to separate from the historical record. Rockne never mentioned the conversation to anyone outside the locker room until he wrote about it in an article for Collier's magazine ten years after Gipp's death. In that article, Rockne wrote that Gipp told him the following: "Sometime, Rock, when the team is up against it, when things are going wrong and the breaks are beating the boys—tell them to go in there with all they've got and win just one for the Gipper. I don't know where I'll be then, Rock, but I'll know about it, and I'll be happy."[21]

In the *Collier's* article, Rockne explained how he had saved that message from Gipp for eight years, until relaying it in a halftime speech as Army was beating Notre Dame at Yankee Stadium in 1928. After recounting Gipp's statement, Rockne told his players, "The day before he died, George Gipp asked me to wait until the situation seemed hopeless—then ask a Notre Dame team to go out and beat Army for him. This is the day, and you are the team."

The pep talk worked. The inspired Notre Dame team defeated Army 12–6.

No one witnessed the conversation between Knute Rockne and George Gipp, and many have speculated that Rockne invented the deathbed scene for the sake of his 1928 team, or for the audience of *Collier's*, or both. During the making of the 1940 film *Knute Rockne: All American*, a young actor named Ronald Reagan, who was playing Gipp, sought out Rockne's widow, Bonnie, on the set, looking for some corroboration of the famous speech. She told Reagan that Rockne had kept a detailed daily diary all his life. Although she had destroyed the diaries upon the coach's death, she clearly remembered that they confirmed the details of the "win one for the Gipper" story.[22]

Whether George Gipp uttered those exact words or not, it is certain that there was a lot of drama at his hospital bedside and in the aftermath of his death. Much of that drama was the result of hostility between Gipp's family and the University of Notre Dame.

Several factors led to the antagonism. The Gipp family felt that Notre Dame had exploited their son's athletic gifts. They also claimed that the university had not been energetic enough in securing Gipp's medical care. Later, there would be disputes about unpaid doctors' bills. At the heart of the hostility, however, was Gipp's deathbed conversion to Catholicism.

The Gipps, devout Baptists, were horrified that the delirious George had been converted to Catholicism just nine hours before his death by his friend and Sorin Hall rector Fr. Patrick Haggerty. The Gipps' anger grew to the point that Vice President Matthew Walsh was tasked with conducting a formal investigation. In his official report, Walsh stated that George Gipp expressed several times during his years at Notre Dame that he might like to become a Catholic. Walsh wrote that several times after becoming ill, Gipp brought it up "without the matter having been suggested to him." Walsh's report did admit that Gipp was delirious when he was baptized.[23]

The indignant Gipp family refused to let any Holy Cross priest or official university delegation attend Gipp's funeral. They forbade the university from erecting any kind of plaque or memorial to their son, and there is none to this day. The Gipps even rejected a collection gathered by Notre Dame students to help offset the funeral expenses. The Gipp family, especially George's brother Matthew Gipp, began describing Gipp's deathbed conversion in the familiar language of anti-Catholicism, complete with tales of sinister priests and strange rituals.

Despite the controversy surrounding Gipp's death, the football program continued to bring in much-needed revenue. An upsurge in enrollment also benefited the university's finances. Returning war veterans were registering at Notre Dame in large numbers. American Catholics, continuing their rise into the middle class, were eager for their children to obtain a Catholic higher education. In 1919, Fr. Burns's first year as president, about a thousand students enrolled in the university. In 1921, the enrollment would rise to fifteen hundred.[24]

In February 1921, the General Education Board, a forerunner of the Rockefeller Foundation, announced that it had picked Notre Dame to receive a $250,000 grant with which to build a lay faculty endowment. It was the first such grant the organization had ever offered to a Catholic school. The money came with several strings attached. First, the university had to raise the gigantic sum of $750,000 on its own to qualify for the grant, and the money had to be collected by June 30, 1925. A second stipulation was that the university had to be completely free of debt. Last of all, none of the revenue generated by the endowment could be used for religious instruction. Almost immediately, Fr. Burns formed a board of lay trustees in order to assure the foundation that the money it gave to Notre Dame would not be controlled by priests. It was a measure of how badly Burns wanted the grant.[25]

The debt-free stipulation created an unexpected problem for Notre Dame. Before the grant was announced, Fr. Burns and Fr. Walsh had been planning to build desperately needed residence halls on campus. The residence halls the university had could not accommodate all the new students, and almost six hundred of the fifteen hundred students who enrolled in the university in 1921 had to find lodging in South Bend. Without borrowing the money, however, the university could not build the halls. Burns and Cavanaugh were forced to postpone construction until the General Education Board's grant money was in hand.

Walsh watched in wonder as Burns threw himself into the task of raising the $750,000. Burns concentrated his efforts on the South Bend area and on alumni in other parts of the state, while Walsh opened an office in the Congress Hotel in Chicago. He had stationery printed up that said "The $500,000 Campaign for Notre Dame"—a reference to the share of the money that Burns expected him to raise in his hometown. Burns frequently told Walsh, and anyone else who would listen, that in the pursuit of the grant, the life of Notre Dame was at stake. Walsh was a competent fund-raiser, but Burns was an absolute genius at extracting the maximum donation from every interested Catholic he could speak to. Burns believed that the fund-raising campaign was a holy calling.

He so sincerely believed this that he decided to step down as president after only three years in office in order to focus his energies completely on the fund-raising drive. He made his surprise

announcement during the scheduled meeting of the provincial chapter at Notre Dame on June 30, 1922.

Burns's successor was an obvious choice. Like Burns, Matthew
Walsh held a PhD. He was a war hero and was widely respected by
the faculty, the students, and the congregation leadership. Walsh,
however, was hesitant. He had become comfortable in his role as the
behind-the-scenes functionary for two gregarious presidents. He tried
to picture himself in the speech-making, glad-handing position he
had seen Cavanaugh and Burns fill so effectively, and he couldn't. In
the end, though, only Walsh doubted the wisdom of the selection.
Within hours of Burns's resignation, the provincial chapter promoted
Matthew Walsh. The longest-serving vice president in Notre Dame's
history was now president.

———

Downstate, D. C. Stephenson was getting comfortable in his own
new position, as recruiter for the Klan. He had recruited people
before, for the army and for the Socialists before that. But he had
grand plans for this new endeavor: he envisioned an army of Klan
recruiters organized along strict military lines—with him at the top
of the organizational chart. For now, though, D. C. Stephenson was
the entire Klan in Evansville, the four-star general and the pot-
scrubbing private.

For his first recruiting effort, Stephenson thought big. He came up
with the idea of a daylong Klan picnic and spent the next few weeks
planning it. On the eve of the picnic, he had only to write his
speech. He worked late into the night in his room at the Vendome,
trying to get every word just right. His speech was to be a dissertation
on the Constitution and the foundations of democracy. He wrote and
rewrote for hours. Next to him, a full glass of whiskey sat on top of
an older, rejected version of the speech.

Stephenson was writing down a reference to Cicero when Violet interrupted him. "Are you coming to bed?" she asked.

Stephenson ignored her and kept writing. His annoyance with her had been growing steadily since their wedding day. She stepped closer, and Stephenson felt his shoulders tighten.

"Is that liquor?" she asked. Stephenson continued writing.

"Answer me, darn it!" she said.

Stephenson laughed without looking up. "Yes, my dear, it's whiskey. Now please leave so I can finish my speech."

When she didn't leave, Stephenson became angry. He finally turned to look at her.

"I told you to leave," he said. He could tell that she was frightened—she knew how he could get when he was drinking. He was glad to see that she was still frightened of him, but it bothered him greatly that she had ignored a direct order. "Leave," he said again.

"Maybe I should just leave for good," she said, her voice shaking. "Maybe I should go back to Akron."

Stephenson burst out laughing. "Are you threatening to divorce me? Woman, I'd give up my right arm for a divorce."

She stepped toward him, furious. "I told you not to bring liquor into our home," she said. With feline quickness, she backhanded his glass of whiskey to the floor. The medicinal smell filled the room.

Stephenson stood. He and Violet looked at each other expectantly. Then he slammed his fist into her face. She fell across the desk and to the floor. When she looked up, her eye was already turning black. She ran crying to the corner of the room. Stephenson gathered up the notes that she had knocked to the ground during her fall, arranged them neatly on the desk, and resumed his work. He had learned how to block out her cries.

The next day, Stephenson arrived early at the park where the picnic was to be held.[26] It was already warm—the afternoon would be a scorcher. Stephenson had reserved the park for the afternoon with the help of Mayor Bosse's nephew, his landlord. He had convinced one of his clients from the typesetting business to print out hundreds of broadsheets for the cost of the paper and the ink. Stephenson had carefully worded the posters: "KU KLUX KLAN HOMECOMING . . . BRASS BANDS . . . A BIG BARBECUE . . . ONE DAZZLING DAY OF DIVERSIFIED DELIGHT!"[27] He spread the posters all over town and in the rural villages that surrounded Evansville. He had also placed advertisements in all three Evansville newspapers, negotiating steeply discounted rates from his friends in the front offices.

He wasn't able to get a similar deal from the high school marching band, which he had hired to perform patriotic marches for one hour. The band director said that his kids needed new uniforms, and he wouldn't bring them out for free. The hour-long performance would cost Stephenson ten dollars. In addition, Stephenson had to pay for the gigantic free barbecue. It bothered him to put up his own money, but he hoped that he would sell enough of the ten-dollar memberships to break even for the day.

The featured speaker at the picnic would be one of Evansville's most respected and most fire-breathing preachers. Stephenson had made the preacher one of the Klan's first officers in Evansville in return for his services and promised to pay him seventy-five dollars a week to give pro-Klan sermons once the whole operation got rolling.

Stephenson stated explicitly in the broadsheets and in every discussion he had with Evansville residents that anyone could join the Klan—any white, native-born man, that is. The civic clubs around town had rigid social barriers, with the Rotarians being near the top, the Kiwanis somewhere in the middle, and the Lions at the bottom. The fraternal clubs, like the Masons and the Knights of Pythias, were closer to Stephenson's idea of the Klan, but they, too, limited their membership. They were also secretive to the point of meaninglessness. Why would you want to join the Masons? Well, you have to join to find out. Only white, native-born men could join the Klan, and nearly everyone in Evansville was white and native born. Stephenson emphasized the openness of the organization while downplaying any violent associations that people had with the Klan. He wanted his picnic to look no more menacing than a county fair.[28]

The band arrived in uniform and began tuning their instruments. The butcher and his crew showed up with three giant cooked hogs splayed across wooden planks. The mouthwatering smell of slow-cooked pork wafted across the park as the men in white aprons skillfully sliced the pigs open with their long knives. Pots of baked beans and bowls of coleslaw sat at one end of each table; pitchers of lemonade sat at the other. The citizens of Evansville began trickling into the park. Stephenson watched them carefully and listened to their conversations. Most of them were curious: *Why would anyone join the Klan? Where are the men in robes?* Stephenson cued the band director, and the band began to play "The Washington Post March."

When the song ended, the crowd turned toward the podium as Stephenson walked to the front. *It's no great trick to get people to show up for free food and music,* he told himself. *The hard part is separating them from their ten-dollar initiation fee.* At the podium, Stephenson fumbled in his coat pockets for the speech he had worked on all night.

"Are you all having a good time?" he asked the crowd. There was a polite cheer. He checked his pants pockets for the speech. He wondered if Violet had somehow stolen the speech to get back at him— he would kill her if it was so.

"I want to thank you for coming," he said. "You are all good Americans, I can see that." There was another polite cheer. He finally located the speech in his vest pocket. The speech was soaked; his flask, in the same pocket, had leaked moonshine all over it. The speech was almost completely illegible, except for the one-word descriptions he had written in big letters at the start of each section. He was going to have to wing it. The crowd buzzed impatiently in front of him. Stephenson wiped his damp forehead with his handkerchief.

"I see a lot of good Christian Americans out here today," he said. The word *Christian* was the only legible word on the ruined first page.

"The good reverend will be with us shortly," he noted, nodding to the preacher at the end of the platform.

"I hope you see what I see: Evansville is a good Christian city, the best that Indiana has to offer." The crowd cheered a little more enthusiastically. "We've got good parks, good schools, good churches. Good barbecue," he added, pointing to the picnic tables. The crowd chuckled courteously. "We have a lot to thank the good Lord for today. Evansville, Indiana, is a good Christian city.

"But there are people who want to change all that," he said, the tone of his voice changing abruptly. Stephenson was an experienced public speaker; he knew that he was moving in for the kill too soon. Without the speech that he had worked and reworked until early in the morning, his rhythm was off. He continued as best he could. "Oh, yes. There are people who don't like the churches we have here. There are people who don't like the separation of church and state that is guaranteed in our sacred Constitution, people who worship a church that is a state." He paused, letting his meaning sink in.

"These people can't be completely loyal Americans—they're loyal to a foreign power! A satrapy, a potentate! But even as they proclaim their fealty to a foreign ruler, they're right here, taking advantage of the freedoms that this great country allows them, taking jobs in our factories and votes from our Christian candidates." The crowd grumbled in agreement. Stephenson tried to remember anything he had prepared to say; his notes were illegible pulp, a good speech ruined by good whiskey.

"I know that everyone I see in front of me today is a good, law-abiding citizen. But did you know that the rule of law is in danger, right here in Evansville? Right now, in those hills there"— Stephenson pointed north, away from the river—"there are bootleggers laughing at the law of the land, purveying their poison to the good people of Evansville." There was a gasp in the crowd, even though the bootlegging in the hills outside of town was one of Evansville's worst-kept secrets.

"Sometimes good citizens have to step up and help the police enforce the law. Two weeks ago, a man asked me to join the Ku Klux Klan. I said to him, 'Why would I join the Ku Klux Klan? I live in Indiana, friend; we don't have a Negro problem here.'" The crowd laughed, as Stephenson had perfectly articulated their thoughts. "Then he told me about the forces at work in this country, the foreigners and their schemes to take over, to turn America—to turn Evansville—into something like the countries they left behind. 'Don't believe it?' he asked me. 'Look around: they are already taking over the schools, flouting our laws, changing the very nature of the United States, a Protestant country at its birth.'" Stephenson paused and lowered his voice. "Now, people, I am ashamed to admit that I already knew all this—just like you know it. I knew that this country was heading down the wrong path, and I wasn't doing a thing about it—didn't know there was anything I could do about it. Until this man told me the Klan is going to stop them. 'Can you name another group that is?' That's what he asked me, people. 'Can you name another group that is willing to fight for Christian virtue, for Protestant values, for America as we know it should be? Can you?'

"I proudly gave the man ten dollars—I would have gladly given him twice that. I joined the Klan because I am determined to fight for these things—Christian virtue, law and order, pure Americanism—and I'm not going to let some outsiders come and take them away without a fight! I'll die fighting if I have to. Thanks to the Klan, I will not have to fight alone. Thank God for the Ku Klux Klan!"

The crowd cheered loudly. Stephenson waved with one hand as he wiped the sweat from his forehead with the other. He was dying to sneak behind a tree and drink whatever whiskey remained in his flask. He had spoken for less than ten minutes. He had planned on speaking for an hour. He stepped down from the podium, disgusted with himself for inadvertently destroying the speech. He calculated the loss in his head—between the food, the band, and the advertisements, he had just blown about $175 of his own money. The band director was waiting for him at the bottom of the steps.

"I already paid you, didn't I?" asked Stephenson, irritated. "I don't have any cash on me, anyway."

"No," said the man, laughing. He handed Stephenson ten dollars. "I want to sign up."

Stephenson sold more than a hundred memberships that day, more than recouping his minor investment in barbecued pork and broadsheets. The next day, a Sunday, he took four of his new members, dressed in the Klan robes he had also sold them at a profit, into downtown Evansville's First Christian Church in the middle of services. The core group of the Evansville Ku Klux Klan marched silently to the altar and deposited twenty-five dollars in the collection basket. Stephenson made sure that a photographer from the *Evansville Courier* was on hand to document their generosity. The newspaper made a favorable mention of the Klan's donation, as did the preacher in his sermon that day.

Stephenson's picnics became more and more elaborate, evolving into all-day patriotic celebrations. With the money from all the memberships he was selling, Stephenson hired jousting knights, tightrope daredevils, and stilt walkers. Music played and preachers preached all day long, and people lined up to join the Klan. Stephenson signed up preachers, teachers, policemen, and farmers. He soon began to neglect his typesetting business—recruiting for the Klan was just too lucrative. Within six months of meeting Joe Huffington, he had sold five thousand memberships, netting twenty thousand dollars at a time when the average American man made twelve hundred dollars in a year. The Ku Klux Klan was making him rich.

Buoyed by his success, Stephenson decided to run for Congress in the spring of 1922. In those frothy times, it did not seem that strange for a man who had lived in the state for only two years to run for one of its highest political offices. William Wilson, the Democratic

Party's nominal candidate, had decided not to run, opening the door for Stephenson.

The door, however, didn't stay open for long. Wilson changed his mind at the last minute and decided to run. Like a good party man, Stephenson quickly withdrew from the race and endorsed Wilson, although it was too late for Stephenson to remove his name from the ballot. An obscure labor group, the Labor Political Support Association, continued to back Stephenson. In a published statement, the group said that Stephenson was the only candidate who stood for "the farmer and the working man." Stephenson lost, as expected, but he had gained the support of the "common" Hoosiers of the area.[29]

Although Stephenson didn't win a seat in Congress, the Klan leadership in Atlanta promoted him to King Kleagle of the state. He and Violet moved to Indianapolis so he could continue his conquest of Indiana.

Stephenson loved life in the capital city. The restaurants were better, the moonshine was smoother, and the streetcars were faster. So were the women: everywhere were worldly, cigarette-smoking city gals who helped take his mind off his wife.

Violet was less enchanted with life in Indianapolis. She had half hoped that the change of scenery might save their marriage, but she saw that her husband's descent into debauchery only accelerated in the big city. The drinking was worse; the hitting was worse. After just a month in Indianapolis, she told him she was leaving.

He didn't laugh this time or dare her to do it. He could see that she was serious. He had come home late from his office at the Kresge Building to find her sitting on the edge of their bed with a determined grimace on her face. She was wearing a nice new dress and her suitcase was packed and at her side.

"The hell you are," he said. "You're my wife; you're staying right here."

She stood and tried to walk past him, but he pushed her back. She tried again.

"Don't you walk out on me, bitch—I'll kill you first." He threw her to the ground. She screamed. Stephenson grabbed her collar and ripped her dress open as she squirmed beneath him. He began clawing at her bare stomach and face, drawing blood. Suddenly he was aware of pounding at the door.

The neighbors had heard the screaming and called the police. After pulling Stephenson off Violet, the cop guarded him in the study as she changed her dress in the bedroom. Stephenson ranted at her: "Go back to Akron. It'll be the best thing that ever happened to me!" There was dried blood under his manicured fingernails. Violet left, and the cop watched Stephenson until he felt that she had gone a safe distance. He took Stephenson's moonshine with him when he left.[30]

Alone now, Stephenson was able to focus completely on the Klan. He continued the process of professionalizing the sales force that Edward Clarke and Elizabeth Tyler had begun. He hired tough sales professionals to blanket the state, showing a particular fondness for real-estate salesmen. He fired underperformers and sent trouble-shooters to problem areas. He demanded forecasts, reports, and loyalty. When he felt the need, women were easy enough to come by, especially for a smooth-talking, good-looking man with money.

Stephenson made frequent trips to Atlanta during this period to update the Klan leadership on his success. He was unimpressed with Clarke and Tyler, and especially with the doddering Imperial Wizard Simmons. He felt that they did not recognize the potential that he had only begun to tap in Indiana.

On one of his trips to Atlanta, Stephenson met Hiram Evans, a pudgy, nearsighted Exalted Cyclops from Dallas. Evans was a dentist, but he didn't behave like a professional. He advocated the kind of violent tactics that Stephenson had worked hard to distance the

Indiana Klan from. Evans told Stephenson about the vigilante "black squads" he was forming in Texas to keep blacks "in line." He even reminisced to a repulsed Stephenson about a lynching he had witnessed as a child. Evans made Stephenson's skin crawl, but Stephenson recognized in him a potentially valuable ally, and Evans saw the same in him. They had one thing in common other than their ambition—their disgust with Simmons. The old man was becoming feebleminded, and the rapid growth of the Klan demanded more capable leadership. Evans approached Stephenson with a plan to seize control of the national Klan. Simmons had already called for a "klonvocation" in Atlanta to mark the Klan's seventh birthday— Thanksgiving Day 1922. The agenda included a purely ceremonial "election" of Simmons to another term as Imperial Wizard. Stephenson took a private railcar to Atlanta for the gathering.

While the delegates gathered in Atlanta, Evans and Stephenson duped the addled Simmons into believing that a group of rebel Klansmen would become violent if Simmons nominated himself for Imperial Wizard. They suggested that he nominate Evans for Imperial Wizard instead and create the new office of Emperor for himself. Simmons agreed to the plan, grateful to his lieutenants for looking out for his safety. Evans was elected Imperial Wizard, and Simmons soon discovered that the post of Emperor was meaningless. In short order, Evans kicked Simmons out of his Atlanta office.

In reward for his loyalty during the coup, Evans gave Stephenson responsibility for twenty-three northern states. He also promised to promote Stephenson to Grand Dragon if his stellar performance continued.

Stephenson had no reason to think that he wouldn't soon get that promotion. Other than his marriage, everything he did in Indiana worked. The week before the Thanksgiving Day coup, Stephenson had signed up 2,264 new members.[31] His vague message about defending pure Americanism struck a chord with Hoosiers. His linking of conservative Protestantism and patriotic values was magical.

Hoosiers saw their Klan as the white knights of *Birth of a Nation*, riding to the rescue at the last possible minute, restoring order, justice, and a lost way of life. In a single year of recruiting, from 1920 to 1921, Stephenson grew Indiana into the biggest Klan realm in the country, with more members than in Georgia, Mississippi, and Alabama combined. The *New York Times* reported that "out in Indiana, everyone seems to belong."[32]

To counter newspapers like the *New York Times* and the *South Bend Tribune* that were anti-Klan, Stephenson took over the Indianapolis Klan's modest newsletter, the *Fiery Cross*. Under his leadership, the paper became one of the most widely distributed and influential publications in the Midwest. Shortly after Stephenson took over, an army of nine hundred newspaper boys was selling the paper as far away as Iowa. The paper's three hundred thousand readers were provided with accounts of midwestern rallies, transcripts of pro-Klan sermons, and breathless reports of the Klan's rapid growth. They were informed of pro-Klan businesses to patronize (Liberty Bell Coffee) and Catholic-owned businesses to avoid (Fuller Brush). Editorials by Stephenson reinforced the twin notions that there was something wrong with America and only the Klan was doing something about it.

With his characteristic flair for drama, Stephenson maintained his anonymity in the pages of the *Fiery Cross* by referring to himself only as "the Old Man." He was thirty-one years old.

5

THE KLAN
TAKES OVER INDIANA

WAITING NERVOUSLY ON THE HARD PLASTIC CHAIR outside Dr. David Smith's office, I felt like a sophomore again, looking to appeal a bad grade. I had scheduled a meeting with Dr. Smith, a professor of clinical psychology at Notre Dame, to discuss the mind of D. C. Stephenson. Dr. Smith's office was in Haggar Hall, and as I sat there I was reminded of a persistent rumor about the building from my student years. We used to tell each other that the basement was filled with cadavers. It didn't make any sense—Haggar Hall was the psychology building, and Notre Dame didn't have a medical school. The rumor lived on nonetheless.

Professor Smith showed up a few minutes late, apologized, and led me into his office. I had contacted Dr. Smith because of his expertise and sterling credentials. He received his PhD in clinical psychology from the State University of New York at Stonybrook in 1991. He did an internship at Bellevue Hospital and worked for a time at Kirby Forensic Psychiatric Center on Ward's Island, in Manhattan's East River. After that, he taught briefly at Ohio State before accepting a job in 1997 at Notre Dame, the alma mater of his father, grandfather, and older brother. Smith had two "nonoverlapping" areas of expertise, marital discord and schizophrenia.

Prior to our meeting, I had e-mailed Dr. Smith a list of D. C. Stephenson's traits, thinking it might help him make a diagnosis. I mentioned that Stephenson had grown up poor, that his father was in his fifties when he was born, and that he was abusive toward women, drank a lot, and was vain. I had read something about narcissistic personality disorder, and I wondered if that might explain Stephenson's behavior. As Dr. Smith and I began to talk, I summarized these facts for him and showed him a photo of Stephenson in his prime. I hoped for a diagnosis, but I thought it might be expecting too much. The "patient" had been dead for decades, and Dr. Smith had never met him.

Surprising me, the doctor ventured a possible diagnosis. "What jumped to my mind," he said, "was psychopathic personality disorder. It's kind of an interesting diagnosis."

Dr. Smith went on to explain. Psychopathic personality disorder was struck from the *Diagnostic and Statistical Manual of Mental Disorders (DSM)*—the bible of his profession—in 1980, when it was in its third revision. The *DSM*, a periodically controversial publication of the American Psychiatric Association (APA), was designed to standardize every psychological diagnosis by providing clear, objective criteria. The first version of the *DSM* was published in 1952. At the time, psychopathic personality disorder was widely recognized and already had its own set of criteria, known as the "Cleckley criteria," designed by psychiatrist Hervey Cleckley (who would achieve popular fame for *The Three Faces of Eve*, his book with coauthor Corbett Thigpen, in 1957).

While the Cleckley criteria were acknowledged as valid within the profession, the APA deemed them too inferential and too subjective for subsequent editions of the *DSM*. For example, one of the Cleckley criteria is the presence of "superficial charm."[1] While perhaps easy to identify in a person who has it, superficial charm is hard to objectively define. When the APA published the *DSM-III* in 1980, it replaced psychopathic personality disorder with the far more generalized antisocial personality disorder. For its diagnosis, the *DSM* provides objective questions such as Is the patient often truant? cruel to animals? engaged in fire setting?[2] Dr. Smith pointed out that almost any career criminal can be described as antisocial according to these criteria; a true psychopath belongs to a much more exclusive club. Psychopathic personality disorder is still diagnosed, but doctors and law enforcement officials get no help in this from the *DSM*. They are left to the criteria of Hervey Cleckley and his disciples.

A quick reading of Cleckley's criteria showed me why Dr. Smith was ready to attempt a diagnosis of Stephenson. The criteria described Stephenson to a T: superficial charm; lack of remorse; pathological egocentricity; fantastic and uninviting behavior with drink; impersonal, trivial, and poorly integrated sex life. Almost all of the criteria were just indicators of the core characteristic of the psychopath: a total lack of empathy. It can also be described as a complete lack of conscience.

When I heard the word *psychopath*, I pictured a person in a straitjacket frothing at the mouth, not someone capable of building a business empire. Didn't Stephenson's success in building the Klan, and in sales ventures before that, indicate that he was not a psychopath? Dr. Smith assured me that worldly success is not at all unusual for psychopaths. For one thing, they often possess great charisma and seem especially charismatic to those who don't know them well—think Ted Bundy. The psychopath's complete focus on self-gratification can translate into tremendous career success under the right circumstances.

So how does a psychopath become a psychopath? I asked Dr. Smith. On this, he told me, the profession is much less self-assured than it is in its diagnosis. Psychopaths come from all social groups and across all demographic lines. In addition, many psychopaths come from "normal" homes that produce other children who turn out to be perfectly well-adjusted. The disorder can be detected very early in life, which may indicate a genetic component. On the other hand, in the cases of identical twins raised apart where one twin turns out to be a psychopath, the other twin is only slightly more likely to be a psychopath than the average person on the street—this indicates only a small genetic component. Scientists speculate that some spectacularly ill-timed event in utero might cause the brain development of the future psychopath to go off its tracks. The only consensus is that very little is known about the cause of the disorder.

Dr. Smith added that psychopaths can't be cured. Their collateral conditions—such as alcoholism and depression—can be eliminated, but the complete lack of conscience is innate and can't be eradicated in the true psychopath.

Dr. Smith and I had spoken for more than two hours. As our discussion ended, he gave me some articles he had photocopied to help me better understand the psychology of D. C. Stephenson. I thanked Smith for his time, overwhelmed by his generosity. I was eager to read the articles he had given me. It was exciting to think that science might give me insight into Stephenson's actions, which at times seemed inexplicable.

As I was preparing to leave, Dr. Smith revealed that he had a personal connection to the Klan: his grandfather, who had graduated from Notre Dame in 1922, had been a charter member of a Knights of Columbus group that was formed to counter the Klan presence in his hometown of Bemidji, Minnesota. Bemidji was one of the Klan's northernmost outposts—the town is about a hundred miles south of Manitoba. In general, the Klan's nativist message didn't do well in Minnesota, with its large German and Scandinavian populations. Nevertheless, at the peak of its renaissance, the Klan managed to fill a meeting hall in the tiny town of Bemidji.

The local Catholic parish formed a Knights of Columbus branch to oppose the Klan. David Smith's grandfather volunteered to stake out the Klan meeting and note who was going in and out. Hiding in the bushes outside the hall, Dr. Smith's grandfather watched as friends and neighbors he had known all his life entered a meeting hall where they pledged to fight for America by fighting against Catholics.

Just as in Indiana, the Klan had a meteoric rise and fall in Minnesota. After the Bemidji Klan collapsed, not many of the former Klansmen were proud of having belonged. For the local Catholics too, the Bemidji Klan's short life was not a pleasant memory. Most were surprised at how close to the surface the anti-Catholic feelings had been. As Dr. Smith's grandfather wrote in his memoirs decades later, "One of the more difficult things in my life was to forget who those people were."

I had taken up far more time than the doctor had originally set aside for me. Still, he offered to make a few more copies of relevant articles for me, embarrassing me with his hospitality. As I waited for him to gather the books, I remembered the rumor from my college days about Haggar Hall.

"You know, when I was a student here," I said, "we always told each other that there were dead bodies in the basement of this building."

"Oh, there are," he said. "There absolutely are."

I was stunned. "What for?"

"The Indiana University Medical School uses them for their anatomy classes. I've seen the hearses pull up in back and drop them off."

"I always thought that was a myth," I said.

"No. It's 100 percent true. On hot days, you can smell the formaldehyde in my office."

It had been an informative interview. I had a possible diagnosis for Stephenson as well as criteria with which to look at his life in a new way. Along with the Cleckley criteria, Dr. Smith had given me Dr. Robert D. Hare's Revised Psychopathy Checklist. Hare wrote in the first page of his book *Without Conscience*, "Psychopaths are social predators who charm, manipulate, and ruthlessly plow their way through life, leaving a broad trail of broken hearts, shattered expectations, and empty wallets."[3] It was as good a description of Stephenson as I'd ever read.

Valparaiso, Indiana, the county seat of Porter County, is located in the northern tier of Indiana that contained almost of all of the state's Catholics in the 1920s. Porter County is bordered on the north by Lake Michigan and on the west by Lake County, the home of Gary, Indiana. While the state was around 5 percent foreign born, Porter County was 11 percent foreign born.[4] It was here that D. C. Stephenson held his next big Klan rally, on May 19, 1923. If the Klan's move into the northern part of the state was a move into hostile territory, though, it certainly wasn't obvious at the Valparaiso rally.

The rally represented Stephenson at his best. He had planned a day that included twenty brass bands, tightrope walkers in full Klan regalia, Texas cowboys brandishing six-shooters and lassos, fireworks, and, of course, free barbecue. He had chartered a twenty-two-car train to bring Chicago Klansmen to and from the rally. He was especially pleased with the generally favorable press the event received. He had carefully fostered both a benign image of the Klan and friendly relationships with key Indiana newspapers. One journalist wrote that the whole rally appeared no more sinister than "a political rally, a county fair, a Fourth of July festival, or a circus."[5] It was exactly the image Stephenson intended to portray.

Stephenson had special plans for Valparaiso. The town was home to Valparaiso University, a small but well-known and well-regarded private university. The school was a frequent athletic opponent of Notre Dame—the two were a little more than fifty miles apart. Despite its good reputation, the school suffered from the postwar dearth of enrollees—and unlike its neighbor, it did not have a famous football program to pull it out of its financial straits. At the time of Stephenson's rally, the school had fewer than one thousand students enrolled and was desperate. After the rally, Stephenson approached the school's trustees with a purchase offer: $340,000 plus a $1 million endowment to maintain the school.[6] Stephenson gave the school a thirty-thousand-dollar down payment. The trustees, while apprehensive about selling the school to the Klan, felt they had no choice in the matter. The life of the school was at stake. They accepted Stephenson's offer.

Stephenson trumpeted the deal in the *Fiery Cross*. Valparaiso University, under the Klan's leadership, would become "the poor man's Harvard," offering a "100 percent American curriculum."[7] Stephenson announced that he would also buy up the land around the school and put in a park with a huge lake, around which he would build housing for students and their parents. Stephenson's handpicked faculty would teach the Klan leaders of tomorrow in an intellectually and morally pure environment.

At the last minute, Imperial Wizard Evans pulled the plug on the deal. It was too expensive, he told Stephenson, and he couldn't justify spending that kind of national Klan money on an Indiana project. Stephenson knew that Evans was more concerned about augmenting Stephenson's already considerable power. Without money from Atlanta, the purchase was impossible. The project had been killed by the man Stephenson had helped get into the Imperial Wizard's office. He ranted against Evans, but there was nothing he could do.

Soon after the collapse of the deal, embarrassed Valparaiso University officials denied that they had ever considered selling their school to the Klan. Reports from the university indicated that the headlines in the *Fiery Cross* were just further examples of Stephenson's megalomania. In 1925, another buyer approached the school's officials looking to build a university on a solid moral foundation. This time, the buyer was able to complete the transaction. The Lutheran University Association purchased Valparaiso University that year, and the school is Lutheran still today.

A week after the Valparaiso rally, while Stephenson was just beginning to dream about purchasing the university and the legitimacy it would provide the Klan, a large, jovial group in Steubenville, Ohio, known as the Sons of Italy gathered in its meeting hall. Its membership was growing rapidly as the local steel mills continued to attract legions of Italians to the area. The hall and the Catholic church formed the foci of Italian community life in Steubenville. Building a bigger, nicer structure for meetings was one of the topics the group discussed that night before getting down to the serious business of eating, singing, gossiping, and discreetly exchanging homemade wine.

As they were dining inside, a black truck with its lights off pulled up in front of the meeting hall. Two disguised men in the back of the truck and a man in the passenger seat pointed guns at the hall and fired. Confused and terrified, the people gathered inside screamed as glass shattered around them. Two men were fatally wounded, their blood mixing with the red wine that had spilled onto the floor. Those with guns of their own ran outside and fired a few shots, but the truck was already roaring away. They tried to make out the faces of the men in back, but it was a moonless night, and the men were wearing black robes.

The attackers were Klansmen, and their bragging about the incident soon made it to an outraged Stephenson. The episode had Evans's fingerprints all over it. It was all over the papers—even the *Indianapolis Times* speculated that the attack was the work of the Klan and asked Stephenson to comment on these "Black Robes." Stephenson had spent long hours convincing Hoosiers and other midwesterners that the new Klan was about parades, old-time religion, and Americanism—not lynchings and violence. Not only had Evans come into his territory, but he had also undone months of work with one stupid episode.

The incident brought into stark relief how different Stephenson's and Evans's goals for the Klan were. Stephenson had big plans for the Klan: he envisioned it operating as something like a political party, with himself working behind the scenes, pulling the strings of the men in office. He even imagined the Klan's ideal of pure Americanism growing into a grand social movement like abolition or temperance. To this end, he had been lobbying Evans for months to create a national Klan policy, a platform that would spell out the political and social aims of the group. But the small-minded Evans ignored him, content to let the Klan remain just another fraternal order, one that was never political and occasionally violent.

Stephenson was surprised, then, when Evans called a meeting to develop the Klan's national platform. The two Klan leaders would meet in the Willard Hotel in Washington, D.C., two blocks from the White House, during the first week of June 1923. While the purpose of the meeting was to formalize the Klan's national platform, Stephenson had been saving up a lot of things to say to Evans and looked forward to the opportunity to confront him face-to-face.

The week of the conference, Stephenson and Evans managed to avoid each other as their delegates relayed messages back and forth between them. Stephenson's messages outlined in lengthy detail all of his ideas for the national platform, which included mandatory Bible reading in public schools, requiring public school teachers to have been educated in public schools, the abolition of parochial schools, American flag displays in schools, and the censorship of immoral motion pictures. Finally, after three days, Stephenson received an invitation to Evans's room. Evans was ready to unveil the Klan's national platform.

When Stephenson arrived at Evans's suite, room 702, the Imperial Wizard appeared too deeply involved in a conversation with a buck-toothed lieutenant to acknowledge Stephenson's presence. Evans sat on one side of a gleaming walnut conference table; Stephenson thought he looked out of place among the room's luxurious appointments, although there were also handguns and moonshine everywhere. Evans's assistants in their cheap suits and bad haircuts alternated between ignoring Stephenson and glaring at him with cartoonish menace that almost made Stephenson laugh. Stephenson could barely contain his disgust for Evans and his men. He decided to start the meeting off with a bang.

"What do you know about a group calling themselves the 'Black Robes'?" Stephenson asked, almost shouting. Everyone in the room stopped talking and stared at him. Stephenson wondered how many Black Robes were in the room.

Evans slowly looked up at him. He smirked. "What about them?" he asked.

"They killed two men at an Italian meeting last month in Steubenville, Ohio. That's what I know about them."

Evans looked around the room and traded grins with his associates. "Too bad they didn't kill every one of those wops," he said.

Stephenson tried to keep his cool. "There will be a very negative reaction to incidents like that," he said.

"The only reaction will be fear," said Evans. "And I want people to be afraid of us."

Stephenson slammed his fist down on the table. "Do you have any idea how stupid that is? The newspapers are just waiting for a reason to write stories about 'the violent Klan.' I'm giving money to churches every week, having picnics and barbecues, and all that good will evaporate with one act of violence committed by your stupid thugs. For every lunatic you recruit with that nonsense, we turn ten men away!"

Evans was stunned. He was not used to being called stupid, especially in front of his troops.

"We are not here to discuss my Black Robes," he said, seething but trying to regain his composure. "I'll be sure to let you know when I need your help with them. We are here to unveil the Klan's national policy."

For a moment, there was silence in the room as the two men glared at each other. Stephenson took a deep breath. There would be a brief truce in room 702. "Good. Fine. Maybe we'll get something accomplished here after all. Let's hear it," he said.

One of Evans's lieutenants handed him a folder. The Imperial Wizard adjusted his reading glasses and took out a single sheet of stationery. He read, "From this point on, the national Klan will have a policy of talking to the newspapers from time to time." He put the paper down and looked across the table at Stephenson. He was clearly proud of the document.

Stephenson stared at him, waiting for more. "That's it?" he asked. He began laughing. "That's our national policy? Talk to the newspapers from time to time?" His laughter grew loud and mocking. Tears ran down his flushed face. He stood and walked to the door, still roaring with laughter.[8]

"Don't you walk out on me, Stephenson," Evans demanded. Stephenson didn't turn around.

"Get back in here!" Evans yelled. "I am the head of this organization!"

"Oh, God help us," said Stephenson, still laughing, as he showed himself the door.

Four days later, Stephenson was sitting in his office in the Kresge Building in Indianapolis, holding an unopened telegram from Evans. He had wondered what the consequences of their stormy meeting in Washington would be. He had angered the man mightily by mocking him in front of his men. Evans was a brutal tactician, and Stephenson had half expected his punishment to be delivered by men in black robes. At the very least, he thought, Evans would demote him or excommunicate him from the Klan. Or Evans could surprise him with some retaliation that Stephenson hadn't even dreamed of. He opened the telegram.

"Congratulations," it began. Stephenson read with disbelief that Evans was promoting him. He was following through on his promise to elevate Stephenson to Grand Dragon of the entire northern realm.

Stephenson's coronation would take place on July 4, 1923, at one of Stephenson's mammoth all-day outdoor rallies, in Kokomo, Indiana, an event that he had been planning for months. Evans himself would bestow the honor on Stephenson. Maybe fulfilling the promise was Evans's attempt to appease his best recruiter. Maybe he thought that by promoting Stephenson he could better control him. Maybe it was just the recognition Stephenson deserved for the work he had done in the Hoosier State. Whatever Evans's reason, the announcement generated a great deal of excitement around a rally that was already promising to be huge.

The event was advertised as a tristate rally for Klansmen from Indiana, Ohio, and Kentucky. In truth, the rally attracted Klansmen from as far away as Florida and California to Kokomo, a medium-sized city of about thirty thousand located between Indianapolis and South Bend. Stephenson's coronation, the holiday, the presence of the Imperial Wizard, and the growing reputation of the Hoosier Klan rallies all contributed to the excitement. It would be Stephenson's biggest show yet.

On July 4, Stephenson flew into Kokomo in the backseat of an open-cockpit biplane piloted by his friend and bodyguard Court Asher. Farmers waved up at them as the bright-yellow plane made its way to the city; the mere sight of an airplane was still a rarity in rural areas in 1923. After overcoming his initial terror, Stephenson was fascinated by the view from above. The impossibly flat Indiana plain unfolded beneath him like one of the battlefield maps he had studied as a child. Everything was green—the grass, the trees, the young corn. Small streams and rivers fed every field. It was a fertile place, a land that was meant to grow things.

As they approached Kokomo's Melfalfa Park, the site of the rally, Stephenson could see cars stopped on the clogged roads below. Many Klansmen were giving up, abandoning their cars to walk the remaining mile or two to the park. As they flew over the train station, Stephenson saw that it too was backed up—special trains with added cars waited to make their way to the platform. When they flew over the park, the expanse of vegetation gave way to a sea of people in straw hats and summer shirts. Stephenson had bragged that two hundred thousand Klansmen would come to Kokomo, and from the plane it certainly appeared to be true. The mass undulated as groups of people parted and came together like flocks of migrating swallows. The motion stopped momentarily as the plane flew overhead; Stephenson thought he could hear the people chanting his name over the drone of the plane's engine. At the far end of the park, a huge American flag was suspended in the air between three large kites. Stephenson smiled. Indiana had never seen anything like this.

The plane began its descent. It went lower and lower until it thumped to the ground. Stephenson caught his breath as the plane came to a sudden stop. A group of Kokomo Klansmen rushed toward the plane to escort him to the stage.

Stephenson had missed some of the preliminaries—anti-immigrant sermons, brass-band performances, and patriotic sing-alongs. As he approached the platform, Stephenson could see Evans standing there in his Imperial Wizard robe. He had half expected Evans to pull the plug at the last minute, as he had with the Valparaiso University deal, but it looked as if he would be true to his word today.

As Stephenson climbed on stage, Evans took the podium. After reading a brief but seemingly sincere speech that praised Stephenson's efforts to grow the Indiana Klan, Evans handed Stephenson the orange robe and hood associated with the office of Grand Dragon. The crowd erupted in cheers. Stephenson accepted a gold medallion from the Klansmen of Indiana that commemorated the promotion. Overhead, Asher buzzed the stage repeatedly in his yellow biplane. "Evansville KKK No. 1" was painted on the underside of the bottom wing.

After the coronation, Stephenson took the podium and gave a long, meandering acceptance speech that he had entitled "Back to the Constitution." The crowd listened politely, although the speech was not the rousing call to arms that they wanted. Stephenson avoided the direct attacks on Catholics and foreigners that the Klansmen had grown used to hearing from their local leadership. Instead, he gave a windy dissertation on the flaws of the electoral college. He advocated the creation of the position of "public printer" in the federal government; the person who filled this position would be tasked with documenting all governmental activities. The crowd listened, nodded their heads, and wiped the sweat from their foreheads as Stephenson talked, and talked, and talked.[9]

Stephenson's speech ended just before sundown. One of the Klan's favorite activities followed—a parade. From his position of honor on stage, Stephenson watched the passing of floats that depicted predatory blacks, militant papists, and booze-swilling foreigners.

At thirty-two years old, Stephenson was the Grand Dragon of Indiana and twenty-two other northern states. He had amassed a fortune that exceeded three million dollars and had bought a mansion in Indianapolis and a seventy-five-thousand-dollar yacht. He had been in the Klan for thirty-two months.

As a boy, Stephenson had lived in what was essentially a hole in the ground, waiting for winter to end on the Oklahoma prairie. He had read tattered histories of Napoleon and impressed his teachers as his father relentlessly attacked his dreaminess. Stephenson had comforted himself then with the notion that something great awaited him. From that stage in Kokomo, he could almost see it. He would reach that destination, whatever it was. Nothing else and no one else mattered.

———

While Stephenson's recruiting machine continued to roll smoothly across the Midwest, his personal life was getting out of control. Women threw themselves at him, but he found himself most attracted to those who were not impressed with his money or power. When he was able to draw these women into his life, he was often abusive toward them, attacking them in strange and horrible ways. He would hit them or claw them or, even worse, sometimes bite them savagely all over their bodies.[10]

His men became skilled at talking women into walking away without calling the police after Stephenson had assaulted them. The women, frightened and ashamed, usually accepted this course of action when it was suggested. Occasionally, Stephenson would narrowly escape arrest, such as when he attacked the manicurist at a hotel in Columbus, Ohio. She agreed not to call the police only after the hotel manager convinced her that such a charge would bring bad publicity to the hotel. Once, at a lavish party at his house, Stephenson pulled a woman into his garage and pushed her to the ground, slapping and biting her as she tried to escape. Stephenson was just drunk enough for her to get away. His bodyguards successfully calmed her down and persuaded her not to bring in the police. Despite these close calls, Stephenson continued to lure women into his embrace and violently attack them, raging against the women who denied him. He never worried for a second that one of these victims would bring about his downfall.

6

IN THE CROSSHAIRS
OF THE KLAN

WHEN MATTHEW WALSH TOOK OVER AS PRESIDENT OF Notre Dame in 1922, eleven hundred of the school's sixteen hundred students lived off campus.[1] When asked, half of the off-campus students said they lived in town because there was no room for them on campus. Fr. Burns had not constructed a single new residence hall during his tenure, at least partially because of the General Education Board's "no debt" requirement. Closing the prep school had made space for about four hundred more students on campus, but still not all of the students could be accommodated.

Many students, however, lived in town to avoid the strict rules imposed on resident students. The rules against drinking, smoking, and staying awake past 10:00 PM were unenforceable in town. So were the mandatory morning and evening prayers and study period that began at 4:00 PM and ended with dinner. At Notre Dame in 1922, many students were veterans of the Great War and so were older than traditional college students. It did not surprise Walsh that many of these young men had jumped at the chance to live off campus, away from Notre Dame's occasionally monastic rules.

At the same time, it was true that almost all of the students with disciplinary problems lived off campus. Off-campus students were more likely to fail classes and miss classes than those who lived on campus—90 percent of the students who were suspended for excessive absences in 1922 lived off campus.[2] It bothered Walsh that some students lived in rented rooms at the South Bend YMCA, a Protestant organization that allowed Catholics in its doors but not in its leadership positions. He couldn't even make the YMCA off-limits, however, because the Notre Dame basketball team played its games there and had nowhere else to go.

In addition to placing young men in moral peril, the shortage of on-campus housing represented a huge financial loss to the university. Every dime that students paid to the landlords of South Bend was a dime they could have paid to the University of Notre Dame. The same was true of their food dollars. When Walsh took office in 1922, only 135 students were paying the debt-ridden university for their meals.[3]

Walsh saw what he had to do. An ambitious building program designed to bring Notre Dame's students back to campus became the first major initiative of his presidency. He commissioned the design of a grand dining room modeled on the medieval guildhalls. A famed but eccentric architect named Ralph Adams Cram, who had designed buildings at Princeton and West Point, agreed to design the dining room for free, saving the school at least the cost of an architect. Walsh also planned a trio of residence halls for the western end of the campus. Fiscal conservativeness having been drummed into him, Walsh resolved to wait until all the necessary money was in hand before building anything. That, unfortunately, would take several football seasons. Walsh had to do something in the meantime.

While his plans for three new brick-and-stone residence halls were filed away, Walsh authorized the construction of two temporary wood structures on the northern end of campus. The plans for the barracks-like buildings were inspired by Walsh's time in the army—both were plain and hastily built. Walsh gave them the prosaic names of Freshman Hall and Sophomore Hall, but the students preferred to call them "cardboard palaces." Freshman Hall was completed in 1922, Sophomore Hall a year later. The two buildings were constructed for a total of $108,600.[4] Each residence hall held about two hundred men. That meant four hundred fewer students would be giving their rent dollars to South Bend landlords, and four hundred fewer students would be exposed to the more roaring aspects of the Roaring Twenties. The dormitories also helped distance students from a city where Klansmen, and opponents of the Klan, were becoming increasingly bold.

———

Bill Foohey stood at the back of Place Hall in downtown South Bend and waited for the speaker to arrive. It was March 13, 1923. He knew that he should be back in his room in Freshman Hall, completing his chemistry assignment, but he had let his friends drag him downtown to listen to "Mad" Patrick O'Donnell rant against the Klan. Foohey was studying chemical engineering and so had less free time than some of his friends who were studying history and business. His freshman year was almost over, and he had made it through with decent grades. More important, he had come to the attention of Dr. Henry Froning, the head of the Chemistry Department and his favorite professor. He desperately did not want to disappoint the man. Nonetheless, Foohey had given in to his friends and set his work aside to go hear O'Donnell. The end of the long, dark South Bend winter seemed to bring out the worst kind of frenzied energy in his pals—it was as if their mischievous tendencies had hibernated all winter and had now emerged ravenous. They were late to the event and had to stand in the back of the crowded hall. Many of the Notre Dame men in the audience took advantage of being off campus by contributing to the auditorium's growing cloud of cigarette smoke.

Foohey was in most ways a typical Notre Dame man. He was a midwesterner, from Fort Wayne, Indiana, just a hundred miles from South Bend. (When Foohey began his sophomore year a few months later, more than half of Notre Dame's 1,992 students would be from the three neighboring states of Indiana, Illinois, and Ohio.)[5] Like most students at the university, he wasn't exactly rich—and he didn't need to be, as a semester's tuition at the time was a tidy $100, board for the same period was $187.50, and a semester's books cost him $23.79.[6] The medical exam he had to take when he first got to the university cost him 50¢. This was at a time when the average man in the United States earned $1,303 a year. In other words, the average American father would spend less than one month's pay on his son's tuition at Notre Dame for one semester.

If Foohey was not rich, he was part of a decided elite—college was an extremely rare achievement at the time. Only 20 percent of the adult population at the time had more than a fifth-grade education. About 17 percent had high school diplomas. Less than 4 percent had college degrees.[7] Foohey had done well in high school, and his teachers had encouraged his father to send him to college—Foohey would be the first in his family to get a university education. The Fooheys were a Catholic family and Bill attended Catholic school. When his teachers, his priest, and his family contemplated higher education for him, nearby Notre Dame was an easy choice.

Around 75 percent of Foohey's peers at Notre Dame were also Catholic. Notre Dame has never required students to be Catholic; such a requirement would have been unthinkable for much of the school's early history, when it depended on the tuition dollars of the predominantly Protestant families in the area. At the time of Foohey's enrollment, Notre Dame accepted almost every applicant, regardless of his religion—or high school academic record, for that matter. Modern Notre Dame has numerous multicultural offices, bureaus, committees, and task forces, but Matthew Walsh's campus beat it in at least this one area of diversity—today's Notre Dame is 83 percent Catholic.[8]

Like many of his classmates, Bill Foohey had Irish roots, but his connection to Ireland was more direct than most. His father, Timothy Foohey, had fled poverty and oppression in Castlelyons, County Cork, in 1859 at the age of seventeen. He arrived in New York City but labored his way across the Midwest, digging canals and working in foundries and eventually rising into management. He had nine children and attained a kind of financial success that would have been impossible in Ireland. He remained grateful all his life for the opportunities he had been given in the United States. He told his children that they lived in the best country on earth, God's country. His love for America was matched only by his hatred of the English. Success and middle age had tempered his passion somewhat, but until the day he died he angered when recalling how the English had allowed Ireland to starve and how Sir John Perrott, their landlord and a "cold-blooded scoundrel" had evicted him and his mother from their fertile farm in County Cork.[9]

Bill Foohey, like many Notre Dame men, had heard anti-Catholic nonsense all his life, stories of secret papal armies and sinister priests, accusations of idolatry and drunkenness. The rumors spread by the reborn Klan were nothing new. Foohey was inclined to ignore the Klan and its rhetoric; his father had always told him, "Fight if you have to; walk away if you can." It was hard for Foohey to believe that the Klan, with their white robes and ridiculous titles, was anything worth fighting. It all just seemed too silly.

A Chicago attorney named Patrick O'Donnell, however, felt differently. He had founded the American Unity League (AUL) to take on the Klan. Worn copies of the AUL's newsletter, *Tolerance,* were often passed around by Foohey and his buddies. Foohey was amazed at the confrontational tone of it—it was unlike any newspaper he had ever seen. He marveled at headlines like "Cheer up, Klansmen! The worst is yet to come"[10] and "Why Kluxers commit suicide."[11] In the most recent issue of *Tolerance,* O'Donnell had announced his South Bend speech and published an invitation to former Notre Dame president Fr. Cavanaugh to preside over the event. Most of the rest of the issue was devoted to the publication of stolen Klan membership rosters. Exposing Klansmen was a central part of O'Donnell's mission. The front page trumpeted the names of prominent businessmen and politicians in the group in individual, illustrated stories. The following pages were filled with densely printed lists of the names of hundreds of Klansmen who were not as well known—it sometimes seemed as if every Protestant in the country had joined. A final page contained retractions and apologies to men who had been erroneously accused of being in the Klan in earlier issues. Foohey tended to think as his father and the leadership of Notre Dame thought: the best thing to do in the face of insults from groups like the Klan was to ignore them. To Foohey, O'Donnell's tactics seemed reckless and possibly counterproductive. Still, it was hard for him to resist the chance to listen to the man speak in person.

The crowd in Place Hall was impatiently hooting and yelling when two men finally took the stage. The first man was wearing a clerical collar and introduced himself as Fr. William J. McNamee of St. Patrick's Church in Chicago. The burly priest gave a brief benediction that served mainly to shut up the rowdy audience. Foohey noted that not only had Fr. Cavanaugh turned down the invitation to appear, but not a single Notre Dame priest was in the room. After the brief prayer, O'Donnell walked toward the podium.

He was as wild-eyed and jittery as Foohey had imagined he would be; he seemed to float to the podium on a cloud of nervous energy. He had slicked-back black hair and distinctly Irish features. The houselights dimmed and the footlights came on, sending yellow beams through the cloud of cigarette smoke and across the stage. Each footlight cast its own shadow of the man, creating a Greek chorus of dark O'Donnells that moved in unison behind him. He was waving his arms and yelling before he even reached the podium, sounding a call to arms.

"Indiana will be the next battleground between Catholics and the Klan!" he said. "What side are you on? Will you fight alongside me in this holy war? What side are you on?" He waited for an answer, but no one said a word. Like Foohey, they all probably feared being singled out by the madman at the podium.[12]

"Our work will be difficult, because your government will not be neutral in this battle," O'Donnell continued. "Your government has been taken over by the Klan! Indiana has seceded from the Union! You people now live in a Klan Republic."

Some people in the audience applauded enthusiastically. In addition to the Notre Dame men in the room, South Bend's Polish and Hungarian Catholics were well represented. They were hardworking, tough-looking men who appeared ready to battle it out with the Klan right then and there. The Notre Dame students in attendance, however, seemed dismissive of O'Donnell—a few even got up the nerve to hoot at him. Foohey made eye contact with some of his friends. *This guy is crazy,* they all seemed to be thinking.

"Oh, so some of you don't believe me," he said when he heard the catcalls. He was smiling; Foohey could tell that the audience's response was something he was used to. He pointed into the crowd. Foohey sucked in his breath, certain for an instant that O'Donnell was pointing at him. With his other hand, O'Donnell raised a sheaf of papers and shook it over his head.

"Over four hundred thousand of your fellow citizens in Indiana have sworn the Klan oath against Catholics," he said. "They have vowed to close your schools, persecute your priests and sisters, close your businesses. Over sixty Klansmen sit in your state legislature right now—and their numbers are growing. I am quite sure that there are Klansmen among us in this room, marking my words, noting your names." The rowdy Notre Dame men immediately quieted down, now afraid of being marked as Klan spies. Everyone looked around, trying to identify the undercover Klansmen among them. O'Donnell lowered his voice.

"But we're going to take the fight to them, men," he said, receiving murmurs of approval. "We're going to take the fight to them," he said again, louder, "and rip away their cowardly hoods and expose these men to the righteous light of day!"

He gestured toward the priest on stage with him. "Fr. McNamee is from St. Patrick's. We are going to drive the Klan out of Indiana just as St. Patrick drove the snakes out of Ireland. Together, we are going to redeem Indiana and reannex it to the American Union!" O'Donnell was pounding on the podium, his eyes ablaze. Foohey could sense that the crowd was with him now, following his words.

"Mark what I tell you!" he continued. "If they are not exposed and driven from Indiana, they, the Ku Klux Klan, will corrupt your juries, dominate your elections, elect their puppets to power and place, undermine your laws, and violate the principles of your constitution! We cannot let that happen!"[13]

The crowd, including every one of the Notre Dame men—even Foohey—stood and cheered. Foohey was caught up in the moment, thrilled by O'Donnell's skill as an orator, but even as he applauded he doubted that any of it was true. O'Donnell's assistants materialized and began passing collection plates through the crowd. The Klan taking over Indiana? It was just too hard for Foohey to believe. He had lived alongside Protestants in Indiana all his life. His favorite professor, Dr. Froning, was a Protestant. He couldn't assume now that all of them were his sworn enemies. Foohey went back to his dorm room and managed to finish his chemistry homework. That night and in the following days, Foohey tried to put Mad Pat's speech out of his mind, but it kept invading his thoughts. What if O'Donnell was right? What if the Klan was taking over the state while Foohey and the rest of them just sat back and waited for people to come to their senses?

A few weeks later, another speaker advertised a talk at Place Hall in South Bend. The Invisible Empire had dispatched an unnamed speaker from its headquarters in Indianapolis to offer a rebuttal of O'Donnell's speech. Foohey again let himself be talked into going, even though he had more important things to do. The words of O'Donnell had stuck with him. If the Klan was taking over his state, he wanted to know about it. He and his chums took the streetcar downtown and walked into Place Hall once again.

The auditorium was slightly less crowded than it had been for O'Donnell; Foohey and his friends were able to sit down. Many of the same Notre Dame men who had filled the room for O'Donnell's speech had come to hear the Klansman. There were others in the crowd too, earnest-looking shopkeepers and clerks in bow ties and wrinkled suits. A few of them had brought pads of paper on which to take notes. Foohey wondered if they were Klansmen. The other noticeable difference in Place Hall was the police presence. Police officers, many with Irish surnames on their uniforms, were conspicuously positioned near the stage. Foohey was glad to see them there; he knew that some of his Notre Dame friends had smuggled in potatoes from the dining hall and might take the opportunity to show off their throwing arms.

The houselights were left on, and the Klan speaker, unlike O'Donnell, began precisely on time. Foohey was disappointed that the man was not dressed in his robe and hood—he looked more like an accountant than some bloodthirsty vigilante. The speaker was small, neat, and precise, a profoundly unthreatening presence.[14]

"I didn't come to South Bend to pick a fight with anyone," he began amiably.[15] "I hope no one came here to pick one with me. Our recruitment in South Bend has grown by leaps and bounds since Mr. O'Donnell's speech. He always helps publicize the Klan's goals and ideals. We are about 100 percent Americanism—who can disagree with that?"

He then gave a well-rehearsed speech on the beauty of the American system. It was a thoroughly inoffensive speech, Foohey thought, one that his own patriotic father would have been comfortable giving. Foohey listened for explicitly anti-Catholic language, but the speech and the speaker were so innocuous that he found his attention wandering as the man went on and on. The speech would not have raised an eyebrow at any Fourth of July rally anywhere in America. Foohey believed that had he not known that the man was in the Klan, he might have signed on with him in his pursuit of Americanism, wholesomeness, and righteousness.

When the Klansman finished his speech, he gamely opened the floor to questions.

"You and your associates seem very devoted to the Constitution, sir," began one Notre Dame man who had stood up and was projecting to the whole room. Foohey recognized him; he was a senior who appeared in every campus theater production. His voice had a practiced clarity and resonance. "Do you believe then also in the separation of church and state?"

A satisfied murmur rolled through the audience. Foohey saw a couple of the cops look at one another, as if the trouble they were expecting was about to begin.

"Of course we believe in the separation of church and state," said the Klansman calmly, smiling. "It's one of the reasons we oppose church-owned schools."

The murmuring in the room increased in volume, threatening to overpower the man, but he confidently plodded forward and regained control of the discussion. "On the other hand," he said, "we believe America is a Christian nation, blessed by God, and we believe that the Bible should be on every teacher's desk in every classroom in the country. We believe that students should hear from the Good Book every day. Religion should be the foundation of public education."

The auditorium was silent. A room full of Notre Dame students certainly wasn't going to boo the Bible and religious education. The next question from the audience was more pointed.

"What, sir, is your opinion of immigration to this country?" another upperclassman asked. He had just a hint of the accent of the Boston Irish. Foohey wondered if he himself would ever be so confident in front of a crowd, if a few years at Notre Dame would make him so. He hoped that it would.

"We believe immigration is out of control," said the Klansman. "Every country on earth limits immigration in some form, except us. There's no reason we should be allowing new people into the country when there aren't enough jobs for the people who are already here. We should impose some sort of minimal residency requirement on citizenship so that people get to know the people and institutions of America a little before they start voting. We are just looking for some kind of reasonable immigration policy. Right now we have no policy, other than leaving the doors wide open."

Again, the crowd was silent.

"How do you feel about Catholics?" asked another member of the audience. "Can Catholics be good Americans?" The questioner was not a Notre Dame student. He had not waited for the speaker to call on him and he did not stand to ask his questions. He had a detectable Hungarian accent and seemed impatient with both the speaker and the debate-team manners of the Notre Dame men.

The Klansman did not answer right away. The grin never left his face, but he paused, as if contemplating the response his answer would bring.

"We believe Catholics can be very good people," he said, "but we do not believe they can be good Americans."

The crowd did not make a sound. It was the first out-and-out bigoted statement they had heard from the man, and it was shocking after such a calm, reasoned discussion.

"We advocate 100 percent Americanism—you've heard me say it several times today," the man continued. "Catholics have a sworn loyalty to a foreign power: the pope and the Vatican. Catholics are a foreign power within our borders and can never be 100 percent American."

The crowd laid into him with that. Someone in the audience hurled a potato at the stage, and it slammed into the front of the podium. Another potato flew over the speaker's head. The Klansman thanked the crowd, hurriedly gathered his notes, and rushed offstage. Two of the cops left the room to escort him to safety. Foohey and his friends walked back to campus. They all expressed general disappointment that the man had not worn a Klan robe and that the potatoes had missed their mark. Foohey returned to his books in Freshman Hall.

Two days later, an editorial appeared in the student magazine, *Scholastic*, that summed up Foohey's feelings exactly. It said that neither O'Donnell nor the Klan was worthy of admiration. The article focused most of its scorn on O'Donnell, accusing him of recklessness and a general lack of couth. Foohey did think the writers were being overly dramatic when they said that they were not opposed in principle to confronting the Klan. "If the vicinity of Notre Dame and South Bend were to become the battleground of the Klan," they wrote, "we see no reason why the Klan could not be met here as effectively as elsewhere."[16] It still seemed unlikely to Foohey that such a confrontation would ever occur. He just didn't believe that the Klan was worth worrying about.

On May 6, 1923, as the school year reached its final days, one of Foohey's friends excitedly shoved an issue of *Tolerance* onto his desk. "Shocking South Bend Klan membership roles revealed," read the headline. Foohey started reading.[17]

According to *Tolerance*, Notre Dame and South Bend were absolutely infested with Klansmen. Among the accused were Albert Erskine, the president of Studebaker and the chairman of Notre Dame's Board of Lay Trustees, and several other trustees. The university barber, who kept shop in the basement of Washington Hall, was also labeled a Klansman. Foohey could hear his friends arguing about the accuracy of *Tolerance*'s newest list in the background as he read; some of them thought that O'Donnell would publish anything to get people talking. Even with that in mind, Foohey's heart sank as he read the last name in the list: Henry Froning, chairman of the Chemistry Department.

A group of students talked themselves into taking action against the barber. Foohey declined to take part. He sat quietly at his desk as they charged across campus, smashed the windows of the barber's shop, and destroyed every piece of the man's equipment. The barber never returned to campus.[18]

Nothing so dramatic was attempted against Dr. Froning. The next day, four other chemistry professors issued a statement that said they were confident that Froning was not a member of the Klan. Still, Bill Foohey's friends in the Cardboard Palace sat around speculating about all the colorful ways Froning might be evicted from the university. Foohey started to defend his professor, but in the end, he didn't. He couldn't speak up for the man if there was a chance that he might actually be a Klansman.

Across campus, in his office beneath the Golden Dome, Matthew Walsh was also considering what to do about Dr. Henry Froning. He still felt out of place and a little ridiculous in the vast president's office, with its gleaming wood floor, expansive desk, and majestic windows. Other than a simple crucifix, there were no adornments on the walls, although Walsh had some army memorabilia in a box in the closet that he planned to display eventually. Sometimes when working late at night, he felt as if Fr. Cavanaugh might walk in at any minute and demand that he get out from behind his desk. There were times when he would have welcomed the invitation. The latest issue of *Tolerance* was spread open in the center of his clean desk. Open next to it was the neatly labeled file that held his considerable correspondence with "Mad" Pat O'Donnell, organized by date.

Walsh had been corresponding with O'Donnell for months, reading the man's frantic warnings about the Klan in Indiana and responding with polite encouragement. O'Donnell was spending more and more of his time in Indiana as the Klan focused more of its energy on the state. Notre Dame's official response to anti-Catholicism had always been to ignore it. O'Donnell argued vehemently that in the face of a rapidly growing Klan, a more aggressive posture was needed. Although the two men's personalities could not have been more different, Walsh liked O'Donnell and his rash defense of Catholics—Chicago's Irish Catholics, in particular. Walsh supported O'Donnell not only because he liked him, but also because his craziest claims occasionally turned out to be true. The Klan was growing like wildfire in Indiana—the *South Bend Tribune*'s estimates of the state Klan's size were getting closer and closer to O'Donnell's supposedly far-fetched estimates every day. In March of 1923,

Lawrence Lyons, the chairman of the Indiana Republican Party, shocked many in the state by admitting that he had joined the Klan, confirming a *Tolerance* article from months before. O'Donnell might be a loose cannon and a radical, Walsh thought, but that didn't mean he was always wrong.

Still, O'Donnell was not a terribly deliberative journalist. He once accused William Wrigley Jr., the famous Chicago businessman, of being a Klansman on the front page of *Tolerance*, and a flurry of lawsuits and retractions followed. It seemed that the Klan was now cleverly allowing O'Donnell and his operatives to "steal" false membership lists salted with the names of powerful men who had the means to defend themselves in court. The Klan could count on the rampaging O'Donnell to publish the information with little or no verification. Albert Erskine had to be one of the Klan's planted names, Walsh thought. He could not believe the man was in the Klan. A Protestant, Erskine was one of the university's most generous and devoted benefactors. He even strongly encouraged his independent Studebaker dealers to give money to the university. The accusation would certainly invoke his anger, and he was more than capable of defending himself. Walsh was sure that he would sic his lawyers on the American Unity League, just as Wrigley had.

While Walsh was sure of Erskine's innocence, he couldn't bring himself to leap to Professor Froning's defense. Froning, while Protestant, had certainly never done anything to indicate that he was in the Klan. He was part of that new breed of faculty brought in by Fr. Burns, a former chemist himself who enjoyed the research lab more than the lecture hall and hired professors accordingly. Burns had seen the hiring of research scientists like Froning as the march of progress; Walsh saw it as a necessary evil. Walsh had strained relationships with almost all of the lay professors—he was uncomfortable with their independence and their expense. That Froning was a lay professor was just one factor that kept Walsh from publicly defending the man. He knew that while O'Donnell was occasionally wrong about who was a member of the Klan, he was correct more times than not. That fact as well made Walsh hesitate.

Froning, for his part, suffered silently under the weight of the accusation. After eleven weeks of not hearing one word of support from the president's office, he decided he couldn't take it anymore and resigned.

Walsh accepted Froning's resignation, but Cavanaugh and Burns stepped into action. They persuaded Froning to return, although Walsh remained silent on the issue, offering no endorsement or vote of confidence. Cavanaugh and Burns appealed to Walsh and convinced him that O'Donnell had once again defamed an innocent man. Walsh, ever respectful of his mentors, agreed to support Froning's return. His resignation and reinstatement took place during the summer recess, so the students were not affected by the disruption. The relationship between Walsh and Froning, however, had been irreparably damaged.

For Fr. Cavanaugh, the May 6 issue of *Tolerance* was the last straw. Unlike Walsh, he had never seen any roguish charm in O'Donnell. He believed that O'Donnell's manner, unstable and bellicose, actually validated the worst Irish stereotypes. The Klan had said all along that the activities of the AUL actually increased its membership, and Cavanaugh believed it. He had been content just to maintain an official distance from O'Donnell and his group. Now, though, O'Donnell seemed to have gone out of his way to embarrass the university, and that was intolerable. Walsh watched with some regret as Cavanaugh focused his considerable energy on ridding South Bend of "Mad" Pat O'Donnell and crippling his organization.

Always forthright, Cavanaugh wrote to O'Donnell and told him that he was going to make his work in South Bend extremely difficult. He strongly suggested that O'Donnell return to Chicago. O'Donnell was incredulous—weren't they all on the same side? The Klan was set to take over Indiana. Wasn't the time right for some rough play? But Cavanaugh had already made up his mind.

He urged all Notre Dame alumni in South Bend and Chicago to stop making donations to the American Unity League. He told them that the group was acting immorally and that no good Notre Dame man should support it. Cavanaugh's message had an immediate effect: O'Donnell's revenues dried up. In addition, the libel suits quickly exhausted the small cash reserve he had in the bank. O'Donnell wrote a pleading letter to Walsh, his sole friend in the administration, describing the "furious opposition" of Cavanaugh and the "disastrous effect" his campaign was having on the AUL.[19] Walsh could not stop Cavanaugh and didn't try. The Klan's most organized and energetic opponent in Indiana was weakened. Cavanaugh had neutralized O'Donnell more effectively than the Klan ever could have.

Soon after the publication of the May 6 issue of *Tolerance*, the issue that defamed Froning and the university barber, Fr. Walsh and Fr. Cavanaugh were invited to a meeting of the South Bend Chamber of Commerce.[20] Unbeknownst to them, the city's Protestant leaders had called them to the meeting in order to hold them accountable for the accusations in *Tolerance* and for the unseemly activism of the American Unity League. Ignorant of Cavanaugh's vigorous but behind-the-scenes efforts to exile O'Donnell, they assumed that as Catholic organizations, Notre Dame and the AUL were working together. Walsh suspected an ambush as soon as they entered the room—it was suspiciously packed with local Protestant clergymen. Walsh and Cavanaugh were led to seats in the front of the room.

Immediately the Protestant clergymen in the room began firing questions at the two priests: "What do you think of *Tolerance*?" "What is your relationship to this O'Donnell?" Walsh fielded the questions while Cavanaugh fumed at the not-so-veiled accusations. Soon, the hypocrisy of the Protestant clergy proved to be too much, and Cavanaugh lashed out. Scowling at them from the front of the room, he reminded them of the libel contained in the pages of the

Klan's *Fiery Cross*, libel that the Protestant church leaders had always managed to ignore. Walsh wasn't sure what angered the man more—the attitude of the Protestant clergymen or the fact that they had forced him to publicly defend O'Donnell. Walsh hid a smile as he followed the enraged Cavanaugh out of the room.

Over the next few weeks, it became harder and harder for Walsh to follow his official policy of ignoring the Klan. In July, the Klan held its gigantic rally in Kokomo, barely one hundred miles to the south of South Bend. The event was well covered by the local papers, who described it in neutral and even positive tones. The Indiana Republican Party chairman's revelation that he was a member of the Klan was just one indication of how thoroughly the Klan had infiltrated the state's Republican Party, Indiana's perennial party in power. Cross burnings were becoming common events all over the state, including in St. Joseph County, the home of Notre Dame. Even if Walsh could have somehow ignored all that, O'Donnell continued to hound him from Chicago, sending letters that were as frequent as they were frantic. He was determined to move forward in his efforts to expose the Klan, even as the American Unity League was sinking under his feet.

Five days after the Kokomo rally, on July 9, 1923, O'Donnell wrote to Walsh, "Don't press unfavorably Erskine . . . until you see us. We have some recent and very important information."[21] He then told Walsh about the Klan's soaring membership, its infiltration into the government at all levels, and its charismatic leader, David Curtis Stephenson.

Three days later, O'Donnell wrote to Erskine and sent a copy of the letter to Walsh. After promising to never again publish his name in *Tolerance*, O'Donnell went on to warn him that many men in his plants were Klansmen. O'Donnell had proof, he said, but Erskine would have to travel to Chicago to see it, as O'Donnell was unwilling to "take our records into your jurisdiction, as you may well understand."[22] Erskine, still stinging from O'Donnell's accusation, declined to make the trip.

O'Donnell also duly reported to Walsh on the growing rift between Stephenson and the national Klan. Walsh heard about this from O'Donnell months before almost anyone in the Indiana Klan knew about it. One of O'Donnell's letters to Walsh included the minutes from a meeting of the Indiana Klan that had been intercepted on their way to William Simmons, the Klan's deposed Imperial Wizard, who apparently still had internal spies working on his behalf. It was, O'Donnell wrote, "the most secret document that has yet been obtained." While upheaval in the Klan's upper echelons could have been good news, the report also contained some sobering numbers. According to the Klan's estimates, Indiana was home to 425,000 Klansmen. It was, as O'Donnell put it, "food for serious thought and prayerful reflection."[23]

O'Donnell's prophecies about the northern march of the Klan continued to come true. Two hundred Klansmen were initiated at a cross-burning ceremony in Mishawaka, South Bend's neighboring city. A Klan parade delighted the citizens of Plymouth, Indiana, just south of South Bend. Nearby Walkerton and Elkhart enthusiastically chartered Klaverns of their own. For months, O'Donnell's strategy had been to combat the Klan by exposing its members. More and more, though, it appeared that public officials were proud to admit their membership in the state's largest social organization. Gordon Ostot, an Indiana state trooper from Elkhart, began appearing at area cross burnings in uniform, with at least the tacit approval of his superiors. Politicians too were beginning to see Klan membership as a political asset instead of an embarrassing secret.

As the Klan's growth continued unabated, with politicians and policemen publicly proclaiming their membership, its opponents grew more militant.

7

D. C. STEPHENSON'S
GRAB FOR POWER

IN 1923, CARNEGIE, PENNSYLVANIA, WAS A SMALL, SMOKY
town located between Chartiers Creek and the rolling hills south-
west of Pittsburgh. For generations, Carnegie had been home to
weary miners who worked twelve-hour shifts in the coal mines just
outside of town. The town had asked Andrew Carnegie, the Scottish
immigrant and steel tycoon, if it could name itself after him in 1901.
He gave the town his approval and two hundred thousand dollars to
build one of the libraries for which he was famous. By 1923, the
plentiful coal in the area had led to the opening of half a dozen steel
mills in Carnegie, bringing a modest prosperity to the town as well
as a tireless immigrant workforce. Many of Carnegie's townspeople
watched nervously as the newcomers took over neighborhoods and
celebrated their new lives in boisterous social clubs.

The townspeople decided to open a club of their own. Carnegie,
Pennsylvania, became one of the Klan's thriving northern outposts, its
growth fueled by fear of the Catholics who made up the fastest-growing
part of the town's population. As one sign of the Carnegie Klavern's
success, it had as its guest of honor the Imperial Wizard himself, Hiram
Evans, for its summer festival and parade on August 25, 1923.

On the misty morning of the parade, Evans watched with pleasure
as Klansmen gathered in the staging area just outside of town. Ten
thousand Klansmen from all over the state shook hands, lined up,

adjusted their robes, and traded rumors about violent Catholic mobs waiting for them in town. Such talk was not unusual—trading stories of Catholic conspiracies was practically a scheduled event at Klan gatherings. In Carnegie, though, the stories seemed to have more of a basis in reality than usual. Carnegie was about 50 percent Catholic, unlike the southern towns Evans was used to, where you could go your whole life without meeting a Catholic. It didn't surprise him to hear that the local Catholics might oppose the parade, nor did it bother him. Unlike D. C. Stephenson, Evans believed that fear was what drew people to the Klan. In the South, most people joined the Klan because they were afraid of blacks. In Carnegie, as in most of the North, people were joining because they were afraid of the swelling immigrant population that was threatening to take over their town. If the local Catholics of Carnegie were to become violent during the Klan's parade, feeding these fears, then so much the better for the Klan.

As the Klansmen assembled and as Evans and Sam Rich, the Klan's leader in Pennsylvania, posed for photographs, a driver skidded his car to a halt in front of them. Evans could see the man's robe in a bundle in the passenger seat. He handed Sam Rich a note.

Rich turned to Evans with a look of shock on his face. "The damn mayor," he said. "He's rejected our parade permit."

Evans looked back at the hooded mass behind them. He had listened to them talk about the Catholic menace all morning; he knew that the weak among them would be relieved to hear that the parade had been canceled.

"What do you think we should do?" Evans asked Rich in a high Texas drawl, a smile on his face. "There's ten thousand of us waiting for your decision."

Sam Rich looked at Evans and then down the road that led into town. He was a law-abiding citizen—that was one of the reasons he had joined the Klan to begin with. Before the Klan came to town, it had infuriated him how the bootleggers and boozers laughed at the

Eighteenth Amendment, the law of the land. Everyone in town knew where the stills were and who could deliver the best homemade wine. The Klan promised to smash the stills and pour the poison into the street. Rich had happily done so himself on a dozen midnight Klan raids into the hills. He considered the Klan to be almost an auxiliary police force. A year ago, he never would have considered marching through town in direct violation of the law. Of course, a year ago he never would have imagined the mayor capitulating to the foreigners. If Rich called the parade off, he would lose face not only in front of the Imperial Wizard, but also in front of ten thousand God-fearing Pennsylvania Klansmen.

"Let's have our parade," said Rich. "Let 'em try and stop us."

Evans slapped him on the back, happy with the decision. "That a boy," he said.

One of Rich's lieutenants blew a whistle, and the jovial murmuring of the men behind them stopped. Orders were shouted up and down the line, and the Klansmen lined up ten abreast. As they stepped off, a hooded band in their ranks began a clumsy but enthusiastic Sousa march.

They came to the Main Street Bridge, their path into town, only to find it barricaded with boards, barbed wire, and several junked cars stacked into an elaborate structure. It would take hours to dismantle it. Rich directed the whole group to the next bridge down the road. This one too had been barricaded, but the barricade was more hastily built, less imposing. The Klansmen, impatient now, tore through it easily and continued their march into town.

Two blocks past the bridge, the Klansmen entered town and passed between the two banks that were Carnegie's tallest buildings. As they made their way, townspeople on the roofs of both buildings began pelting the Klansmen with rocks and bottles. A man next to Evans was knocked unconscious by a flying bottle. Other bottles smashed to the ground at his feet. Broken glass piled up like snowdrifts along the curbs. Evans was amazed at the anger the Klansmen had incurred—amazed and pleased. Some of the Klansmen around him began picking up rocks and throwing them back at their attackers, but the buildings were six stories high; their errant rocks smashed through windows instead. All semblance of a parade was now lost. The Klansmen were moving like an invading army, hunched and cautious but advancing steadily up the street. Under the bruising rain of rocks and debris, they moved one block. The Carnegie police force, about ten terrified-looking men in uniform, yelled ineffectually at both groups from the sidewalk. Ten thousand marching Klansmen and hundreds of furious Catholics ignored them.

Evans could see that the opposition had put together a small ground force to meet the Klansmen who managed to make it through the rock-and-bottle gauntlet. The Klansmen had advanced another half block and were almost within throwing distance of the protesters on the ground when shots rang out.

Evans, like the rest of the Klansmen, threw himself to the ground at the sound of the gunfire. At first, he looked around to see which Klansman had drawn a pistol. As shots continued to be fired, it dawned on him that the gunfire was not coming from the Klansmen— they were the targets. He heard a shout and saw a Klansman slump to the ground, his white robe instantly crimson with blood.[1]

Evans watched three men hurriedly drag the Klansman into a nearby doctor's office. He felt like telling them to take their time. He had enough experience in these matters to recognize a fatal gunshot wound when he saw one. As the men took the man's body away, the rest of the Klansmen ran back the way they had come, suddenly less determined to complete their advance on Carnegie. Evans stood up, brushed the dirt off his robe, and walked slowly back out of town as the Pennsylvania Klan passed him in headlong panic. He stepped carefully over an abandoned tuba. He made a mental note to send the dead man's family a note of condolence.

Back in Indianapolis, Stephenson received word of the disrupted parade the day it happened and immediately got in his car and drove to Carnegie. By the time he arrived, two days later, Evans and most visible signs of the riot were long gone. All the downtown windows had been repaired or boarded up, and the local paper carried only an oblique reference to the parade in an editorial about the importance of brotherhood. Stephenson consoled the dead Klansman's family and blamed the lawless nature of the foreigners for his death, but in his own mind, he blamed Evans. Violence followed the man around.

The only lasting effect of the violence was a pronounced upswing in Pennsylvania Klan membership. Stephenson had always tried to steer the Klan clear of committing violent acts, believing that it was bad for business. In Carnegie, however, the Klan had been attacked, and a Klansman had been killed. The Klansmen were the victims. The early newspaper editorials, clipped for Stephenson by a badly shaken Sam Rich, universally condemned the Klan's opponents and praised the Klansmen for retreating after the shooting. Rich reported to Stephenson that the Pennsylvania Klan would exceed all its recruiting goals for the quarter. And this was Pennsylvania, a state whose support for the Klan had always been lukewarm compared to Indiana's. Stephenson wouldn't give Evans any credit for the good the riot did for the Pennsylvania Klan. In Stephenson's mind, the beneficial result had to be purely accidental, as Evans was not capable of that kind of strategic thought. Still, Stephenson wondered how and when he might instigate a similar kind of anti-Klan incident in his home state.

While Stephenson was plotting, Evans was considering how he might rid himself of his Grand Dragon. Stephenson's growing power and prestige within the Klan were a direct threat to Evans. In addition, Evans was hearing steady reports about Stephenson's womanizing, drinking, and occasionally erratic behavior. A private investigator Evans had hired reported on Stephenson's roadside arrest in Franklin County, Ohio, where he had been found in a compromising position with a woman who was not his wife. In the puritanical code of the Klan, it was unacceptable for a Grand Dragon to be caught literally with his pants down. Evans was also beset by rumors that Stephenson was planning to secede from the national organization, taking the Klan's most lucrative state with him. It all got to be too much for Evans. Rather than wait for Stephenson to make his next move, Evans decided to force his hand. In October, barely three months after promoting the man to Grand Dragon, Evans asked Stephenson to resign. Evans braced himself for Stephenson's response, ready—almost eager—for a full-blown war.

This time, it was Stephenson's turn to surprise Evans. He responded promptly and politely, resigned his position, and installed Evans's man, Walter Bossert, as his successor. He announced his resignation amiably in a small item in the *Fiery Cross* and explained to his close friends that he was stepping down because of "conflicts of jurisdiction."[2] To Evans, Stephenson's agreeability was uncharacteristic to the point of being ominous. He thought that forcing Stephenson to resign would solve his problems. He instead found himself walking the halls of Klankrest late into the night, worrying about what his former best recruiter was up to.

Evans's fears were justified. Stephenson had his eyes on a huge prize in Indiana, and he was willing to postpone his fight with Evans until after he had secured it. Indiana's governor, Warren T. McCray, was in serious trouble, and Stephenson was ecstatic.

Warren McCray grew up and grew rich in Newton County, Indiana, located just below Lake County in the northwestern quadrant of the state. While the region boasted some of the most fertile cropland in the world, McCray made his fortune in livestock, especially Herefords. Perfection Fairfax, a champion show bull at his Orchard Lake Stock Farm, was said to be the most famous resident of Newton County in 1920.

McCray worked his way into Indiana politics by chairing farmers' organizations, charitable groups, and service clubs. His wealth allowed him to make contributions to the right people and the right party—the GOP, the dominant party in the state. He ran for governor in 1920 and won, helped in no small part by the fortune and fame he had gained as a cattleman.

William Foohey, a Notre Dame student, posing in the Klan robe he captured during the May 17, 1924, riot. (*University of Notre Dame Archives*)

Fr. Edward Frederick Sorin in the 1840s. He founded Notre Dame in 1842 at the age of twenty-eight. *(University of Notre Dame Archives)*

Fr. Sorin in the 1880s. *(University of Notre Dame Archives)*

Matthew Walsh, third from the left in the front row. The occasion was his eighth grade graduation from St. Columbkille's in Chicago in 1897. He would leave for Notre Dame and the seminary that year, at the age of fifteen. (*University of Notre Dame Archives*)

Fr. Matthew Walsh at the United States Army Chaplains' School, Fort Monroe, Virginia, 1918. Walsh is at the far left. *(University of Notre Dame Archives)*

Walsh presiding over a military funeral. *(University of Notre Dame Archives)*

Top: Klan funeral, around 1923. Like most fraternal societies of the day, the Klan inserted itself into many public rites, including baptisms, weddings, and funerals. (*Indiana Historical Society*)

Middle: Muncie Klan, 1923. Muncie's chief of police, the Delaware County sheriff, and eight city councilmen were in the Klan at that time. (*Ball State University*)

Left: Nathan Bedford Forrest. The brilliant Confederate general was not the founder of the Klan, as is often stated, but was invited to become the first Grand Wizard in 1867. He quit and attempted to disband the Klan two years later when the group became too violent. (*Corbis*)

Top: Battle scene from *The Birth of a Nation*. D. W. Griffith's 1915 masterpiece helped revive the Klan with its depictions of heroic robed Klansmen rescuing the South from the anarchy of Reconstruction. (*Corbis*)

Right: Lillian Gish. The most famous actress of her day, she embodied feminine virtue in Griffith's film. (*Corbis*)

Photograph from Matthew Walsh's American Expeditionary Force (AEF) military ID card. He would be awarded the Distinguished Service Cross for his actions in France. (*University of Notre Dame Archives*)

D. C. Stephenson during his murder trial in 1925. He had reason to be smug—the trial had been moved to Noblesville, Indiana, a Klan stronghold, and the governor of the state was a friend and avowed Klansman. (*Indianapolis Star*)

Cross-burning ceremony in Indiana, around 1924. While there are open fires in the picture, the crosses are made from electric bulbs, like the one that "burned" in downtown South Bend on May 17, 1924. (*Indiana Historical Society*)

Klan parade in Hartford City, Indiana, in 1924. The parade took place near the peak of the Klan's power in Indiana, when one out of three white Hoosiers was a member. (*Indiana Historical Society*)

EDWARD JACKSON
Governor

Governor Ed Jackson of Indiana. The unabashed Klansman was elected in a
landslide in 1924, cementing David Curtis (D. C.) Stephenson's power.
(*Indiana Historical Society*)

Stephenson with his attorneys and other friends at his murder trial in 1925. From left to right: Sheriff (and Klansman) Charles Gooding, Earl Gentry, attorney Ira Holmes, D. C. Stephenson, attorney Ralph Waltz, and Earl Klinck. (*Corbis*)

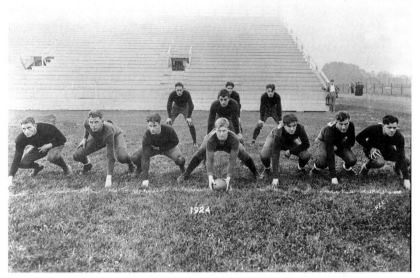

Notre Dame's 1924 offensive starters posing for a photograph at Cartier Field. They would win Notre Dame's first national championship. (*University of Notre Dame Archives*)

George Strickler's famous photograph of the Four Horsemen. They are, from left to right, Don Miller, Elmer Layden, Jim Crowley, and Harry Stuhldreher. (*University of Notre Dame Archives*)

Knute Rockne posing at Cartier Field around 1925. His lifetime winning percentage of .881 remains the greatest for any football coach, college or professional. *(University of Notre Dame Archives)*

Rockne and Babe Ruth, the two greatest sports figures of their day. (*University of Notre Dame Archives*)

Top: Notre Dame Stadium today. An outer ring of about twenty thousand seats was added in 1997. (*University of Notre Dame Archives*)

Left: Fr. Monk Malloy in his office beneath the Golden Dome. Notre Dame has had only two presidents, Malloy and Fr. Theodore Hesburgh, in the last fifty years. (*Todd Tucker*)

At a time when most Republicans were beginning to quietly solicit the support of the Klan, McCray came down mildly against them early in his term. He tried to ban Klan parades, arguing that groups should not take to the streets in disguise. When the group applied for a state charter in 1921, McCray refused to allow it because none of the applicants from the Invisible Empire would sign their names to the document. McCray was eventually overruled in the matter by his secretary of state, Edward Jackson, a war hero, an ambitious politician, and an unapologetic member of the Klan. McCray's anti-Klan initiatives were ineffective and served only to make him an enemy of the state's largest political organization.

Almost immediately after his election, McCray saw the bottom fall out of the beef market in the farm depression of 1921. The governor began borrowing money in an effort to save his business, but the market refused to improve, and legitimate bank loans became impossible to secure. A desperate McCray forged promissory notes in order to borrow against cattle sales that had never taken place. Finally, he borrowed $155,000 from Indiana's agricultural board to satisfy his mounting debts. Inevitably, his financial troubles caught up with him.

In October 1923, the same month in which Evans asked Stephenson to resign as Grand Dragon, a Marion County grand jury in Indianapolis opened an investigation into McCray's loan from the state. In November, he was indicted for embezzling. The Marion County prosecutor, William Evans, who happened to be the governor's son-in-law, resigned in shame and to forestall any charges of a conflict of interest in the impending trial.

Stephenson watched it all unfold from the sidelines and plotted his next move. The governor's woes represented a potential windfall. Stephenson arranged a meeting with Ed Jackson, the Klansman secretary of state who had granted the Klan a state charter in 1921. The meeting took place on December 8, 1923. Stephenson brought with him a briefcase containing ten thousand dollars in cash.[3]

After the two men reviewed Stephenson's plan in Jackson's office, the secretary of state took Stephenson's briefcase into the governor's office. He walked in without knocking and shut the door behind him. The governor was sitting at his desk with the slightly perplexed look on his face that was becoming his normal visage. As Stephenson had suggested, Jackson took the briefcase to the governor's desk and opened it up to reveal the cash before saying a word.

"There's ten thousand dollars in there, governor," he said. "You can have it."

The governor listened with a sad expression on his face—he knew that briefcases full of cash didn't come without conditions attached.

"We want you to have this," Jackson continued. "In return, you'll appoint James McDonald to replace Bill as Marion County prosecutor. He'll slow down the case against you. Eventually, we'll grant you immunity."

"What's in it for you?" asked the governor.

"We'll have a friend in the prosecutor's office. That will eventually come in handy, we're sure," Jackson replied.

The governor leaned forward. "Ed, who is this 'we' you keep referring to?"

Jackson flushed. "Is it a deal or not?"

"Ed, keep your money. I've already appointed a replacement for Bill," McCray said.

"Who?" Jackson asked.

"Will Remy, the chief deputy."

Jackson knew Remy—he was young and tough. Jackson thought he remembered some long-ago run-in between the Klan and Remy.

"You won't reconsider?" Jackson asked.

"Take your money and get out," said the governor in a tired voice. He took off his glasses and rubbed his eyes.

Jackson returned to his office and reported the news to Stephenson.

"So he won't put our man in the prosecutor's office," Stephenson replied, unfazed. "He can't stop us from putting our man in his office."

Having refused the Klan's bribe and offer of immunity, McCray was doomed. At the state trial, his attorneys tried to argue that he was a simple farmer guilty of financial ineptitude, not criminal fraud. To a degree, the defense worked in Indiana. His trial in Marion County Criminal Court resulted in a hung jury, with the charges being dismissed on April 11, 1924. McCray's tactic was less successful in federal court, where he was being tried on the charge of mail fraud for the promissory notes he had faked. He was convicted on April 28, 1924, and sentenced to ten years in prison.

Before his sentencing, McCray was allowed to make one more trip to the governor's office under guard in order to submit his letter of resignation. Emmett Branch, his lieutenant governor, would serve the remaining eight months of his term. McCray's letter of resignation was accepted by Secretary of State Ed Jackson.

Stephenson was delighted by the turmoil that rocked the Indiana Republican Party. Ed Jackson was at the top of a Klan slate of candidates that Stephenson intended to push through the Republican primary. By now, Imperial Wizard Evans was aware of Stephenson's designs on the governor's office. Both men knew that putting a Klansman in the governor's mansion would be the Klan's greatest triumph yet. Stephenson would be a hero to every Klansman in the country, recognized everywhere as the man who had taken over an entire state. He would be untouchable. The Imperial Wizard was desperate to discredit Stephenson before it happened.

Evans announced Stephenson's official banishment from the Klan on April 7, 1924, but everyone in Indiana, including Stephenson, ignored the decree. Despite having resigned as Grand Dragon, Stephenson was still giving orders to Indiana Klansmen, and his orders were still being obeyed. Evans kept trying to force a confrontation before Election Day, and Stephenson steadfastly refused to take the bait. Soon Stephenson's man would be unpacking his bags in the governor's mansion, and then Evans and his cronies in Atlanta would be forced to work with him.

Jackson had been campaigning for governor even before McCray's disgrace. He was a formidable candidate. A lawyer from Henry County,

Indiana, Jackson had first been elected secretary of state in 1916, but he resigned soon after to fight with distinction in the Great War. The voters rewarded his heroism by electing him to a second term in 1920. He was a smooth, good-looking man who was confident and low-key on the campaign trail.

He was also an unabashed Klansman. When Pat O'Donnell began publishing names from stolen Hoosier Klan rosters in 1923, Ed Jackson's name was one of his biggest trophies. It merited a front-page headline in *Tolerance*: "Secretary of state on roll."[4] Unlike most politicians, Jackson didn't run from the Klan after his membership was publicly revealed. He wondered out loud why all those other politicians were so eager to distance themselves from the state's most popular membership organization.

In the Republican primary, Jackson faced Samuel Lewis "Lew" Shank, the flamboyant anti-Klan mayor of Indianapolis. Shank had honed his speaking skills as a vaudevillian and an auctioneer—like Stephenson, he was a master of the stump speech. Although a Protestant, Shank seemed to harbor a genuine personal dislike of the Klan. He frequently and publicly challenged the courage of those who hid their identities behind robes and masks. When he appointed a Catholic—and a Democrat, no less—to be the city's fire chief, it was widely seen as a slap in the face of the Klan. For three years as mayor, "Leather Lung" Lew devoted his considerable oratorical skills to disparaging the Klan.

The 1924 Republican primary in Indiana was quickly shaping up to be a referendum on the Klan, with Jackson for and Shank against. Stephenson threw all of his resources and energy into the fight. He invited Jackson to hobnob with VIPs on his yacht on Lake Erie, donated thousands of dollars to his campaign, and even lent Jackson his fine Lexington Touring Car, complete with chauffeur, in which to travel the state.

Stephenson also transformed his Indiana recruiting machine into a campaign army for Jackson. He ordered the leader of every local klavern to draw up a map of his territory and assign each city block and rural precinct to an individual Klansman. Stephenson's goal was for a Klansman to personally contact every single Indiana Republican. Some klaverns bristled at Stephenson's rigid control. Others simply failed to live up to his militaristic ideal. Nevertheless, the Klan was by far the most active and organized political force in the state. From his headquarters in Indianapolis, Stephenson mailed out six hundred thousand letters to Indiana Republicans, urging them to nominate Ed Jackson, "a Christian Gentleman and a good citizen who loves his country and his God."[5]

Stephenson also had Klansmen canvassers go to every registered voter's home in the state and ask a series of questions designed to determine whether or not the voter favored the Klan platform and the Klan candidate. The polls confirmed that one area of concern for the Klan was Indiana's second-biggest city—South Bend. It was one of the few cities in the state that was heavily Catholic. Stephenson, however, did not see this as an obstacle. He knew that with the proper handling, the strong Catholic presence could actually strengthen Klan support in the area. The Protestants of South Bend had Catholic neighbors, business leaders, and politicians, and the city was home to the most well-known Catholic university—and football team—in the country. In some respects, it would be easier to sell the Klan's program of pure Americanism and Protestant values in South Bend than in those many areas of Indiana where the people had never even seen a priest or a Catholic steeple.

There were positive signs for the Klan in the South Bend area. The Elkhart klavern was becoming one of the state's most active. Pat Emmons, the leader of the South Bend Klan, was a dynamic and capable recruiter who consistently met his recruiting quotas. Stephenson decided that the time had come to have one of his legendary rallies in South Bend, in the tradition of Valparaiso and Kokomo. The Klan would parade right through that most Catholic Indiana city. If the people protested, it would be all the better for the Klan. Stephenson hadn't forgotten the violence in Carnegie and the subsequent upswing in Klan support there. He scheduled a South Bend rally for May 17, 1924—eleven days after the Republican primary.

As the primary neared, Stephenson decided that he needed to come up with a way to remind the voters of who was on the Klan's slate of candidates. There were the newspapers, of course, and Stephenson remained an adept newspaperman, but he wanted an even more direct connection to the electorate, something that didn't seem possible in 1924. To this end, Stephenson invented the clothespin campaign.

He put the entire Klan slate onto a single sheet of yellow paper and printed thousands of copies. Each sheet was folded and pressed into a wooden clothespin. Late at night on Monday, May 5, the day before the primary, Stephenson and his men tossed one clothespin onto every Hoosier doorstep. Stephenson's clothespin message was the last thing that thousands of Hoosiers read before leaving for the polls on Tuesday morning.

Lew Shank never had a chance against Stephenson's juggernaut. When the votes were counted on the day of the primary election, May 6, Jackson had thrashed him 213,625 votes to 90,506.[6] Shank's political career was over. Indiana's Republican Party was now undeniably in the hands of the Klan. The general election was six months away.

Swaggering forth from this victory, Stephenson at last took up the fight with Imperial Wizard Hiram Evans. He fired his first salvo on Monday, May 12, 1924. The venue was the Cadle Tabernacle in Indianapolis, a ten-thousand-seat interdenominational church that had long been a favorite venue of the Klan. Stephenson had summoned all the state Klan leaders, and they had all obeyed—after the primary, Stephenson was the most powerful man in the Klan. Stephenson also called to the Cadle Tabernacle every reporter he knew, promising them something juicy to write about if they came.

An *Indianapolis News* headline said that Stephenson was sounding a "war cry" before the meeting had even taken place.[7]

Standing in the wings of the auditorium, Stephenson watched as reporters and Klan leaders filled every seat in the church, all of them eager to hear the Old Man speak. He took the stage.

"Good afternoon, Klansmen," he said from the podium. "I am happy to be with you today as we celebrate the Klan's greatest political victory—so far. I look forward to seeing you all again for an even greater victory celebration in November.[8]

"Some of you are here, no doubt, because you have questions about the leadership of the Klan right now. I must confess, there have been times recently when the situation has confused me. We now have four hundred thousand sworn Klansmen in Indiana—more men than Napoleon took into Austerlitz. Our members include seven of Muncie's city councilmen, as well as their chief of police. Our members make up the entire Indianapolis City Council. Indeed, there are Klansmen in elected positions in every county in the state. Now, a Klansman is the Republican nominee for our governor. Still, I often hear from down south that the Klan's leadership in Indiana is incompetent. It is a confusing situation," he said sarcastically. "A confusing situation indeed. So allow me, for a change, to tell you about the Klan's leadership in Atlanta.

"Hiram Evans has prostituted the Klan for political purposes and is seeking to govern the organization by the imperialistic methods of the defeated Germany," he said, his tone becoming more heated. "Faithful sons of Hoosierdom! The hour of fate is struck. The venality and the jealousy of the men who carried the rebel flag in '61 are now invading Indiana. It is a cowardly attempt on the part of a few yellow-livered southerners who hate everything that is pure throughout the state of Indiana. Today we declare our independence from the southern Klan. From now on, we are going to elect our own leaders, and we are going to keep Indiana Klan money in Indiana."[9]

Stephenson let his words sink in. He knew that among the men crammed into the Cadle were a few Evans loyalists charged with reporting his words back to the Imperial Wizard. Stephenson didn't want to send them home empty-handed. He also wanted them to be able to describe to Evans the cheers that his words generated.

"The present national head," he continued, "is an ignorant, uneducated, uncouth individual who picks his nose at the table and eats peas with his knife. He has neither courage nor culture. He cannot talk intelligently, and he cannot keep a coherent conversation going on any subject for five minutes.[10]

"Evans can't take the Indiana Klan where she needs to go! He doesn't have the horsepower! He sees a southern social club—I see one of the greatest movements of the age. Either the Klan is a damnable mockery and ought to be disbanded or it represents the militant will of the Master!"[11]

The crowd was with him. Stephenson felt the familiar glow that came with a successful speech and an enthusiastic audience. He pounded on the podium. "There's been a lot of talk going around, and there's going to be a lot more! The fiery cross is going to burn at every crossroads in Indiana as long as there is a white man left in the state! We are going to Klux Indiana as she has never been Kluxed before!"[12]

The crowd stood and cheered. Everyone in the room was his. The Indiana Klan was his, the Indiana Republican Party was his, and soon the governor would be his. Stephenson had attacked Evans and declared the independence of the Indiana Klan. He knew, as he basked in the applause, that Evans's reaction would be immediate and explosive. Stephenson wouldn't have to wait long to see him in person. Evans had called for a meeting in Indianapolis on Sunday, May 18, where he would attempt to reassert his control over the renegade state. Stephenson expected to see him one day earlier. Word had it that Evans was planning to attend the rally in South Bend.

8

THE RALLY AND THE RIOT

F R. MATTHEW WALSH SAT IN HIS OFFICE AND GLUMLY read the primary-election results in the *South Bend Tribune* that was spread open on his desk. "Klan is big feature" read one headline.[1] "Klan victory precipitates party fights" read another.[2] The fight for control of the Republican Party, the party of Lincoln, appeared to be over. By November, Walsh reflected, the Klan might very well be running the state. "Mad" Pat O'Donnell had been right all along. Notre Dame was surrounded by people who hated Catholics.

Even in St. Joseph County, the election hadn't been all that close. Thousands of South Bend voters opened their front doors on the morning of May 6 to find a single yellow sheet of paper folded into a clothespin on their doorsteps. The slate was labeled only "The right ticket to vote."[3] Many had apparently believed it. Harry Taylor, the Klan candidate for St. Joseph County prosecutor, had defeated the popular incumbent Frank Coughlin, a Catholic. A Klansman and a Coughlin supporter had actually come to blows at the polling place on LaSalle Street, resulting in the arrest of the Klansman.[4] It was one of few places in South Bend where the Klan had any kind of fight on its hands.

The Klansman candidate for governor, Ed Jackson, won St. Joseph County in a runaway, 4,307 votes to Lew Shank's 2,241.[5] In all, the Klan endorsed seven candidates for political offices in

St. Joseph County, and five of them won. Charles Kinney, winner of the primary for surveyor in Goshen, declined the nomination, disgusted at his party's capitulation to the Klan.[6] His small gesture did little to dampen the Klan's exultation.

The Democratic nominee for governor, Carleton McCulloch, stated the obvious when he declared that the Republican Party had been taken over by the Klan and that the Klan would be the central issue of the general election in November. The Republican Party, he said, "has, as a political party, for the present ceased to exist."[7] Walsh took little solace in McCulloch's vigor—the Democrat had captured his party's nomination with 88,921 votes, fewer than half of the primary votes received by Ed Jackson in the overwhelmingly Republican state.[8]

Matthew Walsh was concerned not only for his state, but also for his school. Having taken over the state's Republican Party, the Klan was now on its way to South Bend. The ads in the newspapers called it a tristate rally. Walsh had heard that a similar rally in Kokomo the year before had attracted a hundred thousand Klansmen. While there had been no violence in Kokomo, that city wasn't home to a prominent Catholic university. Things would be different at this rally as well because the Klan was fresh from a huge political triumph and eager to flex its muscle. Walsh had a bad feeling in the pit of his stomach. Ignoring the Klan, his policy and Notre Dame's policy for so long, was no longer an option. Walsh wanted to make sure that the city was prepared for the worst. He directed Fr. J. Hugh O'Donnell, his prefect of discipline, and Fr. George Holderith, his director of off-campus students, to request a meeting with Laurence Lane, South Bend's chief of police. They met on Friday, May 16, the day before the rally. Walsh reluctantly decided not to attend. He didn't want anyone at city hall to see that the president of Notre Dame had finally found the Klan worthy of his personal attention.

Fr. Holderith and Fr. O'Donnell were welcomed at the station as distinguished visitors, with respectful handshakes and deferential nods. Most of the city's policemen, including the chief, were Catholic. The priests were escorted to Chief Lane's office.[9]

"Thank you for seeing us, Chief Lane," said Fr. O'Donnell as Lane shut his office door behind them. O'Donnell was strapping and occasionally intimidating, as befit the man in charge of disciplining Notre Dame's two thousand students. During his undergraduate years, when he was known as "Pepper," he had been the starting center on the Notre Dame football team. Despite his subsequent ordination and doctorate, he retained much of the swagger of a star athlete.

"My pleasure," said the chief pleasantly. "Anything I can do to help the university. I understand you are concerned about the Klan gathering tomorrow?" His tone indicated that he did not share their concern. The chief, although appointed by the mayor, had the unctuousness of an elected official.

Fr. O'Donnell cleared his throat. He was trying to walk a careful line. While he didn't want the chief to underestimate the possibility for trouble, he also didn't want to imply that the Notre Dame men were uncontrollable hooligans. Nor did he want to appear to be telling the chief how to do his job.

"You can appreciate my position, Chief Lane," he said, "in trying to keep two thousand red-blooded young men on the campus when an occasion like this presents itself."

"I'm sure that will be difficult," said the chief. In fact, it would be impossible. Four hundred and ninety-two of Notre Dame's 1,992 students lived not within the campus's safe confines, but in South Bend.[10]

"Not that our boys are wild men," said O'Donnell.

"Of course not," said the chief.

"I believe we have a very representative and orderly student body," said O'Donnell.

"As do I," said the chief. "They've been perfect gentlemen during my term as chief—except for the occasional run-in with a streetcar operator!" He laughed to indicate that the ongoing feud between the students and the South Bend streetcar company was merely a minor annoyance to him. "I have no doubt that you gentlemen will be able to control them this weekend."

"Nonetheless—" began O'Donnell.

The chief interrupted him. "Gentlemen, forgive me—I have been withholding good news," he said. "As you know, the Board of Safety has held a series of meetings about these Klan yahoos. As a result of these meetings, Mayor Seebirt told me this morning that he will refuse outright the Klan's parade permit. There will be no Klan parade through the middle of our city."

O'Donnell and Holderith exchanged relieved glances. They both knew that a parade would be a flash point for trouble.

"Oh, thank you, chief. That is good news. No parade," said Fr. Holderith.

"That's right," said the chief. "And if they do try to parade, I will deputize enough men to stop it. Moreover, I will make preparations for a machine-gun-and-tear-gas attack if necessary."

The priests' smiles faded as they envisioned the chief's worst-case scenario. They thanked Lane again and returned to campus, where they dutifully reported to Walsh that the parade had been canceled and that the chief was prepared to use guns and tear gas if necessary.

As Walsh, O'Donnell, and Holderith were meeting that Friday evening, some of the early Klansmen were rolling into South Bend. They were shocked at the welcome they received on the train platform from the locals, menacing bands of jeering young men who encouraged them to go back home. Many of the Klansmen were veterans of the rallies at Kokomo and Valparaiso; they were accustomed to being welcomed with open arms, as if they were visiting Rotarians or fairgoers. In the South Bend Klan headquarters at the corner of Michigan and Wayne streets, the local Klansmen erected a "fiery" cross made of red lightbulbs in their third-floor window. The sun set Friday night on a nervous but relatively peaceful South Bend.

On Saturday, May 17, 1924, Notre Dame's off-campus students awoke to the strange sight of men in white robes directing traffic from every South Bend street corner. The students had been anticipating the rally for weeks; nonetheless, it was shocking to see men in the famous robes and hoods standing in the streets of South Bend in broad daylight, American flags on their cars, Maltese crosses on their chests. As their brethren poured in from the hinterlands, the Klansmen on the streets courteously directed them to the park where they were to gather. Still rubbing their eyes, the Notre Dame men drifted out of their apartments and boardinghouses. Outside, they overheard conversations confirming that the Klan was planning to parade through town, permit or no. The Notre Dame men, curious and somewhat angry, watched as Klansmen filled the streets of the city. They wondered how the first beautiful day of the year would end.

The balmy weather begged for boisterous outdoor activity; if the Klan hadn't been in town, the young men of Notre Dame might have spent the day tossing footballs across the quad. Walsh resisted the fair weather's call to optimism. In a departure from his practiced public obliviousness to the Klan, he issued a statement imploring his young charges to stay on campus. The typed, single-spaced bulletin was posted around campus and in every residence hall early on Saturday morning. It read

It has been rumored that the Ku Klux Klan is to hold some sort of gathering in the vicinity of South Bend, this evening. There is also a rumor to the effect that there may be a parade of the Klan in South Bend.

Notre Dame is interested in the proposed meeting of the Klan, but not to the extent of wishing to interfere with whatever plans may have been made for a demonstration. Similar attempts of the Klan to flaunt its strength have resulted in riotous situations, sometimes in the loss of life.

However aggravating the appearance of the Klan may be, remember that lawlessness begets lawlessness. Young blood and thoughtlessness may consider it a duty to show what a real American thinks of the Klan. There is only one duty that presents itself to Notre Dame men, under the circumstances, and that is to ignore whatever demonstration may take place today. This suggestion should be taken in all seriousness. It is my wish that the Klan be ignored, as they deserve to be ignored, and that the students avoid any occasion of coming into contact with our Klan brethren during their visit to South Bend. Let the South Bend authorities take care of the situation. The place for Notre Dame men, this afternoon and tonight, is on the Notre Dame campus. Any injury, or even a more serious mishap, to a single Notre Dame man would be too great a price to pay for a protest, which in the nature of things is unnecessary and highly undesirable to the authorities of both the University and South Bend.[11]

He signed the bulletin "Fr. Matthew Walsh, CSC, President." It was the kind of notice that a young Matthew Walsh would have obeyed without question. It was a logical, clear order from a legitimate authority. To the majority of his students, though, the document made the situation in town even more irresistible. A parade without a permit? Riotous situations? Loss of life? Walsh was a war hero, yet even he seemed to think that something spectacular was about to occur in South Bend. How could they not at least go into town and check things out?

Many of Notre Dame's Catholic students had grown up hearing lies about their faith and challenges to their patriotism. Now the greatest expression of anti-Catholicism, the Klan, was preparing to march right by their university. Unlike Walsh, the students of Notre Dame were not inclined to ignore the Klan. Meanwhile, two miles south of Notre Dame, the Klansmen were converging. The Klan stood for an older America, an America that would soon be gone if not defended. In Indiana, the Klan had maintained a holding action against what it perceived to be an onslaught of foreigners in its country, and it was on the verge of creating a Klan-ruled society. The Klan would celebrate its achievement in South Bend. By the time Walsh issued his bulletin on Saturday morning, the antagonists in this battle were already running toward each other at full speed. A collision in downtown South Bend was unavoidable.

———

Bill Foohey awoke Saturday morning in Sophomore Hall to rumors and agitation: the Klan was burning a cross somewhere on campus. Foohey joined one of the squads of angry Notre Dame men that mobilized with each report, running breathlessly across campus in an attempt to find and extinguish the fiery cross. By the end of the day, they would find it.

As they made their frantic forays across campus in search of the cross, Foohey and the others stopped to listen to the reports of the off-campus students who had made their way to Notre Dame. They told them that throngs of Klansmen were already in the city and were still going to have their parade, despite the fact that they had no permit from the city. Most incredible of all were the descriptions of robed Klansmen on the street corners directing traffic. It was as if they had appropriated this duty from the police. The students began gathering their courage and plotting a trip into town.

A few coolheaded men spoke in favor of obeying Walsh's order to remain on campus. To most of the men, however, Walsh's warnings only confirmed that whatever was happening could not be missed. Their eventual mass movement into town was not the result of any organized offensive or motivational speech given from the steps of the Golden Dome. They simply raged against the Klan until charging into South Bend was inevitable. They ran the two miles into town as if responding to some silent alarm. No one waited for a streetcar. The campus emptied.

When they arrived in the city, breathless and excited, they saw for themselves what they had been hearing rumors of all morning. Cars drove into the city from all directions, and visitors carrying robes in bundles at their sides filled the train platforms. Everywhere Klansmen were looking for Island Park, the downtown park by the St. Joseph River that would be the site of their rally. The Notre Dame students gladly directed the Klansmen down alleys where other Notre Damers, like Foohey, were waiting to scare the daylights out of them, take their robes, and rough them up if necessary. The confused Klansmen, most of whom thought they were attending an event no more controversial than a state fair, began instinctively gathering in small groups for safety.

In response, the Notre Dame students also began acting in a more organized fashion. When Foohey emerged from the alley with his captured robe, he saw a flying wedge of Notre Damers crash into a cell of terrified Klansmen across the street—it was a maneuver they had learned from their football heroes. They tore the robes off two of the Klansmen; the shirtless men ran into a nearby gas station while the Notre Dame men congratulated one another.[12]

Although to Foohey and the other Notre Dame students it was all just great fun, the potential for real violence loomed large. Many of the Klansmen in town carried weapons—from the large boards their signs were nailed to and the handguns they held conveniently beneath their flowing white robes to even a small cannon. (Klansman Herbert Fisher of Hammond, Indiana, was arrested with the weapon at the corner of Main and LaSalle streets.)[13]

The threat of violence caused Deputy Sheriff John Cully to panic. Inexplicably, St. Joseph County sheriff Michael Hanley was out of town. When the first squads of Notre Dame men began running through the streets, Cully, a known Klansman, phoned Governor

Emmett Branch's office to request that he mobilize Company D of the 152nd Infantry of the Indiana National Guard. The governor, wary of the high political cost of intervening on either side, refused.[14]

Later reports of the riot would simplify the law-enforcement situation into a pro–Notre Dame police department opposing a pro-Klan sheriff's department. Certainly the students saw it this way. The *South Bend Mirror* reported that students rushing to the scene shouted that they needed to "help Larry out," a reference to police chief Laurence Lane.[15] Whatever the sympathies of individual officers may have been, law enforcement on May 17, 1924, in South Bend was most notable for its almost complete absence from the scene. While D. C. Stephenson bragged that he was the law in Indiana, on the morning of May 17, a raucous band of Notre Dame students ruled the streets of South Bend.

The *South Bend Tribune* reported that by 11:30 AM, "not a Klansmen could be seen in the business district."[16] The battered Klansmen were in full retreat, and the Notre Dame men knew it. Before pressing their advantage, Foohey and some of the others paused to celebrate by holding an impromptu parade of their own in the robes they had confiscated.

The local Klan leadership, still not quite sure what had hit them, held a meeting with Chief of Police Larry Lane and Mayor Eli Seebirt to request a parade permit for the second time. Again they were denied. The Klan was now forced to face the fact that not only would it be unwelcome in South Bend, but it would also be denied the deferential treatment from local politicians that it had grown accustomed to.

When the Notre Dame students found themselves alone on the streets, they began migrating toward the Klan's headquarters at Michigan and Wayne, where many Klansmen had retreated for safety. The electric fiery cross still burned defiantly in the third-floor window. As the students approached the building, four mounted policemen broke up the group. The policemen soon moved on, and the students quickly re-formed. They had found their fiery target at last, and they weren't about to walk away from it.

Fortunately for the students, the first floor of the Klan's building housed a grocery, and barrels of potatoes sat outside the store. The first potato shattered the third-floor window that shielded the cross, showering a few pedestrians with glass as they ran for shelter. A fusillade of potatoes followed. Each time one hit its target, a red bulb would burst with a pop and a shower of golden sparks. Occasionally an angry-looking Klansman would peek out through a window, but a barrage would quickly drive him back into the shadows. Soon, only the top bulb of the cross remained glowing. Throw after throw fell short. The men had exhausted their arms trying to hit the bulb, and their throws were becoming weaker and wilder. The remaining red bulb mocked them from above.

"Harry!" Foohey heard someone shout. He turned. Notre Dame's quarterback, Harry Stuhldreher, made his way through the middle of the mob. Stuhldreher was a year older than Foohey, but he knew him by sight—he had been the starting quarterback since his own sophomore year. Foohey hadn't noticed him in the crowd before, but he felt sorry for any Klansman who crossed paths with the muscular star athlete from Massillon, Ohio. Someone in the crowd handed Stuhldreher a potato. He took it and looked up at the lone red bulb. The crowd grew silent as he sized up the distance between him and the target.

Stuhldreher reared back and hurled the potato. Foohey and the rest of the crowd watched it trace a perfect arc to the bulb. It exploded into powder and sparks, a victim of Stuhldreher's uncannily accurate throw. The crowd cheered for their quarterback, as happy as if he had thrown a game-winning touchdown against Michigan. It had taken nearly an hour and two full barrels of potatoes to finish the job. Foohey looked around him, amazed that the police hadn't stopped them.

With the cross destroyed and law enforcement still nowhere to be seen, the Notre Damers' confidence soared. A group of students—Foohey estimated that there were about a hundred of them—decided to take the building itself. Nothing seemed impossible. They charged through the door and up the stairs. Foohey found himself at the front of the group.

At the top of the first flight of stairs, a wild-eyed man jumped out at them and stuck a pistol in Foohey's chest. Foohey felt his body go cold as he raised his hands in the air. He was terrified that the mob behind him would push him into the twitchy gunman. He couldn't speak.

"I am the Reverend Jack Horton of the Calvary Baptist Church," the man shouted at all of them, "and I demand that you leave this building immediately!" Foohey slowly backed down the stairs, his hands still in the air, grateful that the men behind him were also moving in the same direction. It was their first retreat that day.[17]

Chastened by the appearance of a real weapon at their donnybrook, the Notre Dame men gathered outside to determine what to do next. Foohey sat on the curb and tried to catch his breath. He saw four seniors form a delegation to go into the building under the white flag and meet with the local Klan leaders. They earnestly filed into the building. Foohey was glad that he wasn't asked to be part of the peace delegation. He didn't want to face the wild-eyed preacher again.

After about an hour, one of the student leaders stuck his head out of a third-floor window and announced the deal they had struck to the crowd below.

"We will let them parade," he shouted, "if they are not in their robes, and if they leave their revolvers behind."[18]

Foohey and the others nodded their heads. The deal seemed reasonable. They had made their point; the Klansmen were scared. Briefly, there was calm. A small breeze gave Foohey a chill as clouds began to fill the once-clear sky.

———

At about 2:00 PM, as the students were meeting with the Klan leaders downtown, Fr. O'Donnell and Fr. Holderith again called on Chief Lane.[19]

"I told you gentlemen not to worry about this," Lane said. His smile seemed forced, his cheer transparently artificial. Outside his office, the constantly ringing phone went unanswered as a few harried officers scurried about the station. The chief removed his hat to reveal a mess of sweaty, thinning hair. "There is nothing to worry about here. There will be no parade."

The two priests looked at each other. "The downtown streets are virtually shut down," said Fr. O'Donnell, resisting the urge to grab Lane's shoulders and shake him back into reality. "We heard that windows are being smashed and automobiles stopped."

Lane shrugged. "Boys will be boys," he said. O'Donnell's jaw dropped. What was occurring in South Bend went far beyond jumping streetcars and sneaking into dance halls. The chief had talked himself into believing that there would not be trouble, and now he couldn't be talked out of it.

The priests returned to campus without exchanging a word. In the president's office, Walsh sat quietly at his desk while O'Donnell stomped around like a caged bear. Walsh agreed with him that Lane's confidence was downright dangerous, but he wasn't sure what they could do about it.

"We have to get them back here, Matt," said O'Donnell. Walsh remained silent as he processed the descriptions of the chaos that O'Donnell had given him. "If this continues to escalate—"

O'Donnell was interrupted by the sound of something striking the window. The three men turned to see the wind blowing the day's first heavy raindrops against the glass.

———

During the nervous afternoon truce between the Notre Dame students and the local Klan leaders, Klansmen began to assemble at Island Park. The shaken members gathered until they were about two thousand strong. Guards in hoods and robes were posted at the entries to the park, and only those with membership cards or the password were allowed to enter. Despite these precautions, at least one Notre Dame man managed to sneak into the park. When he was discovered, a Klansman shot at him and just missed him as he fled. The Notre Damers outside the park lifted up their proud comrade's sleeve and learned what a powder burn looked like.[20]

While the Klansmen were gathering at Island Park, the Notre Damers assembled at nearby Hullie and Mike's pool hall. One of the seniors who had been in the peace delegation stood atop a chair and pleaded for calm, restating the terms of their agreement with the Klan.

"We will not molest them unless they violate the terms of the agreement," he intoned with overwrought seriousness. "Or unless the police request our aid."[21]

Bill Foohey listened along with the rest of the crowd. While he was having the time of his life, he could not convince himself that he was acting on behalf of law and order. Besides, the city had declined to give the Klan a parade permit. Who were they to allow the parade to take place?

"If the police request our aid, we will respond two thousand strong!" the speaker continued. "Meet at the Jefferson Boulevard Bridge at 6:30—that's the start time for the parade. We'll be in position there to help the police if they ask."

Foohey shouted his agreement along with the others, despite the fact that he thought it very unlikely that the police would request their aid. Then again, it had been a day full of unlikely events.

———

In the midst of this anarchy, D. C. Stephenson arrived in South Bend. As he was being escorted to Island Park by Jack Horton, the pistol-packing pastor, raindrops began to dot the sidewalk. "Any sign of Evans?" Stephenson asked.

"No," said the pastor. "No one is even sure he's here."

Stephenson smirked. He didn't want to say too much in front of the pastor—he didn't know where the man's loyalties lay—but it wouldn't have surprised him if Evans had sidestepped a direct confrontation with him. The man preferred to handle his disputes by proxy, usually in the middle of the night or in a dark alley. Stephenson gave Evans credit for picking a good event to miss. The South Bend rally was not turning out to be a day of diversified delight.

The Klansmen in Island Park huddled together like refugees. Mounted policemen had formed a loose circle around them, but they were not there to protect the Klansman from the marauding students. The policemen faced inward like prison guards, obviously there to keep an eye on the Klansmen. Stephenson saw a noisy mob gathering on a nearby bridge—the group looked even more determined than the policemen to stop them from parading. The dispirited Klansmen in the park seemed to be in no shape to take a stand. Stephenson knew it would be useless to try to inspire them now. A drop of rain hit his nose.

"I demand to see the chief of police. And the mayor!" he shouted to no one in particular. Someone said he would run to city hall and relay his message. A reporter walked by, his notebook in hand and a giant camera around his neck. Stephenson grabbed the man's elbow.

"The city and county officials have utterly failed to protect the law-abiding Klansmen in South Bend! The American flag is being trampled upon in the streets of South Bend!" he said.

"Will you have a parade?" asked the reporter, hurriedly writing down Stephenson's words. Stephenson gestured toward the darkening sky.

"I am canceling the parade—because of the weather. Mark my words, though, we will at some future date have a parade in South Bend. If necessary, we will call in the United States Army for protection!"

A police car pulled up. Chief Lane stepped out and noticed the reporter writing in his notepad as Stephenson ranted.

"Mr. Stephenson, do you intend to parade?" the chief asked him after a brief exchange of pleasantries.

"What do you intend to do about the hooligans who have accosted us today?" Stephenson responded.

"Do you intend to parade?" the chief asked again, louder this time. He seemed to Stephenson to be barely in control of himself. Two policemen came over to stand at either side of the chief.

"The parade has been canceled because of rain," he said. "What about them?" he pointed at the crowd on the bridge. "They are closing down city streets! Knocking old ladies to the ground! I saw them turning over a baby carriage! I demand to know what you are doing about it!" He glanced at the reporter to make sure he was getting everything down.

"Thank you for your cooperation," said Chief Lane. He was muttering "No parade" as he walked away. Stephenson watched him leave. Rainwater was rolling down his cheeks as the chief got in his car and drove away. Lane drove past the mob on the bridge without slowing down.

The reporter continued with his interview. "Do you think this activity has anything to do with the Klan's politics?" he asked Stephenson.

"The Klan has no politics," said Stephenson, stepping away.[22]

He was furious that Chief Lane had been so disrespectful toward him. His anger was tempered only by the fact that the hooliganism appeared to be almost completely one-sided. These college students, the brightest young Catholics in the country, had unlawfully taken over the second-largest city in Indiana, and all the while the Klan had gone peacefully about its business. With the general election approaching, the timing of the publicity was perfect. Not only would this help the campaign, but Stephenson also expected a profitable upsurge in membership in the South Bend Klan. He began writing the *Fiery Cross* story in his mind: "Klan persecuted by petulant papists with potatoes." *I hope you little bastards are having fun*, he thought, looking toward the bridge. *You are playing right into my hands*.

The sporadic drops of rain that had allowed Stephenson to save face and cancel the parade because of weather turned into a steady downpour around 3:30 PM. By 6:00 PM, it was a full-blown deluge. According to the *South Bend Tribune*, "It rained and rained and rained: a driving downpour slackening occasionally only to burst forth with renewed vigor."[23] The Klansmen—disappointed, bruised, and now soaked—began to leave South Bend in droves, by car, charter bus, and train.

For the group of Notre Dame students on the Jefferson Boulevard Bridge, Klan targets were getting harder and harder to come by. The Notre Dame men began to stop every automobile, inspecting each one for any sign of the KKK as if they were guards at a border crossing. They weren't just looking for the obvious robes and hoods; American flags and Masonic pins were also assumed to be the marks of a Klansman. Foohey watched some of his friends smash a windshield. A fender was crumpled on another car. A motorist mouthed off and was dragged out of his car—the police had to pluck him out of the mob and remove him to the relative safety of city hall. A carload of Klan musicians was stopped, their instruments seized and destroyed. Foohey was surprised at how delicate a trombone was; it flattened like paper.[24] Only one Klansman roamed right into their midst on the bridge—he was protected by his Indiana state trooper uniform and the revolver on his hip. As he passed by, he warned the students that their day would come.

"There are fifty thousand Klansman gathered just outside the city," he yelled. "They're just waiting for the Old Man's call."

Neither the rain nor the trooper's warning did anything to dampen the students' jubilation.

A streetcar full of cheering Notre Damers passed Foohey on the bridge. One of the men in the crowd, apparently wanting to get on board, pulled down the electric pole that powered the car, stopping it cold. He was arrested and taken to the police station.

That enthusiastic rioter was one of eight people arrested that day—seven by the police and one by the sheriff's department. Six of the arrests were of anti-Klan protestors: three for assault and battery, two for using profane language, and the one for pulling down the streetcar pole.

Two Klansmen were arrested. One was arrested for carrying a weapon; no other details were reported. The other arrest was more dramatic. Klansman C. A. Denbaugh of Logansport, Indiana, attacked Notre Dame senior Robert O'Neill with a baseball bat. When Deputy Sheriff Walter Doan gave chase, the Klansman and a friend took refuge on one of the charter buses that was leaving the city. Doan boarded the bus, and the Klansman pulled a gun. Doan disarmed and arrested him. Denbaugh's companion tearfully told the police that he had no weapon and that he just wanted to go home, away from the mob. After he showed the police that there was nothing hidden inside his bundled robe, he was allowed to leave.[25]

The actual arrests that day did not conform to the popular conception of law-enforcement loyalties. All six Notre Damers who were arrested were arrested by the supposedly Notre Dame–friendly police department. The sole arrest made by the sheriff's department was of a Klansman.

A sense of temporary calm descended over South Bend as the rain continued and the last of the Klansmen departed. The triumphant Notre Dame men returned to campus. Many, like Foohey, had robes to show off. One of the most prized trophies of the day was a large KKK banner made from a bedsheet. The students ran it up the central flagpole on campus and danced around it shouting obscenities. Foohey caught glimpses of horrified priests and brothers watching them through windows of the buildings on campus. They stayed inside, though; not even Notre Dame's strictest priests would try to stop them that day.[26]

Downtown, the local Klan was licking its wounds, humiliated by what had happened to the parade it was to host. South Bend's law enforcement was embarrassed too, that the students of Notre Dame had so easily taken control of the city's streets. A public backlash against law enforcement's handling of the situation was already beginning. A rattled Deputy Sheriff John Cully reacted by deputizing thirty local Klansmen.

9

THE AMBUSH

ON SUNDAY, MAY 18, MATTHEW WALSH ONCE AGAIN SPENT the morning reading depressing headlines in the South Bend newspapers. "Tense excitement prevails," read one headline.[1] The accompanying article described the previous day's events as "a disturbance as the city has not known in years."[2] The students were portrayed as a howling, potato-throwing mob in every account. Walsh anticipated that it would take years to repair the damage done to the school's reputation and to the school's relations with the city of South Bend. Nonetheless, he read the headlines with a profound sense of relief. No one had been seriously injured on either side. The visiting Klansmen had all gone home. And, best of all, it was over. The campus rested, went to Mass, and prepared for the week to come.

While Walsh was giving thanks for a once again peaceful campus, D. C. Stephenson was rushing headlong into his next battle. The weather and the Notre Dame hooligans had allowed Imperial Wizard Evans to avoid a confrontation with Stephenson in South Bend; he would not be so lucky in Indianapolis. Stephenson drove like a madman on the soaked roads leading out of South Bend. He half expected to see Evans and his cronies behind barricades on the outskirts of South Bend, guns drawn, waiting for the papal army to march southward.[3]

Evans had called the entire Indiana Klan to Indianapolis for the May 18 meeting, believing that by obeying his summons the Klansmen of Indiana would be acknowledging his power. Many Hoosiers were genuinely in Evans's camp, having grown disgusted with Stephenson's profiteering, womanizing, boozing, or some combination of the three. Also well represented at the meeting would be the many Hoosiers who were simply confused about who they were supposed to report to. Conflicting dictums from Stephenson and Evans were piling up in klaverns across the state. Clearing up that confusion was one of Evans's principal goals on May 18.

Stephenson had encouraged his followers to attend the meeting as well. He thought their presence would unnerve Evans and lead him into a boneheaded, heavy-handed power play that would drive the Indiana Klan further away from Atlanta. There was a strong belief in Indiana that the Hoosier Klan was somehow "pure" and that the southern leadership was inherently violent and sinister. Stephenson wanted Evans to affirm that notion. Stephenson also knew that the press would be at the meeting, and he wanted to ensure that not everyone quoted in the papers was pro-Evans. Stephenson anticipated seeing many friendly faces in Indianapolis.

If one of Evans's goals was to clear up confusion among the troops, the meeting went wrong right from the start. Evans had booked the ballroom of the Lincoln Hotel for the event, but it proved far too small for the hordes of Klansmen that were pouring in from every corner of the state, some of them at the behest of D. C. Stephenson. Evans vetoed the next logical location, the spacious Cadle Tabernacle, because it was seen as a Stephenson stronghold. Finally, the Imperial Wizard moved the meeting to Buschmann Hall, the headquarters of the Indiana Klan. The Klansmen spent the morning shuttling between three Indianapolis buildings in search of the meeting that was supposed to eliminate the confusion in Indiana.

When he finally arrived at Buschmann Hall, an agitated Evans immediately banished the press from the room, along with a number of Klansmen whom he arbitrarily judged to be Stephenson partisans. Still, it was standing room only inside the smoky hall. A speaker selected by Evans denounced Stephenson from the podium. He was supposed to be the first in a series, but despite Evans's efforts to control the agenda, a number of Stephenson's supporters shouted their way to the podium. The rival camps drowned each other's speakers out with hoots and boos. To Evans's dismay, the most popular topic of conversation between speeches and in the hallways was the success of the Klan ticket in the Republican primary election—for which Stephenson received almost all of the credit. Backstage, Evans screamed at his lieutenants for allowing so many Stephenson partisans in the room.

While Evans worked himself into a state of red-faced frustration inside Buschmann Hall, Stephenson stayed outside, coolly handling the press that Evans had banished. The southern leadership was trying to tell the Indiana Klan what to do, he told them. With a paucity of information coming from inside the hall, most papers were left to print only Stephenson's version of events.

Evans did release a terse written statement to the press through a subordinate immediately after the meeting. "There is no more dissension among Indiana Klansmen who are in good standing,"[4] it read. The statement went on to explain that Stephenson was no longer a factor in Klan affairs. The statement ignored the fact that the vast majority of Hoosier Klansmen still answered to Stephenson. The current odds-on favorite for governor, a Klansman, was traveling Indiana in Stephenson's Lexington Touring Car. No matter what Evans said, Stephenson's power and prestige in the Indiana Klan had never been greater. Evans had hoped that the Indianapolis meeting would convince Hoosier Klansmen to abandon Stephenson and accept his leadership. It had been a total failure.

On the long train ride back to Atlanta, as the flatness of central Indiana gave way to the rolling hills of the Ohio Valley, Evans regained his composure and contemplated his next move. Despite

Stephenson's frequent accusations, Evans was not a stupid man. He realized that his latest efforts to rein in the Indiana Klan and squeeze Stephenson out had been failures. As he reflected on the debacle, Evans concluded that he had been wrong to try to take power away from Stephenson with meetings, declarations, and mandates. Stephenson wielded power naturally, unthinkingly, like the mountain lions he had seen in Texas as a young boy. You can't tame a predator like that. You have to kill it, or put it in a cage.

———

On Monday, May 19, life returned to relatively normal on the Notre Dame campus. Students returned to class, still slightly giddy from Saturday's excitement and with the knowledge that they had bested the mighty Klan. The few students who had obeyed Walsh's command to remain on campus felt left out as the war stories made the rounds.

Chief of Police Larry Lane was less thrilled by Saturday's events. He was a man finely attuned to public opinion, and the current local opinion of him was decidedly low. Before the events of Saturday, Lane had assumed that the Klan had few friends in South Bend and that if the Notre Dame students taught them a lesson, it wouldn't be such a big deal. He had miscalculated. Even South Bend's Catholics—whose windows had been cracked and whose cars had been dented—were upset over Saturday's anarchy. A newspaper editorial in the *South Bend Mirror* entitled "The city's shame" summed up the general feeling of the public, saying that Chief Lane had allowed "a howling mob of college students" to take over the reins of government. The author described Lane's "nil-administration" of the police department and encouraged him to resign.[5] Lane was furious. He had gone easy on the men from Notre Dame, and in return they had embarrassed him. Given the chance, he would not make the same mistake again.

Late on Monday afternoon, it looked as if Lane would get that second chance. Deputy Sheriff John Cully called him and told him to bring his men to the Klan's headquarters later that night, when the Klan would be finishing up its regular meeting. Cully told Lane to expect more trouble from the Notre Dame students. The deputy sheriff didn't explain how he knew in advance that there would be trouble. He did tell Lane that the police department would have the enthusiastic support of thirty new sheriff's deputies. Lane called in a few off-duty men to augment his night force and briefed them at the station. The Klan's meeting would end at 9:00 PM. They would be in place before then. Lane's incessantly ringing phone kept him occupied during the intervening hours. He assured one angry citizen at a time that law and order once again reigned in South Bend.

Shortly before 9:00, Lane and a dozen of his men walked the short distance from the police station to the Klan's headquarters. They waited in the shadows around the corner from the building, nightsticks drawn, talking in low voices. The streets of South Bend were empty and quiet. No Notre Dame students were visible. The Klansmen were still in their headquarters, completing their weekly meeting. It seemed as if Chief Lane might not get the chance to redeem himself, to show that he was in fact a zealous enforcer of the law. Then the Klansmen raised their repaired fiery cross in the third-floor window. Chief Lane winced at the sight of the bright red bulbs. He knew it would draw Notre Dame students like moths to a flame.

A few minutes passed. Lane heard the sound of hundreds of people approaching on foot—there were so many of them that their feet sounded like hooves on the street. He turned to his men—they were poised and ready.

About five hundred Notre Dame students came into sight. They were running, smiling, almost out of breath. Lane turned to his men. "Wait for my signal," he said.

Just as the Notre Dame students came in sight of the building, the men inside began to exit. It was a marked contrast to Saturday's chaos. The Klansmen filed out of the building casually and assembled in roughly equal numbers on each side of the street. Lane suspected that Cully's deputies were among them. They stood there passively, as if they just wanted to observe what would happen; the now laughing Notre Damers clearly did not regard their presence as threatening. Lane noticed that while none of the Klansmen were in robes, they had tied white handkerchiefs around their arms for identification.[6]

Pressing in hard against the building and pointing at their target— the fiery cross—the Notre Dame students were too focused on their goal to notice something as subtle as an armband. The first potato of the evening was hurled at the building and slammed harmlessly against the brick. The Notre Dame mob hooted at the errant throw.

"All right, boys," Chief Lane said to his officers, "let's show them who's running this town!"

The police charged in on the Notre Dame men from behind. The Notre Dame men were surprised; they didn't expect resistance from the Klan after Saturday's rout, and they certainly didn't expect it from the previously lax police department. Lane jabbed the butt of his club into the ribs of a Notre Dame man and threw him to the ground. He watched one of his men bring his club down hard across the top of a young man's head. The student fell to his knees with a stunned look on his face.

The charging policemen stood in the students' path of retreat while the Klansmen blocked them on each side. As the students were absorbing the fact that the police were attacking them, the Klansmen on the sidelines began to participate in the fray. They hurled bottles and rocks indiscriminately into the crowd. Chief Lane saw one of his men, Sergeant Ben Roberts, collapse after being hit in the face by a large rock, his jaw obviously broken.[7] A bottle flew back out from the crowd and hit a Klansman in the nose; blood ran between the man's fingers as he covered his face with his hands. Lane began to back out of the melee, clearing a path with rapid swings of his club.

At the edge of the fight, he found two of his men arresting a Klansman.

"You can't arrest me! I'm a special deputy!" he was screaming.

"He shot a student!" said one of Lane's men as they dragged him away.[8]

Chief Lane looked back on the scene in front of the building. It was a maelstrom of flying bottles, rocks, and fists. He was supposed to be demonstrating his ability to maintain law and order. Instead, the situation was out of control. The Klansmen were joining the fight more enthusiastically, and the Notre Damers were not retreating. Now someone had been shot.

He raced back to the station, only two blocks away. Without pausing to catch his breath, he called his friend Chief Corwin Hartwick in Mishawaka and asked him to send whatever help he could spare. Hartwick promised to send nine men. Lane then called the chief of the railroad detectives; he could spare two men.[9] It was not nearly enough. Lane heard screams in the distance. There was only one person left to call.

"Fr. Walsh," he said into the phone, his voice breaking. "We need you to come down here."

———

Some of the Notre Dame men managed to break away from the fight in front of the Klan building. They ran from the Klan's headquarters to the courthouse, about three blocks away, and gathered on the lawn. A contingent—including sophomore Bill Foohey—wanted to return to the fight and tried to sway the others to join them. Their pride hurting more than their bruises and cuts, the students began to reenergize. As they were mobilizing, Fr. Walsh and Fr. O'Donnell arrived.

Having seen real warfare in his day, Walsh disliked it when people glibly likened things to the battlefield. Sportswriters' constant comparisons of football to warfare especially irritated him. At the courthouse, though, the analogy seemed apt. There were injured young men everywhere, some of them groaning, most of them trying to downplay their pain. There was fear, of course, the men having realized with a shock that there were people in the world who meant to do them real physical harm. There was a special kind of hungry confusion, as the men were ready to go back and fight but weren't sure what had gone wrong or what would happen next. Most reminiscent of war was a distinctive kind of savage anger among the men, feeding on their fear, growing stronger by the second.

Walsh started to speak to the crowd and saw quickly that no one could hear him. He climbed onto the cannon on the monument behind him and spread his arms to gain his balance. Carved into the limestone of the monument was the word *Gettysburg*, the battle in which Fr. Corby, the gentle man who had welcomed Walsh into religious life, had gained his fame. The irony was not lost on Walsh, student of history. Corby had climbed a rock at Gettysburg in 1863 in order to grant absolution to the men of the Irish Brigade immediately before their charge. Walsh himself had served with honor in World War I, alongside legions of Catholics ready to give up their lives for their country. Now Indiana was full of men who thought them all disloyal Americans. Unlike Corby, Walsh would try to convince his charges to turn away from the battle.

As he steadied himself on the cannon, Walsh noticed that Chief Lane had pulled up in his car. He watched from the shadows with his headlights off.

Walsh wasn't sure about what had already happened. Lane had not explained on the phone but had sounded frighteningly desperate, so Walsh knew the situation was far more urgent than Saturday's public-relations disaster. As Walsh looked across the courthouse lawn at the furious, bleeding young men in front of him, he was certain that if he didn't intervene immediately the night would end in catastrophe and death. Walsh had been in a similar situation once before, at the prison in Paris, when a carefully worded appeal had pulled a mob back from the edge of serious violence. Walsh exhaled and began to speak.

"Whatever challenge may have been offered tonight to your patriotism, whatever insult may have been offered to your religion, you can show your loyalty to Notre Dame and South Bend by ignoring all threats," he began. Walsh was famously reserved in front of the students, in normal times leaving the speech making to more vocal men like Fr. O'Donnell and Fr. Holderith. Few students had ever heard him say ten words, much less a whole speech—the novelty of that alone would have held their attention, and the dramatic image of their president addressing them from a cannon held them transfixed.

"The constituted authorities have only the desire to preserve order and peace and protect everyone," Walsh continued. The students booed loudly at this. Walsh pressed on through the catcalls. "That is their duty! Others can well leave to their hands the maintenance of peace and the punishment of anything that is wrong. If tonight there have been violations of the law, it is not the duty of you and your companions to search out the offenders.

"I know that in the midst of excitement you are swayed by emotions that impel you to answer challenge with force. As I said in the statement issued last Saturday, a single injury to a Notre Dame student would be too great a price to pay for any deed or any program that concerned itself with antagonisms. I should dislike very much to make explanations to the parents of any student who might be injured—even killed—in a disturbance that could arise out of any demonstration such as been started here tonight.

"There is no loyalty that is greater than the patriotism of the Notre Dame student. There is no conception of duty higher than that which a Notre Dame man holds for his religion or for his university. I know that if tonight any of the property of the university or any of its privileges were threatened and I should call upon you, you would rise to a man to protect it. It is with the same loyalty to Notre Dame that I appeal to you to show your respect for South Bend and the authority of the city by dispersing."[10]

Although it is not possible that all of the men downtown that night heard Walsh's speech, the men closest to him heard enough to understand his message. Some of the young men desperately wanted to continue the fight, while others were scared and were looking for an excuse to leave. Still others may have simply been swayed by Walsh's logic. None, however, were willing to disobey Walsh so directly in his presence. The men who could hear Fr. Walsh gave a tired cheer and started walking back to campus. With the retreat of that group, the Notre Damers' urge to fight dissolved. Walsh stayed on top of the cannon until the courthouse lawn was empty. Fr. O'Donnell waited on the ground beside him. When Walsh finally climbed down, he saw Chief Lane drive slowly away.

The reports of a student being shot later proved to be erroneous. South Bend attorney Al Hosinksi, one of the sheriff's "special deputies," did in fact brandish a pistol at the fight, but an investigation after his arrest revealed that he hadn't fired a shot. No one blamed the police officers for arresting him—a shooting seemed imminently possible at the time. After two riots in three days, the citizens of South Bend realized that if nothing had been done, a shooting would probably have been inevitable.

Early on Tuesday morning, Mayor Eli Seebirt announced to the frightened public that he would hold two meetings that day. In the afternoon, he would meet with local Klan leaders. In the morning, he would meet with "prominent Catholics of the community,"[11] including Fr. Matthew Walsh and Fr. J. Hugh O'Donnell. At that meeting, the students of Notre Dame took their second beating in two days.

"These spoiled brats are out of control," said one shop owner.

"They have to be dealt with firmly by all parties," said a bank vice president. "You've been too soft on them. They get to go home in a

few weeks—we have to stay here in South Bend and repair the damage they have done." The mayor nodded somberly in agreement.

Walsh listened to them blame the students and the university's
administration with the calm detachment that he had mastered.
O'Donnell, squirming in the chair next to him, was not nearly as
adept at stoicism. While Walsh certainly didn't hold the students
blameless, he did feel the need to point out that there was plenty of
culpability to go around. Putting a fiery cross in a downtown window
and robed Klansmen on every street corner could certainly be
regarded as provocative. He was just about to say so when Chief Lane
chimed in.

"I too am horrified at the behavior of these students," he said.
"Although I am not surprised. Given their history of boorish behav-
ior in our community, an incident like this was just a matter of time."
He exchanged serious nods with the men in the room.

Walsh stopped just short of responding. He was afraid that any
words that might leave his mouth at that moment would further the
notion that Notre Dame men had violent tempers. The speakers at
the meeting had all agreed that the Notre Dame men were completely responsible for the violence on Saturday. Chief Lane, it was
clear, had decided that the politically expedient course was to jump
on that bandwagon. Walsh was silent for the rest of the meeting. If
he defended his students, the men in the room would likely view it
as the administration being too lenient. Walsh knew that nothing he
could say would change anyone's mind. He forced himself to listen
quietly to the men discuss the hooliganism of his students, considering it his penance for the riot.

Later, Walsh had Fr. O'Donnell and Fr. Holderith write out and
sign a detailed statement about their meetings with Lane over the
weekend—how the chief had said that there was nothing to worry
about and how he seemed more amused than upset by the actions of
the students. The criticism from the town's most prominent
Catholics stung Walsh, but he knew that they were emotional and

that their ire was only temporary. Lane's reversal, on the other hand, was a premeditated betrayal.

After the meeting with the mayor, Walsh rushed back to campus. While he didn't feel compelled to discuss the details during the morning meeting, he was taking decisive action to prevent further violence. He had called a meeting of the entire student body in Washington Hall. The person he had asked to speak to them was the man at Notre Dame who had the greatest proven ability at motivating young men: Knute Rockne. Walsh had had his difficulties with his famous employee, but he recognized that the students worshiped the coach and would listen to every word he had to say.

Walsh stood at Rockne's side as the coach addressed the assembled students from the stage. Rockne gave a passionate if somewhat rambling speech on the virtues of religion, fair play, sportsmanship, and good manners. He finally brought it all back to the situation at hand. "You cannot expect to win a game of football unless the players follow the signals of the quarterback," he said to the rapt students. "Fr. Walsh is your quarterback, and you are the great Notre Dame team. It is your duty to follow the signals of Fr. Walsh, and when you do, you will be in the right, and will not be a party to any disorder." [12]

The students gave a great cheer. Though Walsh noted that Rockne had referred to him as "your quarterback" and not "our quarterback," he was sincerely grateful to the coach for his effort. Walsh stepped to the podium as Rockne finished and looked out at his young men.

And they were young men again. They were grinning in the afterglow of Rockne's speech, elbowing one another and slapping the backs of their friends' heads. One young man in an aisle seat had fallen fast asleep; his chums were stealthily tying his shoelaces together. It was hard for Walsh to believe that these were the same battered, angry soldiers he had confronted at the courthouse the night before.

"None of you should take part in a demonstration against any organization," Walsh began, "regardless of the principles of that organization. It would be possible to curb such demonstrations by keeping all of you on campus. But I will not do that. It is not necessary. I know that you will follow my signal—as your quarterback." He gestured back to Rockne, on the stage behind him. "Remain on campus and away from South Bend when there is any demonstration that does not meet your favor."[13]

The students cheered again. Fr. O'Donnell stepped forward to administer a "no rioting" pledge to the students, modeled on the temperance pledges that periodically made their way through campus.

"Stand up and raise your right hand," O'Donnell said commandingly. Every student obeyed.

"Do you hereby solemnly promise, God helping you, to abstain from all demonstrations against objectionable organizations and to employ all proper means to encourage others to do the same?"[14]

Two thousand young men enthusiastically said, "I do."

Walsh was a realist. He expected the "no rioting" oath to be every bit as effective and lasting as the temperance pledges. Consequently, he took the additional step of instituting patrols around the campus at night. These small groups of unarmed priests and brothers were charged with keeping a lookout for men on either side who were ready to continue the fight. The patrols never ended up intercepting any irate Klansmen or fired-up students, only the occasional clandestine smoker enjoying a contraband cigarette in the moonlight.

While the local press reported favorably on the Rockne speech and the oath, Walsh still had a severe public-relations crisis on his hands. The image of an out-of-control, potato-throwing Catholic mob was one that many newspapers around the country found irresistible. Minnesota's St. Paul Daily News published an article with a two-inch alliterative headline that Stephenson would have been proud of: "Notre Dame collegians clash with Kluxers."[15] Closer to home, the

Chicago Herald-Examiner published a photo of students parading in their captured robes beneath the headline "Students rout Klansmen."[16]

Stephenson wouldn't be outdone by the conventional press. "Notre Dame mob beats women and children" was the classic *Fiery Cross* headline. The paper eventually published its account of the riot in booklet form; it was entitled *The Truth about the Notre Dame Riot on Saturday, May 17, 1924*. It described an American flag being "stoned, torn to ribbons and trampled underfoot by a cursing mob of students."[17] The booklet speculated that "the fact that candidates sponsored by the Klansmen of St. Joseph County swept the primaries here on May 6 has goaded the alien element to desperation." One of many atrocities committed by the "alien element," according to the account, was "the beating of an old white-haired couple that carried small American flags."[18] The pamphlet sold well at ten cents a copy.

After the meeting with the student body, Walsh reverted back to his policy of ignoring the Klan, a stance he still believed in despite the primary election and the riot. This policy, while perhaps sound in the long run, allowed Stephenson most of the early momentum in the public-relations war that followed May 17. For a brief time, there was a petition drive led by the Michigan Klan for Michigan A&M— later known as Michigan State University—to cancel its June 6 baseball game with the Irish. The petition stated that Notre Dame students "attacked women in Klan cars, tore flags from the Klan headquarters and stamped them under their feet, searched every person on the streets carrying a bundle which might contain a Klan robe and drove several visiting Klansmen from the city."[19] Several of those visiting Klansmen were apparently from East Lansing. Walsh never commented on the drive, which ultimately failed. The Irish beat the Aggies on June 6, 4–3.

Walsh's minimization of the riot was equal parts public-relations strategy and embarrassment at what had taken place. The day after Rockne gave his speech and O'Donnell administered the pledge, Walsh asked O'Donnell in a memo to tell the students that there was no need "to be unduly excited over what has happened."[20] A week later, on May 27, he wrote to a friend in Chicago and referred to the riot as "the Klan happenings."[21] While Walsh acknowledged in that letter some of the bad press that the school had received, he stated his belief, and no doubt his sincere hope, that "everything is moving on quietly and the thinking people of South Bend are all with us."[22]

For months after the riot, Walsh received letters condemning him and the students for the violence. Many of the letters were of the "Say it ain't so" variety, begging Walsh to deny the horrible stories the letter writers had read about the unpatriotic, out-of-control Notre Dame students. Other letters were more sinister. One Klansman wrote, "You can thank your lucky stars that you have your buildings intack [sic], for if the Knights of the Ku Klux Klan assembled in South Bend last Sat. [May 17] had been as lawless as your bunch of anarchist students they would have wiped the Notre Dame buildings off the earth." He went on to call the students "ruffnecks," "hoodlums," and, most colorfully of all, "mackerel snapping anarchists." He ended by saying, "We showed you a few tricks at the recent Primary, now we are going to show you several more at the election in the fall. I say down with Catholic domination of every kind in AMARICA [sic]." He signed the letter, "A KLUXER."[23]

A different letter promised "hot lead" for the Notre Dame students.[24] Another Klansman sent Walsh the headline from the May 30 issue of the *Fiery Cross* with a threat scrawled across it in pencil: "YOU DIRTY UNAMERICAN SKUNKS WILL PAY FOR YOUR MOB ACTIONS IN SOUTH BEND."[25]

Walsh took all the threatening letters, all the memos, and all the unflattering newspaper accounts and filed them in a "KKK" file with his official papers. He was still certain that his policy of ignoring the Klan was sound and that the Invisible Empire would eventually collapse under the weight of its own ignorance and hate. A corollary theory of his held that Catholic Americans—hardworking, patriotic, and virtuous—would eventually take their place in the mainstream of American life. Ever the historian, Walsh kept his Klan file to chronicle an important part of the university's history, the challenges it faced during this journey. Walsh would never admit that those articles, which he read from time to time when he was alone in his office, also sometimes made him smile. Despite the danger the students had put themselves and others into, despite the embarrassment they had brought the university, and despite their disobedience on a grand scale, Walsh probably derived some small, secret pleasure in how his students had taken it to the Klan. He never disciplined a single student for participating in the riot.

10

THE ASCENT OF NOTRE DAME

W HILE MATTHEW WALSH HAD OPTED NOT TO PUNISH the students who had participated in the riot, Imperial Wizard Hiram Evans was not nearly as forgiving of D. C. Stephenson. He knew that he needed to neutralize Stephenson, one way or another, and he was running out of time—Stephenson's man would soon be in the governor's mansion. Evans had hoped to discredit Stephenson at Buschmann Hall the day after the riot in South Bend, and that had been a farce. Stephenson was again calling himself Indiana's Grand Dragon. The vast majority of Hoosier Klansmen still accepted him as Grand Dragon. Evans decided to take a different approach.

In June 1924, Evans convened a Klan tribunal to determine the guilt or innocence of Stephenson on six charges: violating the Klan oath, violating the Klan constitution, conspiring against the order, habitual drunkenness, commission of an act unworthy of a Klansman, and disrespect of virtuous womanhood. Evans hired detectives to conduct a detailed investigation and to even depose some of the virtuous women Stephenson had allegedly violated. There were many to choose from.

Predictably, Evans's tribunal found Stephenson guilty of all six charges and sentenced him to "banishment forever and ostracism in any and all things by each and every member of this order" on June 24, 1924.[1] In a further attempt to discredit the best organizer in the history of the Klan, Evans published a complete account of the investigation, including transcripts of the interviews with the women, and distributed it throughout Indiana. Evans thought that the lurid details of Stephenson's assaults and arrests would disgust the average Hoosier, and they did. Still, it wasn't enough to fuel any kind of grassroots effort against the man. Like his hero, Napoleon, Stephenson had attained that rare combination of popularity and power that made him immune to normal political laws. Scandals that would sink any other Hoosier leader did nothing to hurt Stephenson.

Stephenson's relationship with Ed Jackson was the strongest plate in his armor. At the Indiana Republican Convention, which began on May 21, 1924, Stephenson relished his role as power broker from the center of the smoke-filled rooms where the real business of the convention was conducted. On the convention floor, he bestowed power on those whom he deemed worthy by shaking their hands, and he punished those few Evans loyalists in attendance by ignoring them, making them powerless. The *South Bend Tribune* reported that Stephenson "was the central figure in pre-convention arrangements and on the floor of the convention itself."[2] The Evans faction offered up a slate of its own to compete with Stephenson's, a slate that was soundly trounced by Ed Jackson and the rest of the men of the clothespin campaign. The convention was the perfect showcase for the things that Stephenson did better than Evans: he was a better politician, a better salesman, a better speaker, and a better public-relations man. Evans, however, was not one to back down from a fight. He possessed unique skills of his own.

Stephenson owned a fifty-eight-foot yacht, the *Reomar II*, that had been built in 1911 for Ransom E. Olds, the founder of the Oldsmobile automobile company. The name *Reomar* was derived from "R. E. Olds Marine." Stephenson had purchased the boat for the astronomical sum of fifty-five thousand dollars.[3] It was one of his favorite and most conspicuous indulgences, with glassy teak decks and brass fixtures that gleamed thanks to the *Reomar*'s attentive crew. It was the ideal place for both lavish political parties and private evenings with would-be starlets. Stephenson even sailed the yacht to the National Republican Convention, which opened in Cleveland on June 10, 1924. After the convention, Stephenson returned the yacht to its slip on Lake Erie in Bayview Park, Toledo, Ohio.

Before dawn on the morning of June 27, the docks around the *Reomar* were silent and the still waters of Lake Erie were indistinguishable from the black sky. Even if there had been witnesses on the dock, it would have been impossible to see conspirators in black clothing. At 3:30 AM, a massive explosion illuminated the marina like an early sunrise. The fireball quickly consumed itself, but the marina still glowed from the burning pieces of the boat that dropped back into the lake with a hiss. The singed ropes that had secured the yacht to the dock drooped limply into the water, as if surprised by the *Reomar*'s sudden departure. No one was killed in the explosion, and no one was ever charged with the bombing.

Stephenson didn't care if the cops considered the case unsolved; he knew who had done it.[4] Evans had always moved comfortably through the dark worlds of intimidation and violence. Stephenson knew that Evans was wearying of legitimate tactics like the meeting at Buschmann Hall and the tribunal. Stephenson had expected assassination attempts before, and the explosion of the *Reomar* seemed to confirm that his fear was the result of more than a paranoid delusion.

Stephenson hired more bodyguards and then constantly questioned their loyalty. He stashed pistols throughout his home and office. He drank more bootlegged whiskey. He avoided the big central window in his Indianapolis office, convinced that snipers were across the street, waiting to see his profile. With the general election looming, Stephenson was on the verge of his greatest victory. The stakes had never been higher for him—or his enemies. He sat in the darkest corner of his office, drinking, plotting, and watching the violent summer of 1924 give way to autumn.

Despite the sense of renewal and optimism that Matthew Walsh felt as the Notre Dame students returned to campus in September, he was troubled by reminders that anti-Catholicism still thrived in South Bend in the wake of the riot. In September, Helen Jackson, an "escaped nun," and L. J. King, an ex-priest, popular figures on the anti-Catholic lecture circuit, were scheduled to appear in South Bend. Helen Jackson's book, *Convent Cruelties*, was a descendant of Maria Monk's anti-Catholic classic, *Awful Disclosures of Maria Monk*. In keeping with the spirit of the times, Jackson emphasized the "un-American" nature of Catholicism. One of the book's fifteen cartoonish illustrations was of a nun intercepting her mail, "thus violating U.S.A. Postal laws."[5] The book also contained two photographs of Jackson, one in her "convent garb" and another of the escaped Jackson "in her American clothes."[6] Like her book, her lecture promised to detail her "providential delivery from Rome's convent slave pens."[7]

Pat Emmons, the head of the St. Joseph County Klan, surprised Walsh by sending him a bizarre letter denouncing the speakers in advance, telling Walsh that their talks were "in direct conflict with the purposes and ideals of our institution, for ours is one in which prevails only brotherly love for every race, color, creed and lineage."[8] Walsh expressed his doubts about Emmons's sincerity in a neat handwritten note on the top margin of the letter and filed it with the rest of his Klan documents. Perhaps Emmons was hoping to soften Walsh up for a future request for football tickets. Rockne's backfield that fall was especially promising.

In late September, the *Fiery Cross* again began raising blood pressures in Notre Dame's front office. The Klan paper, still run by Stephenson, announced that a second rally would be held in South Bend, on October 18, 1924. The express purpose of the rally was to avenge the events of May. The *Fiery Cross* estimated that two hundred thousand Klansmen would attend, many of them borne on special trains from Oklahoma, one of few states other than Indiana that was dominated at its highest political levels by the Klan.

Walsh reluctantly participated in a series of emergency meetings with local leaders who were panicked at the prospect of another riotous weekend. The mood at the meetings was not nearly as cooperative as it had been in May. Walsh believed that the authorities—especially Chief Lane—had ambushed the Notre Dame men on May 19. He also believed that Notre Dame had unfairly borne the brunt of the criticism in the aftermath of the riot. Walsh refused to tell the assembled dignitaries how he would handle the students during the next rally—until they shared with him the details of the city's plan. Neither side would give in. During this standoff, his newly acquired distaste for the civil authorities of South Bend reached a very personal level. Walsh described the meeting, at which Chief Lane had been present, in a letter to Charles O'Donnell, Andrew Morrissey's successor as provincial: "The palaver of our doughty chief has been nauseating."[9]

The potential for violence seemed so great to O'Donnell that he nearly canceled his October 18 trip to New York City for the Army–Notre Dame game, which he had planned to attend with the archbishop of New York.

Before O'Donnell could do anything that drastic, however, the second South Bend rally fizzled and died. Those officials in the Indiana Republican Party not affiliated with the Klan, especially in South Bend, dreaded the thought of another riot and the publicity it would garner in the weeks before the general election. They heavily pressured the Klan to cancel the second South Bend klonvocation. The *Fiery Cross* announced with its distinctive flair that the meeting had been canceled because the Klan had received intelligence about imported Catholic gunmen who were prepared to terrorize the meeting.

O'Donnell was therefore able to attend the Army–Notre Dame game with the archbishop—it was not one he would have wanted to miss. It was the third game of the season for Notre Dame. Both teams were undefeated. In front of fifty-five thousand fans, including the

U.S. secretary of war and a German zeppelin pilot, the Irish defeated
Army 13–7.

One of the many sportswriters in the press box for that game was
Grantland Rice of the *New York Herald-Tribune*. Fleshing out the
kernel of an idea given to him by George Strickler, a Notre Dame
sophomore and one of Rockne's publicity assistants, Rice took inspiration for his lead from the Rudolph Valentino film *The Four
Horsemen of the Apocalypse*. Rice's opening would become the most
famous lead in the history of sports journalism:

> Outlined against a blue, gray October sky the Four Horsemen
> rode again. In dramatic lore they are known as famine, pesti-
> lence, destruction, and death. These are only aliases. Their
> real names are Stuhldreher, Miller, Crowley, and Layden.
> They formed the crest of the South Bend cyclone before
> which another fighting Army football team was swept over
> the precipice at the Polo Grounds yesterday afternoon as
> 55,000 spectators peered down on the bewildering panorama
> spread on the green plain below.[10]

The passage was reprinted in newspapers across the country,
cementing Notre Dame football's national prominence. Walsh's
ongoing silence on the Klan was predicated on his belief that a
Catholic advance into mainstream American life was inevitable.
American Catholics took a major step forward after the game
against Army, having been advanced downfield by Rockne's
talented backs.

When the team returned from New York, the enterprising
Strickler, who had suggested the Four Horsemen motif to Rice, had
the four newly famous players pose for a photograph atop tired work-
horses from the university farm. He sent copies of the photo to the
wire services; like the article, it was soon printed in papers across the
country. Strickler also printed hundreds of the photos at his own

expense and sold them to sports fans for one dollar apiece. After netting three thousand dollars from the venture, Strickler dropped out of Notre Dame. Perhaps inspired by his brush with Grantland Rice, Strickler spent the rest of his life in journalism.

Shortly after the Four Horsemen phenomenon began, Indiana held its general election, on November 4. The Klansman Ed Jackson thrashed his Democratic opponent by 127,481 votes. Indiana had elected an unabashed Klansman as governor. By then, Notre Dame was 5–0.

Four days after the election, Rockne's team defeated an outclassed Wisconsin team 38–3. The Big Ten Conference had for years denied Notre Dame membership—a decision many believed to be motivated by anti-Catholicism—so Notre Dame fans took particular delight in their team's pummeling of a Big Ten opponent.

The next game for the Irish would be a much tougher contest—the Notre Dame team would face Nebraska on November 15, 1924. Since 1918, when Rockne's remarkable career as head coach began, his team had lost only four games. Two of them were to Nebraska. The two losses had been in Lincoln in front of rabidly anti-Catholic crowds. Rockne badly wanted to teach the Cornhuskers a lesson, as did the Notre Dame fans.

The game was played in South Bend in front of twenty-two thousand fans, filling Cartier Field to capacity for only the third time. It was also the first Notre Dame home game to be broadcast on the radio, by Chicago's WGN. The Notre Dame fans got what they were after, as the Irish crushed Nebraska 34–6, holding the national power to only two first downs. Each of the Four Horsemen scored a touchdown—Don Miller scored two.

The next week, on November 22, Notre Dame played Northwestern at Soldier Field in Chicago. Forty-five thousand fans watched Notre Dame beat another Big Ten team, 13–6. The Irish finished the regular season a week later by destroying Carnegie Tech 40–19. Notre Dame was undefeated and untied.

For their efforts, the Irish received their first-ever bowl invitation. The Rose Bowl invited Notre Dame to California to play Stanford, the Pacific Coast Conference champion. Walsh accepted the invitation only after receiving a thirty-five-thousand-dollar guarantee. He planned to use the money to construct a basketball gym on campus, which would allow the school to cut its ties with the YMCA in South Bend at last.

The football team and its entourage made a three-week trek to Pasadena by Southern Pacific Rail, on a charter train that included a special chapel car for daily communion. The team was hosted by the local Knights of Columbus lodge at every stop, including Chicago, Memphis, and New Orleans, where the players stuffed themselves on so much Creole food that they were unable to practice the next day, much to Rockne's disgust.[11]

Fr. John O'Hara, Notre Dame's prefect of religion, accompanied the team for the entire trip. He expressed the exultation many Catholic Americans felt when he described the journey to the Rose Bowl as a "crusade for the spread of the Holy Communion."[12] In May of the previous year, O'Hara had urged the men of Notre Dame in his bulletin to avoid fights with the Klan. Notre Dame at that time seemed to be an isolated Catholic outpost in increasingly hostile Protestant territory. Seven months later, on January 1, 1925, in front of fifty-three thousand fans, Notre Dame defeated a bruising Stanford team 27–10. At the end of the most fervidly anti-Catholic year in American history, Notre Dame was football's undisputed national champion.

————

It was the first of eleven consensus national championships for Notre Dame, more than any other school has earned. The team earned at least one championship in every decade except the 1950s and, more recently, the dry spell that was the 1990s. I was a junior at Notre Dame for the last one—Coach Lou Holtz's only championship, in

1988. That team also had to travel west to claim its title, to the Fiesta Bowl in the Arizona desert. I took a Greyhound bus to Kansas City, where I met my friend Sean O'Connell. We drove the rest of the way to Tempe in the Tercel that he had somehow convinced his sister to lend us. On the first frosty night of our drive, we pulled into a rest stop in western Kansas. It was, we discovered, the Knute Rockne Memorial Rest Stop. When we asked the attendant why it was called that, he pointed into the blackness that he said contained a cornfield and told us that that was where Rockne's plane had crashed. He spoke with such solemnity that I believed that had it been daylight, I would have seen tendrils of smoke still climbing from the wreckage.

The Knute Rockne Memorial Rest Stop was just one of the things that season that taught me how important Notre Dame football was to the world beyond us ten thousand students, and beyond even the school's legions of living alumni—the world of fans who have no tie to the school other than their fanatical devotion to it. They even have a name—they're the "subway alumni." I saw them every game weekend. Those who didn't have tickets to the game would sit in their vans and watch the game on TV, thrilled just to be within sight of the stadium. They would come up to me when I was away from Notre Dame and wearing Fighting Irish garb, like once in Bangkok, when a man with a thick German accent asked me what I thought about the next season's prospects. I always assumed that those dedicated fans with no official ties to the university loved the team because it represented Catholicism—a puzzling phenomenon to me at the time.

As Notre Dame students, Sean and I and the rest of our friends who had made the journey to Arizona felt that the football gods owed us a championship, while we were still young and still had guaranteed student tickets for every game. Chris Zorich, Todd Lyght, and the rest of Holtz's talented squad didn't disappoint us. Under a cool desert sky in Sun Devil Stadium, the undefeated Notre Dame team beat undefeated West Virginia 34–21 to win the consensus national championship. Notre Dame had gone eleven years without a championship—an eternity, it seemed to me.

As the victorious Notre Dame football players of 1924 made their way back east, they encountered a slight problem in Salt Lake City, Utah. An organ concert in the Mormon Tabernacle was on the team's crowded agenda, but some university officials were concerned that the concert would constitute a visit to a non-Catholic church— a forbidden act at that time. Fr. O'Hara, the mastermind of the team's publicity tour, made the battlefield decision that the tabernacle was not a church. The concert went on as scheduled.[13]

In all, it took the team twelve days to meander home through banquets, receptions, receiving lines, and admiring Catholic throngs at train stations across the country. In Denver, the team stood in a receiving line for more than two hours; even the governor passed through to pay his respects. The trip westward had been a Catholic American pep rally; the trip home was a victory celebration. It was more than a celebration of football prowess—Notre Dame's championship title also offered proof that the University of Notre Dame and Catholic institutions of learning in general could mold successful Americans. O'Hara made the point at every stop. The resultant publicity for the university was invaluable.

Back in South Bend, Fr. Walsh concerned himself with the championship's more tangible rewards. The fifty-two thousand dollars netted from the Rose Bowl far exceeded the thirty-five-thousand-dollar guarantee. The plans for a modest basketball gymnasium were likewise expanded into a six-thousand-seat arena.

D. C. Stephenson was also eager to build on his successes of the past year. Ed Jackson had won the gubernatorial election on November 4, 1924. The senior senator from Indiana, Sam Ralston, was seriously ill. If he died in office, the governor would appoint his replacement—and if Jackson was in office by that time, he might appoint Stephenson.

In the meantime, Stephenson made detailed plans for the pending session of the legislature. Evans's faction was fond of clumsy attacks on parochial education, frontal assaults that were doomed to fail. Stephenson, in contrast, planned to go about the "Kluxing" of Indiana quietly and behind the scenes. His initial plans revolved around the closely linked ventures of lining his pockets and consolidating his power.

Once Jackson was in office, Stephenson would propose through him a number of industry reform bills that he would withdraw only after "donations" from the affected industries had been obtained. He planned to reform the highway commission so that he would have control over millions of dollars in road-construction contracts. Stephenson's legislation was innocuous on its face. Who could argue with a bill that required public schools to teach a course on nutrition? Meanwhile, Stephenson would publish the only textbook allowable for the class.[14]

On a cold, snowy January 12, 1925, Stephenson watched his friend and protégé be sworn in as governor of Indiana. Klansman Ed Jackson took the oath of office inside the statehouse in front of hosts of spectators. To their delight, Jackson followed his oath with an exceptionally brief inaugural address. Then it was on to the party.

The postinaugural party was held in the Indianapolis Athletic Club, normally a Democratic venue. Stephenson arrived, as usual, accompanied by a pretty, young secretary. Never one to let himself be tied down, though, he soon began flirting with another young female employee of the state, who was sitting across from him at dinner. She had dark eyes and short, dark hair that was styled in a modern way. She was not quite attractive, and her insecurity appealed to Stephenson's predatory instincts. Her name was Madge Oberholtzer.

The entertainment at the party was characterized by the kind of all-American wholesomeness that had propelled the Republicans to victory in Indiana. Well-rehearsed, alcohol-free toasts were offered. A local Rotarian promised the support of his club's entire membership. A magician performed tricks.

The highlight of the evening came when poet William Herschell took the podium to read his wildly popular poem "Ain't God Good to Indiana?" After offering a few congratulatory remarks to the governor, Herschell began his recitation:

> Ain't God good to Indiana?
> Folks, a feller never knows
> Just how close he is to Eden
> Till, sometime, he ups an' goes
> Seekin' fairer, greener pastures
> Than he has right here at home,
> Where there's sunshine in the clover
> An' honey in th' comb;
> Where the ripples on th' river
> Kinda chuckles as they flow—
> Ain't God good to Indiana?
> Ain't He, fellers? Ain't He, though?
>
> Ain't God good to Indiana?
> Seems to me He has a way
> Gittin' me all outta humor
> Just to see how long I'll stay
> When I git th' gypsy feelin'
> That I'd like to find a spot
> Where th' clouds ain't quite so restless,
> Or th' sun don't shine so hot.
> But, I don't git far, I'll tell you,
> Till I'm whisperin' soft an' low:
> Ain't God good to Indiana?
> Ain't He, fellers? Ain't He, though?

Ain't God good to Indiana?
Other spots may look as fair,
But they lack th' soothin' somethin'
In th' Hoosier sky and air.
They don't have that snug-up feelin'
Like a mother gives a child;
They don't soothe you, soul an' body,
With their breezes soft an' mild.
They don't know th' joys of Heaven
Have their birthplace here below;
Ain't God Good to Indiana?
Ain't He fellers? Ain't He, though?[15]

As Herschell stepped away from the podium to thunderous applause and enthusiastic cheering, Stephenson reflected on the year. One out of three white Hoosier men were in the Klan. A Klansman—*his* Klansman—was governor. Despite Evans's best efforts, Stephenson was still calling the shots in Indiana. Good booze and beautiful women had never been more available. Was God good to Indiana? Stephenson would have to answer yes. He asked Madge Oberholtzer to dance.

11

THE RUIN OF D. C. STEPHENSON
AND THE COLLAPSE
OF THE KLAN

MADGE OBERHOLTZER LIVED WITH HER PARENTS IN Irvington, a quiet, desirable suburb of Indianapolis. The neighborhood was home to both Butler College, the school she attended for three years, and her new gentleman caller. D. C. Stephenson's home, the replica of Klankrest, was just a few blocks away from the Oberholtzers' home. Oberholtzer's father, George, was a postal clerk. Their house in Irvington was expensive for a civil servant, so the family took in boarders to help make ends meet. Although he was not a Klansman, George Oberholtzer was in some ways typical of the disaffected middle-class Hoosiers who made up their ranks. He was white-collar, moderately educated, not quite prosperous, and not quite happy with his lot in life. The presence of a twenty-eight-year-old unmarried daughter in the house would have confirmed to many at the time that things had not exactly gone the way they were supposed to for George Oberholtzer.

After leaving Butler College without a degree, Madge Oberholtzer wandered from job to job, trying her hand at teaching, clerking for an insurance company, and managing the Indianapolis office of the Acme Motion Picture Company. When she met Stephenson at Ed Jackson's postinauguration party, Oberholtzer was managing the

Indiana Teachers and Young People's Reading Circle, a statewide lending library run by the State Department of Instruction. As a state employee and an enthusiastic Republican Party volunteer, she had been invited to the inauguration.

Stephenson began courting Oberholtzer immediately after the inauguration, taking her to quiet dinners and on walks around Irvington, always treating her like a lady and getting her home at a respectable hour. Her parents were thrilled that she had caught the eye of a man like Stephenson—wealthy, powerful, and charming to boot. Stephenson also flattered Oberholtzer by including her in his professional life, having her deliver messages to his people in the state legislature and even proposing that she write the nutrition text-book that would soon be required in every Indiana school, a book he had already entitled *One Hundred Years of Health*. She began to see a way out of the drudgery she watched her father endure every day, a fate she was sure awaited her. With Stephenson, she saw herself lead-ing a new life of money, glamour, and endless opportunity.

As Stephenson was pushing his agenda through the state legisla-ture and romancing Oberholtzer, he was also gearing up for the approaching Indianapolis mayoral election. He wanted a Klansman in office, but he knew the Republican Party leaders in the city, headed by William A. Armitage, wouldn't back his man—they did not look kindly on the newcomer Stephenson and his pretense of running the Grand Old Party. They would accept the votes of the Klansmen, of course, but accepting a Klansman as their leader was another matter entirely. Armitage designated his own man, Ralph Lemcke, the for-mer city treasurer, to be the Republican nominee for mayor. But Stephenson didn't back down. He felt it was time to push aside the old-line party leaders in the capital city. He searched Indianapolis for a puppet candidate to represent his interests in the mayor's office.

He found that puppet candidate in John Duvall, a relatively unknown banker and attorney who had succeeded Lemcke in the treasurer's post. Duvall appeared sufficiently ambitious and malleable for Stephenson's needs. Stephenson staged a dramatic first meeting with Duvall. The Grand Dragon called on Duvall in his downtown office with thirteen other Klan officers. They filed silently into the office with Stephenson at their center and closed the door behind them.

"We want you to run for mayor," said Stephenson. "If you run, you'll win."

It was a tempting offer for a young politician looking to skip a few steps on the political ladder. Like everyone else in Indiana, Duvall had seen what Stephenson had done for Ed Jackson.

"Let me think about it," he told Stephenson. After two weeks, he called him and agreed to do it.

Duvall's deal with the devil was formalized in February 1925. He knew the score—he got to be mayor, and Stephenson got to call the shots. Nonetheless, he was surprised at how directly Stephenson put the arrangement in writing:

> In return for the political support of D. C. Stephenson, in the event that I am elected mayor of Indianapolis, Ind. I promise not to appoint any person as a member of the Board of Public Works with out they first have the endorsement of D. C. Stephenson.[1]

Duvall signed the contract, agreeing to the same terms that dozens of other Hoosier politicians had agreed to.

Even before the campaign had begun, Stephenson was telling Duvall whom he would appoint to scores of city jobs. One of Stephenson's numerous bodyguards would be a sheriff's deputy. A loyal supporter, Claude Worley, would be named chief of police. When it was clear to Stephenson that Duvall would be compliant with these demands, he threw his campaign machine into motion on Duvall's behalf. Canvassers were sent to every house in Indianapolis, and on the day before the 1925 primary election, clothespins were dropped onto every doorstep. Once again, Stephenson's efforts were successful: his man crushed the old guard's candidate in the primary.

———

At 10:00 PM on Sunday, March 15, 1925, Madge Oberholtzer returned home from an evening out with a friend. Although ill, her mother had stayed awake to deliver an important message to her daughter. D. C. Stephenson's secretary, Fred Butler, had telephoned with an urgent request. Butler apologized on Stephenson's behalf for the late hour but said that Stephenson needed to talk to Oberholtzer right away, before he left on a trip to Chicago. It was about *One Hundred Years of Health*. Oberholtzer was excited—she liked Stephenson, and she liked the idea of authoring the textbook. She called Stephenson, who said he would send a man to escort her down the street. She told her mother of her plans and waited in the parlor. Earl Gentry soon appeared at the door. Together they walked down the deserted sidewalk to Stephenson's house.

When Gentry escorted Madge into the parlor of Stephenson's house, she saw Stephenson sitting in a chair, flanked by his watchful guards. Lamplight barely penetrated the cloud of cigar smoke in the room. Stephenson was the only one sitting down. When he spoke, she understood why.

"Thank you for coming," he slurred. He was too drunk to stand. He extended his hands toward her. Despite her unease, she instinctively put her hands out to meet his. She had never seen Stephenson drink before. In fact, she had often heard him criticize the lax enforcement of prohibition to his political colleagues.

"I . . . I think I want to go home," she said. Stephenson's hands tightened around her wrists.

"You're staying with me," he said, his eyes half-closed.

Oberholtzer broke away and lurched toward the telephone on a table in the hallway. One of Stephenson's omnipresent associates ripped the receiver from her hand before she could begin the call. Two others dragged her into the kitchen. Behind her, Stephenson said, "Let's get her a drink, help her relax."

A man handed her a glass. "Drink it," he said. She hesitated.

"You heard the man," said Stephenson. He was leaning in the doorway, smiling. The eyes of a dozen hard-edged men were upon her. Most were displaying guns in their belts or in holsters under their shoulders. Her hand shook as she took the glass. For a moment, she considered throwing it to the floor, but that kind of courage wasn't in her. She swallowed the drink fast. Everything went black as the burning in her throat overtook all other sensation. She coughed and fought the nausea rising up in her, brought on by both fear and young whiskey. The men made her drink two more. After the third glass, she could no longer stand.

Through her haze, Oberholtzer was aware that she was being taken outside and pushed into an automobile. She mumbled again that she wanted to go home, but she knew by then that they weren't going to let her go. After a short drive, someone pulled her out of the car. She recognized Union Station. Stephenson's thugs carried her through the cavernous building to his private railcar. They shoved her roughly into the lower berth. She had no idea where the train was going or what was happening to her. As the unfamiliar effects of the alcohol worked their way through her system, she was unaware of the train rolling out of the station and accelerating through Indianapolis on its way into the dark Indiana countryside. She lost consciousness.

She awoke as Stephenson climbed into the berth with her. "Now I've got you," he said. He suddenly seemed very focused and alert. Oberholtzer was in a kind of stupor; she couldn't believe what Stephenson was doing to her. She couldn't believe that his men had just let it all happen. Stephenson approached her; the sweet-sour smell of alcohol coming from him was overwhelming. She felt the sandpapery roughness of his cheek against hers as he tried to kiss her. With one motion, Stephenson ripped off the black dress she had put on for her evening out. She heard buttons rolling across the floor of the car and began to cry.

"No one can hear you," he said flatly.

He pinned her arms to her sides. He bit her neck, her legs, her back. She felt blood running down her body. She screamed and thought she couldn't endure any more pain. Then Stephenson raped her.

Shocked and battered, Madge drifted in and out of consciousness. The train made a stop, and Stephenson crawled out of the berth. She heard him tell his bodyguards that he didn't want to cross the state line with her. They removed her from the bed, dressed her, and carried her out of the berth and onto the platform. A sign said that they were in Hammond, Indiana, the last stop on the line before Chicago. Stephenson had his men check them in to the nearby Indiana Hotel; Stephenson and Oberholtzer were checked in as Mr. and Mrs. W. B. Morgan. Madge was crying when they threw her into the bed with Stephenson. Despite her sobbing, Stephenson promptly fell asleep.

Oberholtzer waited until his breathing was steady and shallow; then she climbed slowly out of bed. City lights shone weakly through the window, giving her just enough light to navigate the room. She found Stephenson's gun still inside the belt of his pants, which had been tossed carelessly on the floor. The gun was heavy and her hands were shaking, but she pointed it right at Stephenson as he slept. She was too close to miss. She could no longer hear Stephenson's snoring over her pounding heart.

Instantly, she knew she could not do it, and she loathed herself for her cowardice. The man deserved to die for what he had done to her, but when she imagined the crack of the gun and the blood and carnage, she couldn't bring herself to pull the trigger. She thought about the scandal for her poor parents, the whispers they would have to endure for the rest of their lives if she killed a man in some dingy hotel room. She couldn't shoot the monster, but she knew she couldn't go on living in the same world he lived in either. She turned toward the large mirror over the room's dresser and put the gun to her head.

As she looked at her reflection, she was comforted by the thought of ending her life. She couldn't fathom going back to her everyday life of work, shopping, movies, and dinner with her parents after what had happened. She knew she would think about the things that had happened on the train every day for the rest of her life. Ending her life would bring rest, and peace. Even so, she was again afraid to pull the trigger, and again she hated herself for being weak. She heard a rustling in the bedroom and quickly slipped the gun back into Stephenson's trousers. She spent the rest of the evening in a chair, listening to Stephenson's raspy snore and contemplating the ways she could end her life.

The next day, a sober Stephenson tried to act as if they were on some kind of casual outing together, as if she were his companion and not his captive. It was a seductive charade, thought Oberholtzer. If she went along with it, she could just go on living as if nothing had happened. She wondered how many women before her had decided to push Stephenson's crimes into the back of their minds in an attempt to forget everything. She knew she couldn't do that. Even with Stephenson behaving normally, the charade had definite limits. His men wouldn't let her out of their sight or near a phone. She supposed they were waiting to see how she was going to react to the previous evening's events before letting her go.

She decided to play along. Putting on the cheeriest face she could muster, she asked Stephenson if she could have some money to go to the drugstore to buy some cosmetics. Stephenson looked at her closely, as if he were reading her mind. Oberholtzer had spent enough time with Stephenson to know that he was an expert judge of character, a man whose success was based on his ability to size people up and predict their actions. She tried to smile and looked nervously down at the floor.

Stephenson nodded slowly to one of his men, indicating that he was to accompany her, and handed her fifteen dollars. For the first time in what seemed like an eternity, Oberholtzer felt hopeful. Her plan to kill herself was moving forward.

In the drugstore, Stephenson's bodyguard became distracted by the magazines and the picture postcards as Oberholtzer shopped. She racked her brain trying to think of a poison she might be able to purchase there. She remembered her friends at Butler once gossiping about a sick girl and a scandal. She had ingested a disinfectant, mercury bichloride, in an attempt to induce an abortion but had nearly poisoned herself. Oberholtzer asked the clerk for a box of the tablets, paid for them with Stephenson's money, and hid them in her purse.

Back at the Indiana Hotel, Madge excused herself while the indifferent Stephenson read the newspaper on the couch. In the bathroom, she counted out the tablets. There were eighteen. She arranged them on the washstand in groups of three, thinking that three was the largest number she would be able to swallow at a time. Without stopping to think about it, she took the first set of three with a glass of water. Before she could measure any reaction, she swallowed the second group of three.

She never got to the next set. She immediately began vomiting blood into the sink and collapsed on the floor. Stephenson's guard opened the bathroom door when he heard the thud; the door hit Madge's head. He saw the sink full of blood.

"What have you done?" he asked.

"I've taken poison," she muttered from the floor.

"What kind?"

"Bichloride."

"Oh, my God," he said and ran out of the room.

A few minutes later, Stephenson appeared. "You fool!" he said.

"I want to be dead," she said.

He shoved a bottle of milk in her face. "Drink this!" he told her. Oberholtzer groaned. She was through with taking orders from Stephenson.

Stephenson panicked—this had never happened to him before. Women had become upset with him, of course, but their shame had usually driven them to keep quiet. Stephenson sent for his car, which was still in Indianapolis—they couldn't risk taking the train with Oberholtzer in that condition. Once the car arrived, Oberholtzer sat propped up between Stephenson and Earl Gentry in the backseat while one of Stephenson's bodyguards drove his car at top speed toward Indianapolis. She screamed in pain with every bump in the road. Stephenson tried again to make her drink the milk, thinking it would soothe her stomach. Her ruined stomach couldn't hold the milk; she vomited violently all over the interior of the car and the men on either side of her.

"My God, Earl," Stephenson said over the barely conscious, moaning woman between them. "I really think she is going to die."

————

As Stephenson, Oberholtzer, and his bodyguards were speeding back to Indianapolis, Madge Oberholtzer's parents were becoming increasingly worried about their daughter. She had not come home from her appointment with Stephenson—her mother had waited up all night for her to return. On Monday morning, Matilda Oberholtzer had called Asa Smith, a respected Indianapolis attorney whom some friends had recommended she call. She told him about the late-night phone call and her daughter's trip to Stephenson's mansion. Smith advised the frantic mother not to overreact. Her daughter was twenty-eight years old, after all, old enough to spend the night away from home, regardless of how improper it might be. A loyal Republican, Smith was also wary of throwing around accusations about the state's most powerful political figure, especially over what might just be a clandestine romance between two consenting adults. He counseled caution and said he would help.

Smith called Madge Oberholtzer's friends at the State Board of Instruction. He went to Stephenson's house to ask about her. Neither Stephenson nor Oberholtzer was there, and no one on Stephenson's staff admitted having seen them. He went to Union Station with Matilda Oberholtzer to see if her daughter was on any arriving trains. As the day went on with no word from Madge Oberholtzer, Smith began to wonder if some of her mother's worst fears might be justified.

It was late Monday night when Stephenson and Oberholtzer arrived back in Irvington. Stephenson took the woman to his house and put her in the room over his garage. Madge Oberholtzer was clearly not getting better. He ranted to his bodyguards, trying to come up with a solution. At one point, he suggested that he would marry Oberholtzer and compel her not to testify against him. One look at Oberholtzer, though, convinced him that marriage was not a realistic option. She would be dead before he could arrange it.

It was just the sort of incident that his enemies had been waiting for—he could feel the noose tightening around his neck with each phone call and each knock on the door. Law enforcement was not involved yet, probably only because the family was trying to avoid a public scandal. Finally, at a loss for a better plan, Stephenson detailed the loyal Earl Klinck to stake out the Oberholtzers' home and wait until the parents left. When they were gone, he would get Madge and return her to the house. On Tuesday morning, Asa Smith took Oberholtzer's parents downtown to give a statement to a detective agency. While they were away, Earl Klinck got Madge, put her in the car, drove to her house, and carried her inside. He placed her ravaged body in bed. He hid his face from one of the boarders as he left, explaining only that he was "Mr. Johnson from Kokomo" and that Oberholtzer had been in a car accident.

For weeks, Oberholtzer's parents remained at her bedside as a series of doctors and specialists attended to her. Despite their efforts, Oberholtzer's body and spirit were irreparably broken. She remained bedridden for her few remaining days, long enough to give a detailed, witnessed, signed, and notarized statement to Asa Smith.

Smith turned the statement over to Will Remy, the Marion County prosecutor, even before Oberholtzer's death. Remy quickly prepared a warrant and had Stephenson arrested on kidnapping charges on April 2, 1925. Stephenson talked the arresting policemen into letting him walk to the police headquarters, only a block away from his home. He immediately posted his ten-thousand-dollar bond and was released. News of the arrest spread, and the sensational story began its long run in the Indiana newspapers. Stephenson, skilled public-relations man that he was, countered the headlines by hinting to reporters that the whole matter was a frame-up engineered by Imperial Wizard Evans. "Nothing to it," he stated to the press. "I'll never be indicted."

Stephenson was not as confident as he appeared to be. All of his carefully laid plans seemed to be in danger, and his enemies were poised to press their advantage while he was vulnerable. Adding another dimension to the chaos was the reappearance of Nettie Hamilton, Stephenson's first wife, who had traveled from Oklahoma to sue Stephenson for child support. She told her story to a stream of eager reporters. "We're destitute," she said, "and he's rich!" He had never given them a dime, she complained. She encouraged the newspaper reporters to run photographs of their poor, beautiful daughter, Florence Catherine, now nine years old.

The negative publicity continued to swirl around Stephenson. Then, nearly a month after being abducted and assaulted, Madge Oberholtzer died at home on April 14, 1925. When the charge against Stephenson was changed to second-degree murder, the negative publicity became a torrent.

Late at night on April 16, the day of Madge's funeral, a trail of expensive dark cars drove up Stephenson's long driveway. Stephenson's home had become the scene of intense observation, so several neighbors witnessed the late-night visit. The cars left soon after they arrived. A few moments later, an explosion blew out every window of the house and illuminated Irvington. People rushed into the street in their nightclothes to see the fire. Stephenson was not home—he had secretly moved to a downtown hotel to avoid his ex-wife Hamilton. (She was horrified to learn that she had probably saved his life.) The bombers might have been vigilantes, whipped into a frenzy by Oberholtzer's funeral. They might have been Evans's Black Robes, sent to silence Stephenson once and for all. Or they might have been in the employ of corrupt politicians, men afraid of what Stephenson might reveal about them on the witness stand. Stephenson's enemies had grown so numerous that it was hard for him to say for sure.

Despite his long list of enemies, Stephenson still had friends in high places. The judge at his arraignment—James Collins—was a friend. The coroner who examined Oberholtzer's body, Dr. Paul Robinson, was a Klansman. Robinson declared that Oberholtzer had died from the mercury bichloride, not from anything Stephenson had done. Even with these signs of loyalty, however, Stephenson knew how fast his "friends" would abandon him if he appeared to lose power—he had watched and assisted the rats jumping off of Governor Warren McCray's sinking ship in 1923. Stephenson began squirreling away his "contracts" with politicians and other incriminating documents in safe-deposit boxes across Indiana, insurance against betrayal.

On April 20, 1925, Stephenson was arrested by Marion County sheriff Omer Hawkins—another friend and Klansman. This time, he was charged with murder. This time, there would be no bail.

To many, the murder charge seemed like a stretch, since Oberholtzer had admitted in her statement to attempting suicide. The state contended that it was an infection caused by Stephenson's bites, not the mercury bichloride, that had killed her. The public was riled by the media's accounts of an innocent damsel ruined by a Klansman ogre, and the district attorney was reluctant to charge the villain of the story with anything less than murder.

Stephenson hired a team of pricey veteran lawyers that included Ephraim "Eph" Inman, the best criminal defense lawyer in Indianapolis. Inman immediately requested and was granted a change of venue, from Indianapolis to sleepy Noblesville in rural Hamilton County. In 1923, two hundred Klansmen had burned a cross on the Noblesville courthouse lawn.[2] Only one county in Indiana had a higher percentage of its population in the Klan in 1925.[3] The deck seemed stacked in Stephenson's favor, with his celebrated lawyers, his seemingly inexhaustible funds, the move to Noblesville, and an overreaching murder charge against him.

In court, the team Stephenson had hired would be going up against Will Remy, the small, young-looking Marion County prosecutor. The press quickly dubbed him "the boy prosecutor." Remy had filled the prosecutor's post vacated by the son-in-law of disgraced Governor McCray—a post that Stephenson and Ed Jackson had unsuccessfully tried to bribe McCray into filling with a Klan puppet in 1923.

Imperial Wizard Evans didn't waste any time capitalizing on Stephenson's misfortune. On August 9, Evans spoke at a rally on the Noblesville courthouse square, within earshot of Stephenson's jail cell. While Evans could barely contain his glee at Stephenson's arrest, he was worried that the public would hold the Klan responsible for Stephenson's crimes. The Imperial Wizard reminded everyone that Stephenson was no longer the Grand Dragon of Indiana and that he had been drummed out of the Klan months before the Oberholtzer tragedy.[4] To most Hoosiers, though, Stephenson was the Klan. Stephenson listened to the speech from his bare cell, raged against Evans's dismissal, and criticized him for throwing together such a boring rally, with no music, food, or jousting knights.

After numerous delays and motions by Stephenson's defense team, including a request for a change of judges, the trial began on October 25, 1925. The prosecution declared that the deceased Oberholtzer would be its main witness, "clean of soul, but with her bruised, mangled, poisoned and ravished body."[5] The newspapers helpfully described Oberholtzer as beautiful and elevated her three meandering years at Butler College into graduation with honors.

Other witnesses for the prosecution included Oberholtzer's bereaved parents, the family's elderly boarder, the family doctor who had tried to save her, and the attorney Asa Smith. The night clerk from the Indiana Hotel in Hammond testified that Stephenson and Oberholtzer had been checked in as a married couple. Bellhops and Pullman porters testified as well. Dr. Virgil Moon, an instructor of pathology from Indiana University, offered his expert opinion that Oberholtzer had died as a result of infections from the bite wounds, not from the poison she had swallowed.

The most damning piece of evidence, however, was the lengthy, detailed statement from Oberholtzer herself. Inman tried valiantly to exclude the document, arguing that Asa Smith had actually written it and that Oberholtzer had not truly believed she was dying when she wrote it, a condition for making a deathbed pronouncement admissible in court. His request was rejected, and the statement was entered into evidence. Stephenson's team could do little more than nitpick the details, such as pointing out the odd fact that no one could locate or remember the name of the official who had notarized the statement.

In her statement, Oberholtzer had described her ordeal in brutal, plain language. She not only gave the details of her kidnapping and rape, but also painted a portrait of Stephenson as a drunk—he was inebriated in nearly every scene of the drama. Others had also testified about the central role of alcohol in Stephenson's life—the maid from the Indiana Hotel attested that his room had reeked of liquor—and Remy had described Stephenson in his opening statement as "a drunkard and a persistent destroyer of women's chastity."[6] One of the Klan's main connections to ordinary Hoosiers had long been its promise to defend prohibition as the law of the land. While Stephenson was not on trial for violating the Volstead Act, or for hypocrisy, the tales of his persistent drunkenness did not help him with the Hamilton County jury.

The prosecution finished its case on November 5, 1925. The defense took over, and Eph Inman called Dr. Orville Smiley to the stand. The doctor argued that the poison had killed Madge, not Stephenson's bites. Her death was a suicide, not a homicide, he told the jury. An autopsy witness contradicted everything the jury had heard by testifying that Oberholtzer's bite wounds had not appeared all that severe. An expert witness contradicted the testimony of Dr. Moon, stating that Madge had ingested a fatal dose of mercury bichloride. Inman reminded the jury that Madge had admitted to trying to kill herself. Wasn't it ridiculous to now claim that the poison had in no way contributed to her death? His logic was unemotional and compelling.

Only once did the defense attempt to sully the portrait of Oberholtzer as a virtuous young martyr, "clean of soul." The defense called Cora Householder to the stand to testify that her husband had had an affair with Oberholtzer years before. Judge Will Sparks immediately declared the story inadmissible and ended her testimony. The defense also produced a number of witnesses who said they had seen Oberholtzer and Stephenson together on numerous occasions, contradicting Oberholtzer's assertion in her deathbed statement that she and Stephenson had gone out only a couple of times. It was an ineffective gambit. Everyone wanted to believe that Oberholtzer was a pure soul. Even Cora Householder told a reporter that she was reluctant to smear the reputation of the dead woman.[7]

To many observers, the defense on the whole seemed unenergetic. Inman took a conservative approach, declining to make an opening statement and electing not to make Oberholtzer's character an issue (aside from Householder's testimony, which had been derailed). The savvy lawyer didn't want it to seem as if Stephenson was attacking the young woman a second time. In addition, any attempt to taint Oberholtzer's name might have resulted in a disastrous counterattack, with Remy calling to the stand a succession of seedy Klansmen to testify as to Stephenson's character. Inman was also confident that the evidence showed that the poison had killed Madge, not Stephenson's bites. Stephenson went along with Inman's strategy, although for different reasons. Stephenson's protégé, Ed Jackson, was governor. On the outside chance that a jury from a Klan-friendly town should convict him, he knew that he could count on a pardon.

The jury was made up of twelve white men from Hamilton County. (Women were not allowed to serve on juries at the time.) The jurors, men with names like Harley Huffman and Clyde Clark, wore dark suits into the courtroom every day. Ten of the twelve were farmers.[8] While it was not recorded, it can be reasonably assumed, given the demographics of central Indiana at the time, that the men were overwhelmingly Protestant. In other words, the jury was made up of men who under different circumstances might have been recruited by the Klan at one of Stephenson's all-day rallies. Statistically speaking, any group of twelve randomly selected white men from Hamilton County would have contained four or five Klansmen—35.4 percent of the native-born white men in the county were in the Klan in 1925.[9] Will Remy had done his best to screen out card-carrying Klansmen during jury selection, but the population he was dealing with was one that deeply identified with Klan ideals.

If the men on the jury were Klansmen or Klan sympathizers, however, it didn't help Stephenson. Hoosiers joined the Klan because they thought something was wrong with the country—liquor, immigration, and moral decay were three likely candidates. Stephenson had sold them on the Klan by promising to take a stand against all that and to be the vigorous guardian of their Protestant values. The more likely the jurors were to be Klansmen, the more likely they were disgusted to hear about Stephenson's drinking, whoring, and brutality. Although the move to a Klan stronghold like Hamilton County had at first appeared to be a great victory for the defense, Inman's arguments would have been more convincing and Stephenson's excesses would have seemed less repulsive to a sophisticated urban jury. In the end, the defense's case fell apart. After only five hours of deliberation, the jury convicted Stephenson of second-degree murder on November 14, 1925. Judge Sparks sentenced him to life in prison.

Stephenson remained smug, as always. He was quite willing to do some time in the Indiana State Prison in Michigan City until things cooled down, believing that Ed Jackson would come through with the pardon when the time was right. Stephenson knew that his dream of being appointed to the Senate was probably over and that his empire may have been slightly damaged by recent events. He was confident, however, that he would be able to rebuild whatever had been destroyed.

Stephenson soon discovered that his former disciples, including Ed Jackson, were content to let him rot in his cell. It no longer benefited them to be his friend. They began to disassociate themselves from the Klan right and left in the press. Stephenson was enraged but not entirely surprised. After all, he had planned for such a day. He would not go down alone.

From his prison cell, Stephenson engineered the release of the incriminating documents he had stowed in safe-deposit boxes across the state. The most spectacular revelation was the "contract" with John Duvall. Duvall had won the Indianapolis mayoral election on November 3, 1925, two days before the prosecution finished its case against Stephenson. After the contract was made public, the state charged Duvall with corruption in May 1926. He resigned as mayor when he was convicted in 1927. Duvall was ungrateful to the Ku Klux Klan after his fall. "They never gave me a chance to be Mayor," he wrote to the *Indianapolis Star* in 1955, "and did everything they possibly could to ruin my administration."[10]

Other documents released from Stephenson's stash detailed for Hoosiers the close relationship between their governor and the Klan. Ed Jackson was charged with bribery on September 7, 1926, a result of the offer he and Stephenson had made to Governor McCray in 1923. Stephenson eagerly volunteered to testify at Jackson's 1928 trial. Once on the witness stand, though, he melodramatically took the fifth, claiming that his life had been threatened by mysterious assassins. It was a pathetic last bit of grandstanding by the Grand Dragon. While the criminal charges against Jackson were eventually dropped, Stephenson still got his revenge. Jackson was disgraced, and his political career was ruined.

Jackson and Duvall were not the only politicians Stephenson brought down from his prison cell. The chairman of the Indiana Republican Party went to prison. A judge in Muncie was impeached. The entire Indianapolis City Council resigned.[11]

Hoosiers were profoundly disillusioned by both Stephenson's trial and the subsequent corruption scandals. They abandoned the Klan in droves. At its peak, the Indiana Klan boasted about 350,000 members. Less than a year after Stephenson's trial, membership in the Indiana Klan had dropped to less than fifteen thousand. In a strange way, it validated Stephenson's egomania. Without him, the Indiana Klan was nothing.

———

For Matthew Walsh, the spectacle of D. C. Stephenson's trial and its aftermath had confirmed a long-held belief. The Klan had fallen on its own sword, although in a fashion more spectacular than Walsh could have ever foreseen. Nonetheless, the man who had written his doctoral dissertation on anti-Catholic violence in Colonial Maryland did not expect anti-Catholic hatred to be permanently vanquished in America. The whole episode had also left Walsh with a profound distrust of local politicians and law enforcement. Walsh devoted the rest of his presidency to bringing Notre Dame students who lived in South Bend back to campus. He delayed constructing a new football stadium once again and began an unprecedented building spree.

By 1927, Walsh had constructed a new quad of residence halls. Howard Hall was named for Professor Timothy Howard and was the first building at Notre Dame named for a layman. Lyons Hall was named for Joseph Lyons, a professor at the time of the great fire of 1879, when the school's biggest building was reduced to ashes. Morrissey Hall was named for Fr. Andrew Morrissey, the priest who was standing on the steps of the Main Building when the fifteen-year-old Walsh arrived at Notre Dame in 1897. The three buildings cost $787,000.[12]

Walsh didn't want his students eating their meals in South Bend either. He built the grand South Dining Hall that had been designed for free by Ralph Adams Cram years earlier. By the end of Walsh's presidency in 1928, Notre Dame had twice as many students as it had when his term began, and almost all of them were sleeping and eating on campus. It is one of his most lasting legacies. In 1933, Notre Dame enrolled 2,545 students. Only twenty lived off campus. Today, Notre Dame has 11,311 students, and 77 percent live on campus.[13]

In 1927, near the end of his presidency, Walsh made one more lasting change to the university, formalizing a tradition that had been around for a number of years. With his signature, Notre Dame officially became the home of the Fighting Irish. There is some debate about how the nickname began, but it almost certainly came to life as a slur. Time and the football team's success, however, had transformed a damaging stereotype into a beloved nickname.

———

The year 1928 marked the end of Matthew Walsh's presidency at Notre Dame and the last hurrah of the 1920s Klan. In the presidential race that year, the Protestant Republican candidate, Herbert

Hoover, defeated the Catholic Democratic candidate, Alfred Smith, after a campaign that had revealed the full spectrum of American anti-Catholicism, from cerebral arguments in the *Atlantic Monthly* to a widely published fake letter in which the pope promised to send Smith his toenail clippings to use as sacred relics. When Hoover trounced Smith, the Klan took the credit, although endemic anti-Catholicism and the strong economy alone probably would have led to Smith's defeat.

By 1930, the national Klan had withered down to about forty-five thousand members.[14] The northern Klan had collapsed with Stephenson's conviction. In the Klan's southern strongholds, the Depression was making it ever harder for recruiters to extract the ten-dollar initiation fee from prospective members. In 1936, in order to raise cash, a weary Imperial Wizard Evans sold Klankrest to an insurance company, but it was sold again in 1939—to the Archdiocese of Atlanta. While rank-and-file Klansmen were outraged at the sale, Evans actually accepted an invitation to the building's dedication. He said the Latin ceremony was "one of the most beautiful services I ever saw."[15] Later that year, he retired as Imperial Wizard.

The position then went to a Hoosier—James Colescott of Terre Haute, a sixteen-year veteran of the Klan and a former assistant to Evans. Colescott refocused the Klan on a new boogeyman—Communism. He also slashed the initiation fee to $6.00 and reduced the price of robes from $6.50 to $3.50.[16] Despite these bargains, membership in the northern Klan continued to shrivel. The hard-core remnant klaverns began to flirt with the Nazis, their natural allies in their views on Jews, minorities, and Communists. When World War II began, friendships with Nazis suddenly became unfashionable, and the Klan found itself on the wrong end of a congressional investigation. Congress wanted to know exactly what the relationship was between the Klan and the Nazis. The subsequent testimony revealed just how weak the Klan had become. In Washington, D.C., in 1942,

Colescott testified that there were only ten thousand paid members in the entire Ku Klux Klan.[17]

In 1944, Imperial Wizard Colescott received a bill from the Internal Revenue Service for $685,000 in back taxes on profits the Klan had earned during its heyday. To avoid the liability, Colescott decided to go out of business. On April 23, 1944, he disbanded the Klan, revoking the charter of every klavern in the country. Colescott told reporters, "The Klan is dead—the whole thing is washed up."[18]

The Klan would come to life again, primarily in the South and primarily focused on its original target, the southern African American. If the Klan is perhaps a permanent fixture in America, it is now at least thoroughly relegated to fringe status. Gone are the days when a politician regards an endorsement from the Klan as a good thing. Gone are the days when a Grand Dragon can hand-select city councilmen, mayors, and governors. That Klan is dead.

12

THE AFTERMATH

O N NOVEMBER 20, 1925, SIX DAYS AFTER D. C. Stephenson was convicted of second-degree murder, Knute Rockne was baptized into the Catholic Church. Many in the Notre Dame administration were ecstatic about Rockne's conversion. Critics of Notre Dame had for some time countered the Catholic boosterism that surrounded Notre Dame football with the reminder that not only were many of the players Protestant, but so was their famous coach. Some made the point by suggesting that the team should change its nickname to the "Fighting Scandinavians."[1] Catholic publications had known for years that there were many benefits to a good conversion story, and Rockne's would be one of the best.

The fact that Rockne had not displayed a great deal of interest in any religion in his lifetime led many people to question his motives when he adopted the official religion of his employer. No one, however, believed that the coach had to change religions in order to keep his job. His fame after the 1924 season was in full bloom. If he ever felt a lack of job security because of his religion, which is doubtful, he certainly didn't feel it after winning the national championship. Even if some in the administration had occasionally urged him to become Catholic, Rockne had never been one to bow to pressure from the university on any matter before, large or small.

Rockne may, however, have occasionally bowed to pressure from Bonnie Rockne, his devoted wife and an observant Catholic who was raising their four children in the church. In addition to being exposed to Bonnie's faithful example, Rockne had for years listened to anti-Catholic jeers in places like Lincoln, Nebraska, and Evanston, Illinois. The insults puzzled and amazed him. His boys weren't Communists, anarchists, or drinkers—that was plain to see. They were good American men who played their hearts out for him. A more or less nonreligious man, Rockne had over time simply come to identify with the Catholic religion more than any other. And if becoming Catholic would make Bonnie happy, he could think of no good reason not to do it. Rockne quietly arranged to receive instruction in the faith from Fr. Vincent Mooney, a former Notre Dame baseball player. Rockne had decided to join Matthew Walsh's team. Not even his children knew about his decision.

Knute Rockne Jr. in particular was surprised when he learned of his father's conversion. Rockne Jr. attended Notre Dame's grammar school and, unbeknownst to him, was receiving instruction for first communion at the same time as his father. At the children's first-communion ceremony in the chapel of St. Edward's Hall, the home of Notre Dame's grammar school, Rockne shocked his son by kneeling at the communion rail with him.

Rockne was frequently questioned about his conversion later in life. At times, his answers almost seemed to confirm the opinion that he had shallow, half-baked motives for converting. In a postscript to Rockne's biography, Fr. John Cavanaugh, who had been president of Notre Dame when Rockne was promoted to head coach, recalled the coach's comments on the subject during a lay retreat at Notre Dame in the summer of 1929: Rockne said that it had always bothered him to see his men run off to church at each town they stopped in while he went to the hotel to relax. He also pontificated on the athletic advantages of religious devotion: he said that "when I saw all of them walking up to the communion rail to receive, and realized the hours of sleep they had sacrificed, I understood for the first time what a powerful ally their religion was to them in their work on the football field."[2]

Rockne was a football coach, though, not a theologian. It would be wrong to equate his occasionally imperfect articulations of his deepest spiritual beliefs with insincerity. When H. C. Byrd, the athletic director of the University of Maryland, questioned Rockne about his motives for converting, Rockne gave just about as good an answer as a convert can give. "The way I look at it is that we're all here to try and find, each in his own way, the best road to our ultimate goal," Rockne told him. "I believe I've found my way, and I shall travel it to the end." The end was closer than anyone knew.[3]

Notre Dame football continued on its path to greatness after the collapse of the Klan. Knute Rockne's Fighting Irish finally got a new football stadium in 1930, two years after the end of Matthew Walsh's presidency. The stadium was built by the Osborn Engineering Company of Cleveland, Ohio, the same company that built Yankee Stadium in New York. The company based its plans heavily on input from Rockne, who wanted a somewhat scaled-down version of the University of Michigan's massive stadium. When Notre Dame Stadium was complete, Rockne had the Kentucky bluegrass sod that had served him so well transferred from Cartier Field to the new stadium. The total cost of the project was around nine hundred thousand dollars, more than the cost of all three of Walsh's new residence halls combined. Walsh's stated reasons for delaying the building of a new stadium had always been limited resources and competing priorities. With the immediate sale of 240 ten-year box seats, however, the stadium was built with virtually no debt—just as Rockne had always predicted.

The Irish played their first game in the stadium on October 4, 1930, beating Southern Methodist University by a score of 20–14. Notre Dame would go on to win all ten of its games that year and earn Rockne's third consensus national championship.

After that inaugural season in Notre Dame Stadium, Universal Pictures approached Rockne with an offer of fifty thousand dollars to play a football coach in its new movie *Good News*.[4] It was a busy time for Rockne; he had also just agreed to become the national sales manager for the Studebaker Corporation. Confident that none of these side jobs would impede his coaching and eager to augment his celebrity, Rockne consented to appear in the film.

The leisurely pace of train travel couldn't accommodate Rockne's demanding schedule, so he became a frequent flier at the dawn of commercial aviation. On his way to California, Rockne stopped over for a few hours in Kansas on March 31, 1931, to visit his sons Bill and Knute Jr. at Pembroke, their boarding school. The three weren't able to meet up immediately, though, and Rockne's busy itinerary did not allow for any flexibility. Without seeing his sons, Rockne boarded Transcontinental-Western flight 599 bound from Kansas City to Los Angeles. Just outside Bazaar, Kansas, on the western edge of the state, the plane iced up and crashed. A farmer named R. Z. Blackburn was the first on the scene. He found nine dead bodies and no survivors.[5]

Rockne's death became a cause for national mourning. His funeral service at Sacred Heart Church in South Bend was broadcast nationally by the Columbia Broadcasting Company. President Hoover sent a funeral message to South Bend, as did the king of Norway. The mayors of New York City and Philadelphia attended in person. Bishop Francis Noll received the body in the church.

Fr. Charles O'Donnell, Walsh's successor as president, gave the oration. Rockne was no go-getter, he told the country. He was a "go-giver." Rockne could have gone to any college in the land, O'Donnell observed, "but he chose Our Lady's school, he honored her in the principles he inculcated and the ideals he set up in the lives of the young men under his care. He was her own true son."[6] With O'Donnell's elegy, Rockne's legend—as an inspirer of young men and an unassailable advocate of discipline and clean living—began to take shape.

Matthew Walsh was regarded similarly by many of the men who knew him—the word *remote* is the one most often used. Professor Thomas Stritch, a man who spent sixty years on Notre Dame's campus, called Walsh "the most enigmatic" of the eight presidents he personally knew. "There was something impenetrable about him," he wrote in his book *My Notre Dame*.[7] Students thought him an old-fashioned disciplinarian. One student who was at the school during Walsh's presidency remembered him as "not one to socialize."[8] The same student recalled that when the weather was good, Walsh would sometimes sit on the front porch of the Main Building in a rocking chair to watch the campus settle down for the evening.

Like John Cavanaugh before him, Matthew Walsh was probably slightly grateful when he reached the end of the six-year term imposed on him by congregation rules. He returned to the classroom and taught history, his first love, until he retired in 1947 at the age of sixty-five. Subsequent Notre Dame presidents often sought Walsh's advice. While he gladly counseled his successors, he remained steadfastly unwilling to discuss even the most ancient university controversies with outsiders. One Notre Dame historian wrote that Walsh would break off conversations about old feuds if young priests even walked into the room.[9]

Notably, it took a fellow historian and Notre Dame insider to get Walsh to candidly discuss his students' confrontation with the Klan. Arthur Hope, Holy Cross priest and Notre Dame graduate, consulted Walsh extensively for the centennial history of Notre Dame that he published in 1943. The two men had breakfast together every day in the Corby Hall dining room; as they talked about Walsh's childhood, the history of Notre Dame, and the two days of riots in 1924, the famously remote former president began to open up. By the time Hope had finished the book, the two men were fast friends. Hope thanked Walsh in his preface: "To Fr. Walsh, whose companionship and encouragement helped me through many a difficult day, I offer sincere thanks. Of all the Notre Dame men I know, Fr. Walsh is the richest in the lore of our school. And of those riches, he has given me without stint."[10]

In 1960, Walsh saw one more presidential election with the Catholic faith at its center. John F. Kennedy had to reassure American voters that as president, he would not take orders from the Vatican: "I believe in an America that is officially neither Catholic, Protestant, nor Jewish—where no public official either accepts or requests instructions on public policy from the Pope, the National Council of Churches, or any other ecclesiastical source."[11] The reassurances worked, and unlike in 1928, the Catholic candidate won. America had voted a member of its largest religious denomination into the presidency for the first—and only—time.

Exactly one week after Kennedy's inaugural address, on January 27, 1961, Matthew Walsh underwent heart surgery in Chicago at the age of seventy-eight. While he was able to return to Notre Dame, he moved more or less permanently into the student infirmary. He would be in and out of St. Joseph's Hospital in South Bend for the next two years, but he was on campus when he died at 10:28 AM on January 19, 1963. The tolling bells of Sacred Heart announced his passing to a frozen campus. The headline on the front page of the *South Bend Tribune* declared that he had headed the university during the "Golden Grid Era."[12] The article summarized Walsh's sixty-six years at the university, which began in 1897. Those years included ten years as vice president, a tour with honor in the Great War, and six years as president. His obituary mentioned that during his presidency, the number of both the students and the faculty doubled. The obituary said nothing about the Klan or the riot.

As Stephenson ran out of incriminating information to reveal, the public and the press lost interest in him. He busied himself in prison with studying law so that when his money ran out, he could represent himself in court. He would present more than forty appeals to the state, not a single one of which was ever granted.

Governor Henry Schricker granted Stephenson parole in 1950, on St. Patrick's Day. Soon after his release, Stephenson failed to meet with his parole officer. He was arrested in a Minneapolis suburb, where he had found work in a print shop. He returned to prison in Indiana.

Six years later, Governor George Craig included Stephenson in a Christmas clemency that he granted to sixty prisoners. Most of the sixty were old, sick, or otherwise pitiable. No reporters were on hand to watch the notorious Grand Dragon walk free. No editorials protested his release. Many of the 350,000 men who had been members of Stephenson's Klan were still alive in 1956. They tended to keep quiet about their days in hoods and robes; a typical former Klansman would say in later years that when he joined the Klan he "didn't know what it was about" or that the Klan back then didn't represent the kind of intolerance it represents now. The Klan had risen and fallen so fast in Indiana that it was easy to dismiss as the result of some kind of mass hysteria, an anomaly that need not be analyzed too closely or remembered too well.

At the peak of his success, at the age of thirty-three, Stephenson had insisted on being called "the Old Man." Now, at sixty-five, he really was an old man. The girth that had signaled success in 1924 was now just fat. He wore thick glasses. Almost all of his attractive blond hair was gone.

Yet Stephenson was still smart. He knew that his days as a power broker, kingmaker, and millionaire were over. He would have to find something else to occupy whatever time he had left. He could go back into sales. Through it all, he had always been a good salesman. He had an idea for a new kind of type-cleaning machine that he could sell to newspapers. Certainly, he would find a woman—he had always been good at that too.

As Stephenson left prison unnoticed on December 20, 1956, he could take some solace in the fact that he was still making history. He had just served the longest sentence in Indiana history for second-degree murder.[13]

———

D. C. Stephenson outlived Walsh by three years. After Governor Craig released him from prison in 1956, Stephenson moved to Seymour, Indiana, and quickly married Martha Dickinson. They separated less than a year later. Stephenson then moved to Jonesboro, Tennessee, where he married another woman—Martha Murray Sutton—without bothering to divorce Dickinson. He found work at the *Jonesboro Herald and Tribune,* where his skills at both writing copy and maintaining presses were put to good use. He also sold a type-cleaning machine of his own invention to newspapers and print shops in the region.

The former Grand Dragon had a heart attack on June 28, 1966, while carrying a basket of fruit from his car to his house. He died in his wife's arms. Like Walsh, Stephenson had been reluctant to discuss the glory days of the Indiana Klan. His widow knew nothing about his past until a reporter told her about it twelve years after his death.[14]

———

Bill Foohey, the Notre Dame sophomore who posed proudly in his captured Klan robe, became a portrait of Irish American success. He graduated from Notre Dame with a bachelor's degree in chemical engineering in 1926 and went on to get his master's in the same in

1927. While working toward his doctorate, with the help of a scholarship from DuPont, he taught at Notre Dame, occasionally working alongside Knute Rockne in the Chemistry Department.

Foohey received his PhD in chemical engineering in 1929 and took a job with DuPont in New Jersey, where he would work until his retirement in 1970. He was awarded several patents during his career. After his retirement, he was a sought-after consultant for the pharmaceutical industry.

Foohey's brother, Jim Foohey, graduated from Notre Dame ten years after him, in 1936. Bill Foohey had three children: Sean, William Jr., and Mary Ann. He sent both sons to Notre Dame and one grandson, my friend Mark Foohey, the son of William Jr. After a long and interesting life, Bill Foohey died in 1981 at the age of seventy-seven. Mark Foohey was thirteen years old at the time. He remembers his grandfather as a soft-spoken, gentle man—not at all the type of man one could see participating in a violent riot, throwing punches, dodging bottles, and hurling potatoes at an electric fiery cross. Bill Foohey never shared anything about the riot with his grandson.

No one knows what happened to the robe.

EPILOGUE

ONE QUESTION I CARRIED AROUND WITH ME WHILE researching this book is What does it mean to be an American Catholic? I converted to Catholicism in 1991 when I was in the Nuclear Navy. A sympathetic priest in Windsor, Connecticut, agreed to work my instruction around the rotating twelve-hour shifts that the navy had imposed on me. My motives were clear—I was to marry a Catholic girl in a few months. Fr. William Burns was a practical man, a pharmacist before entering the seminary. He kindly gave me a crash course in Catholicism and sent me to my wedding fully credentialed. Since then, though, I have often wondered what it all means. My favorite history professor at Notre Dame was Robert Kerby, a Korean War veteran. He once told me that he took up the study of history because he wanted to find out why everybody was shooting at him. In that same spirit, I have been trying to figure out what it means to be a Catholic in America, both in 1924 and today.

One of the Klan's more hysterical prophecies has come true: Catholics have become the biggest religious denomination in America. Roman Catholics make up 24.5 percent of the population. Baptists, at 16.3 percent, are a distant second.[1] The Klan's fears about a monolithic Catholic voting bloc, however, were unfounded; Catholics are just as fragmented politically as the rest of America. In the 2000 presidential race, 49 percent of American Catholics voted for Al Gore, while 47 percent voted for George W. Bush.[2]

The Klan's warnings about immigration have also turned out to be overheated. The 2000 census revealed that 28.4 million Americans were born in another country, about 10 percent of the total population.[3] Compare this to the percentage of the population that was foreign born in the 1920 census, at the height of immigration's "golden age": 13 percent. Charted from census to census in the United States, the percentage of Americans born in a country other than the United States makes a relatively straight line. They come from different countries at different times, and they settle in different American cities, but overall the total magnitude of immigration stays fairly constant.

While the makeup of the country in terms of immigration has not changed much since 1924, the makeup of the University of Notre Dame is vastly different. The university today has 11,311 students. Half are women; the school has been coeducational since 1972. Of the three residence halls that Matthew Walsh built on the south quad in the final years of his presidency, two now house Notre Dame's loyal daughters. The school that once couldn't afford fire insurance now has an endowment that is somewhere in the neighborhood of three billion dollars—one of the top twenty largest endowments in the nation, and the largest for any Catholic university. The median SAT score for a freshman at Notre Dame is 1335, and 40 percent of the students ranked in the top five of their high school class. More than twelve thousand high school seniors applied to be part of Notre Dame's class of 2007, the largest applicant pool ever, up 23 percent from just a year before. They were competing for fewer than two thousand spots in the freshman class. Notre Dame is one of a handful of colleges that accepts fewer than half of its applicants and enrolls more than half of those it accepts.[4]

Notre Dame today is very self-conscious about its relative homogeneity. The promotional film that is shown in the school's visitors' center features a Brazilian student who declares that she doesn't really like football. Redheaded Irish students who like the game are not given equal time. The Columbus murals in the Main Building were designed to be an uplifting affirmation of the Catholic role in

America's founding. Now a brochure apologizes for their Eurocentric depiction of Native Americans. The school has an Office of Multi-Cultural Student Affairs, an Interrace Forum, and a Diversity Council. Despite these conspicuous efforts, the school remains most appealing to roughly the same middle-class, midwestern Catholic constituency that flocked to Notre Dame in Walsh's era. Notre Dame today is 84 percent white and 83 percent Catholic.[5] The campus directory lists fifty-three Kellys, fifty-eight Sullivans, and eighty-two Murphys.

The six-year term limit that Walsh met with relief is gone. In the last fifty years, Notre Dame has had just two presidents, Fr. Theodore Hesburgh and Fr. Edward "Monk" Malloy.

Malloy is a reserved man and as such immediately reminded me of the Matthew Walsh I had read so much about. Malloy is also unfailingly gracious and polite; his secretary called me to schedule an interview after a single e-mail. Nonetheless, when I was in his office, Fr. Malloy didn't force himself to laugh at my jokes, and he gave measured answers to my questions.

Malloy came to Notre Dame in 1959 as a star athlete, a basketball player who had been recruited by fifty-five colleges. He entered the seminary in 1963 after graduating. His undergraduate years overlapped Fr. Walsh's final days, but they never met. Malloy was ordained at Sacred Heart Church in 1970 and received his doctorate in Christian ethics from Vanderbilt in 1975.

Besides his occasionally icy reserve, Malloy shares another characteristic with Matthew Walsh—his Irish heritage. His grandfather was from Liverpool, England, by way of western Ireland. In fact, other than Fr. Edward Sorin and Fr. Sorin's nephew, Auguste Lemonnier, every Notre Dame president has been either Irish born or the son of at least one Irish parent.

The most obvious difference between Matthew Walsh and Monk Malloy is the latter's close relationship with the students. For years, Malloy played regular pickup basketball games with students, a tradition that ended only recently with the sixty-two-year-old

Malloy's tendinitis. It is hard to imagine Walsh ever running the pick-and-roll with a group of sweaty undergraduates. Malloy teaches the greenest of undergraduates in a freshman humanities seminar every semester. Perhaps most unusual for a college president today, Malloy lives in a student dormitory. Since 1984, he has lived in room 141 of Sorin Hall.

During our meeting, I asked Fr. Malloy if he ever receives anti-Catholic hate mail. "Once in a while," he said, but not enough for him to remember any specifics. More often than not, he went on to say, the hate mail he gets is from "conservative Catholics not liking something that went on here, or liberal Catholics not liking something that went on here."

I asked how relations were with official South Bend. "As good as they've ever been," he said, a dodge as deft as a point guard's head fake. Fr. Malloy told me that he has met the South Bend police chief, although he didn't provide any details about the circumstances of their meeting. Malloy pointed out that if a kid gets in trouble for underage drinking in town today, the parents' first instinct is to "get a lawyer and get it off their record."

I asked him what he likes most about the job ("the variety") and least ("personnel issues"). I asked him if he thought the near–50 percent Catholic vote for George Bush after his visit to the rabidly anti-Catholic Bob Jones University indicated complete assimilation or dangerous complacency. He diplomatically stated, "For the last twenty years, a rising affluence has led to a greater identification with the Republican Party." It is hard to interview someone like Fr. Malloy, someone who gets interviewed all the time—he has been asked everything before and has polished answers for everything. It is hard to get such a person off balance, off the script, into anything a little interesting and dangerous.

The university is like that too, I think. The school has renovated and polished everything several times over since my graduation. The rickety "Cardboard Palace" in which Bill Foohey nailed up his captured Klan robe is long gone. In its place are new glass-and-brick residence halls named for wealthy benefactors.

Even Rockne's stadium has disappeared. It is hidden beneath an exterior ring that added twenty thousand seats to the stadium in 1997. More than eighty thousand people fill that stadium every game day, rain, shine, or snow. Since 1973, every home game at Notre Dame has sold out. While many of the fans are familiar with George Gipp, the Four Horsemen, and Knute Rockne, few have probably ever heard of the riot that took place in 1924.

You have to go inside the stadium gates now to see the weathered bricks that once made up the outer wall. They are shades darker than the new bricks, both because of their age and because of the shadow cast by the new addition.

NOTES

In citing works from the University of Notre Dame Archives in the notes, some abbreviations have been used. They are as follows:

CMWA   Matthew J. Walsh: Manuscripts collection
UKKK   Ku Klux Klan collection

Epigraph
1. Edward Sorin, CSC, *The Chronicles of Notre Dame du Lac*, trans. John M. Toohey, CSC, ed. James T. Connelly, CSC (Notre Dame, IN: University of Notre Dame Press, 1992), 16.

Prologue: May 19, 1924
1. I. I. Probst, interview by the author, September 5, 2002.
2. "The city's shame," *South Bend Mirror*, May 24, 1924, 4.
3. "Mayor Seebirt moves toward peace in Klan war; holds meeting with Klansmen and opponents," *South Bend Tribune*, May 20, 1924, 2.

Chapter 1
The Antagonists
1. Arthur J. Hope, CSC, *Notre Dame: One Hundred Years*, rev. ed. (South Bend, IN: Icarus Press, 1978), 356. As in many instances in this book, I have here dramatized an incident outlined by Hope. Historians have accused Hope of being a hagiographer, but he wrote this book with the close cooperation of Matthew Walsh, and I have every reason to believe that his anecdotes about Walsh are accurate and come from Walsh himself.
2. Roger Daniels, *Coming to America: A History of Immigration and Ethnicity in American Life* (New York: HarperCollins, 1990), 135.

3. Ibid.

4. Gaelic Dreams.com, "Top 100 Irish Surnames," http://gaelicdreams .tripod.com/id164.htm.

5. Daniel Pilarczyk, "The Changing Image of the Priest," *Origins*, July 3, 1986, 140–41, quoted in Donald B. Cozzens, *The Changing Face of the Priesthood: A Reflection on the Priest's Crisis of Soul* (Collegeville, MN: Liturgical Press, 2000), 3–4.

6. Donald B. Cozzens, *The Changing Face of the Priesthood: A Reflection on the Priest's Crisis of Soul* (Collegeville, MN: Liturgical Press, 2000), 133.

7. "The Parish Record," St. Columbkille's Church, Chicago, 1908, CMWA, box 1, folder 41, University of Notre Dame Archives.

8. Ibid.

9. Hope, *One Hundred Years*, 356–57.

10. Robert E. Burns, *Being Catholic, Being American: The Notre Dame Story*, vol. 1 (Notre Dame, IN: University of Notre Dame Press, 1999), 34.

11. Damaine Vonada, *Notre Dame: The Official Campus Guide* (Notre Dame, IN: University of Notre Dame Press, 1998), 100.

12. Matthew J. Walsh, CSC, "A Leap Year Ride," *Scholastic*, January 31, 1903, 291–92, University of Notre Dame Archives.

13. *The Dome: The Annual of the University of Notre Dame*, 1912, University of Notre Dame Archives.

14. Hope, *One Hundred Years*, 337.

15. Ibid., 335.

16. Burns, *Being Catholic, Being American*, 69.

17. Hope, *One Hundred Years*, 303–5. I have again dramatized a story outlined in Hope.

18. Ibid., 324.

19. M. William Lutholtz, *Grand Dragon: D. C. Stephenson and the Ku Klux Klan in Indiana* (West Lafayette, IN: Purdue University Press, 1991), 11.

20. Ibid.

21. Colin Jarman, comp., *The Guinness Book of Poisonous Quotes* (Chicago: Contemporary Books, 1993), 239.

Chapter 2
Fr. Sorin and the Birth of Notre Dame

1. Edward Sorin, CSC, *The Chronicles of Notre Dame du Lac*, trans. John M. Toohey, CSC, ed. James T. Connelly, CSC (Notre Dame, IN: University of Notre Dame Press, 1992), 4–13.

2. *Veil of Fear: Nineteenth-Century Convent Tales by Rebecca Reed and Maria Monk*, ed. Nancy Lusignan Schultz (West Lafayette, IN: NotaBell Books, 1999), vii.

3. Robert E. Burns, *Being Catholic, Being American: The Notre Dame Story*, vol. 1 (Notre Dame, IN: University of Notre Dame Press, 1999), 13.

4. Arthur J. Hope, CSC, *Notre Dame: One Hundred Years*, rev. ed. (South Bend, IN: Icarus Press, 1978), 27.

5. Sorin, *Notre Dame du Lac*, 16–17.

6. Ibid., 24.

7. This is very frequently quoted. The version used here was taken from a plaque outside the replica of the Log Chapel on campus today.

8. Sorin, *Notre Dame du Lac*, 25.

9. Ibid., 35.

10. Hope, *One Hundred Years*, 59–60.

11. Sorin, *Notre Dame du Lac*, 37, 88.

12. Ibid., 38.

13. Ibid., 90–91.

14. Ibid., 99.

15. Roger Daniels, *Coming to America: A History of Immigration and Ethnicity in American Life* (New York: HarperCollins, 1990), 140.

16. Charles R. Morris, *American Catholic: The Saints and Sinners Who Built America's Most Powerful Church* (New York: Vintage Books, 1998), 62.

17. Ibid., 52.

18. Sorin, *Notre Dame du Lac*, 248.

19. Ibid., 277.

20. Hope, *One Hundred Years*, 123.

21. Ibid., 170.

22. Ibid., 186.

23. Ibid.

24. Thomas J. Schlereth, *A Dome of Learning: The University of Notre Dame's Main Building* (Notre Dame, IN: University of Notre Dame Alumni Association, 1991), 12.

25. Hope, *One Hundred Years*, 201.

26. Schlereth, *Dome of Learning*, 25.

27. Damaine Vonada, *Notre Dame: The Official Campus Guide* (Notre Dame, IN: University of Notre Dame Press, 1998), 23.

28. Burns, *Being Catholic, Being American*, 21.

29. United States Census Data, researched with the assistance of the analysis tool at the Geospatial and Statistical Data Center, University of Virginia Library, http://fisher.lib.virginia.edu.

30. Ibid.

31. Ibid.

32. Ibid.

33. Jill Suzanne Nevel, "Fiery Crosses and Tempers: The Ku Klux Klan in South Bend, Indiana, 1923–1926" (senior history paper, Princeton University, 1977), table 2-1. Read at the Mishawaka Public Library, Mishawaka, Indiana.

34. Ibid.

35. Ibid.

36. Ibid.

Chapter 3
The Reincarnation of the Ku Klux Klan

1. Wyn Craig Wade, *The Fiery Cross: The Ku Klux Klan in America* (New York, Oxford University Press, 1998), 138.

2. Ibid., 133.

3. Ibid., 32.

4. Ibid.

5. Ibid., 34.

6. Ibid., 34–35.

7. Ibid., 32.

8. Thomas D. Dixon, *The Clansman: An Historical Romance of the Ku Klux Klan* (Lexington: University of Kentucky Press, 1970), 326.

9. Wade, *Fiery Cross*, 125.

10. Ibid., 120–25.

11. Ibid., 126. This is a controversial quote that many Wilson apologists have disputed, since Griffith appears to be the only witness. Wade argues convincingly that Griffith's meeting with Wilson is documented and that Griffith was unlikely to fabricate the quote because of his great respect for the president.

12. Ibid., 137. The disavowal was in the form of a letter signed not by Wilson but by Joseph Tumulty, his chief of staff.

13. Arthur J. Hope, CSC, *Notre Dame: One Hundred Years*, rev. ed. (South Bend, IN: Icarus Press, 1978), 305–6. Hope describes it as "the most splendid movie that had yet been made."

14. Wade, *Fiery Cross*, 146.

15. Ibid., 141.

16. Ibid., 142.

17. Ibid., 147.

18. Ibid., 421. Wade reproduces the Klan's entire "Kloran," which includes all the interrogatories, in his appendix.

19. Ibid., 429.

20. Ibid., 157.

Chapter 4
Notre Dame and the Indiana Klan

1. Arthur J. Hope, CSC, *Notre Dame: One Hundred Years*, rev. ed. (South Bend, IN: Icarus Press, 1978), 325. The whole story of the Chaplains' School as I have it here is taken from Hope's account.

2. "Training School for Chaplains," 9, CMWA, box 2, folder 50, University of Notre Dame Archives.

3. *The Chaplain: His Place and Duties* (Washington, DC: Government Printing Office, 1926), 13–14, CMWA, box 2, folder 47, University of Notre Dame Archives.

4. *Practical Hints for Catholic Chaplains* (New York: The Catholic Ordinariate, 1918), 4, CMWA, box 2, folder 45, University of Notre Dame Archives.

5. Matthew Walsh, letter of July 29, 1918, CMWA, box 2, folder "World War I—Correspondence," University of Notre Dame Archives.

6. Ibid. There are three typed copies of the letter in the Notre Dame Archives, one of which says in a note that the original is lost. The original is in the archives, though, in Walsh's handwriting, in pencil, on Knights of Columbus War Activities stationery. None of the copies or the original explicitly identifies a recipient; it is addressed only "Dear Father." An intelligent guess would be that the letter was to Fr. Cavanaugh. It is not to Walsh's actual father, because in the letter Walsh asks that the details of combat be kept from his family. One of the copies has "L. Rosenbloom So. Lafayette St." written lightly on the back.

7. Hope, *One Hundred Years*, 327–28.

8. Ibid., 329–30.

9. Certificate, CMWA, box 2, folder "World War I—Correspondence," University of Notre Dame Archives. "S.S. Buford" is handwritten at the top of the certificate.

10. Discharge certificate, May 6, 1919, CMWA, box 2, folder 40, University of Notre Dame Archives.

11. Grunts.net, "History of the 3rd Infantry Division," http://www.grunts .net/army/3rdid1.html.

12. Hope, *One Hundred Years*, 324.

13. M. William Lutholtz, *Grand Dragon: D. C. Stephenson and the Ku Klux Klan in Indiana* (West Lafayette, IN: Purdue University Press, 1991), 15.

14. Ibid., 20.

15. Wyn Craig Wade, *The Fiery Cross: The Ku Klux Klan in America* (New York: Oxford University Press, 1998), 155.

16. Hope, *One Hundred Years*, 333.

17. Ibid.

18. Robert E. Burns, *Being Catholic, Being American: The Notre Dame Story*, vol. 1 (Notre Dame, IN: University of Notre Dame Press, 1999), 447–49.

19. John Heisler, ed., *1999 Notre Dame Football Media Guide* (Notre Dame, IN: University of Notre Dame Sports Information Department, 1999), 228–33.

20. Burns, *Being Catholic, Being American*, 203.

21. Knute Rockne, "Gipp the Great," *Collier's*, November 22, 1930.

22. Letter from Ronald Reagan to Tony DiMarco, 3 October 1986, personal collection of I. I. Probst.

23. Burns, *Being Catholic, Being American*, 218.

24. Ibid., 149.

25. Ibid., 143.

26. I gave free rein to my imagination in constructing this account of the Evansville rally. It is based on descriptions of other Klan rallies, reports of D. C. Stephenson's speeches on other occasions, and additional documentary material. But, more than other events in this book, it reflects my sense of what *might well have happened* rather than what the record shows *did* happen.

27. Leonard J. Moore, *Citizen Klansmen: The Ku Klux Klan in Indiana, 1921–1928* (Chapel Hill: University of North Carolina Press, 1991), 99. These words are borrowed from an advertisement reproduced in the book for the Valparaiso rally, which would take place in 1923. I make the assumption here that Stephenson would have advertised his first rallies with similar gusto.

28. Ibid., 95–96. One of Moore's theses to explain the success of the Klan in Indiana is its relative openness when compared to the service clubs of the day.

29. Lutholtz, *Grand Dragon*, 37–38. Lutholtz speculates that Stephenson may have written the endorsement himself.

30. Ibid., 41.

31. Ibid., 55.

32. Wade, *Fiery Cross*, 226.

Chapter 5
The Klan Takes Over Indiana

1. Robert D. Hare et al., "The Revised Psychopathy Checklist: Descriptive Statistics, Reliability, and Factor Structure," *Psychological Assessment* 2, no. 3 (1990): 339.

2. *Diagnostic and Statistical Manual of Mental Disorders (DSM-IV-TR)*, 4th ed., text revision. (Washington, DC: American Psychiatric Association, 2000), 706.

3. Robert D. Hare, *Without Conscience: The Disturbing World of the Psychopaths among Us* (New York: Pocket Books, 1993), 1.

4. United States Census Data, researched with the assistance of the analysis tool at the Geospatial and Statistical Data Center, University of Virginia Library, http://fisher.lib.virginia.edu.

5. Robert L. Duffus, "Salesmen of Hate: The Ku Klux Klan," *World's Work* 46 (1923): 31–38, as quoted in M. William Lutholtz, *Grand Dragon: D. C. Stephenson and the Ku Klux Klan in Indiana* (West Lafayette, IN: Purdue University Press, 1991), 74.

6. Richard Baepler, *Flame of Faith, Lamp of Learning: A History of Valparaiso University* (St. Louis, MO: Concordia Publishing House, 2001), 105.

7. M. William Lutholtz, *Grand Dragon: D. C. Stephenson and the Ku Klux Klan in Indiana* (West Lafayette, IN: Purdue University Press, 1991), 76.

8. Ibid., 77. The meeting at the Willard Hotel took place. The ostensible purpose was to discuss the Klan's national platform, and I present here the platform Evans came up with. Stephenson's laughter and most of the dialogue is presumed.

9. Ibid., 86–91.

10. Ibid., 98–102.

Chapter 6
In the Crosshairs of the Klan

1. Robert E. Burns, *Being Catholic, Being American: The Notre Dame Story*, vol. 1 (Notre Dame, IN: University of Notre Dame Press, 1999), 228.
2. Ibid., 230.
3. Ibid., 228.
4. Ibid., 230.
5. *Bulletin of the University of Notre Dame: General Catalogue, 1923–1924* (Notre Dame, IN: University Press, 1924), 376.
6. Ibid., 55.
7. National Center for Education Statistics, *Digest of Education Statistics: 2000* (Washington, DC: U. S. Department of Education, 2000), tables 3 and 8.
8. Mike Borgia, "Admitting Success," *Scholastic*, February 20, 2003, 14.
9. Letter from Timothy Foohey to the Lady Hibernians of Chicago, circa 1920, private collection of Sean Foohey. The letter describes vividly Foohey's life in Ireland and his love for the United States. The last line is "The stars and stripes forever."
10. *Tolerance*, June 24, 1923, 7, UKKK, box 1, folder 8, University of Notre Dame Archives.
11. Ibid., 13.
12. M. William Lutholtz, *Grand Dragon: D. C. Stephenson and the Ku Klux Klan in Indiana* (West Lafayette, IN: Purdue University Press, 1991), 67. The speech Lutholtz quotes is actually a speech O'Donnell gave to the Ancient Order of Hibernians in Indianapolis on St. Patrick's Day 1923, less than a week before the Place Hall event. It is one of the few accounts I could find of an actual speech by O'Donnell, and as it is so close chronologically, I made the assumption here that his language in South Bend was similar.
13. Ibid.
14. Burns, *Being Catholic, Being American*, 288.
15. The Klan did in fact send a speaker to South Bend to rebut O'Donnell. As no good written account exists, I have constructed his speech from other Klan speeches and articles of the day.
16. Editorial, *Scholastic*, February 17, 1923.
17. Arthur J. Hope, CSC, *Notre Dame: One Hundred Years*, rev. ed. (South Bend, IN: Icarus Press, 1978), 372.
18. I. I. Probst, interview by the author, September 5, 2002.

19. Letter from Patrick O'Donnell to Fr. Matthew Walsh, May 26, 1923, UKKK, box 1, folder 2, University of Notre Dame Archives. O'Donnell goes on to say, "Our financial position and our limited power are too precarious to hazard them any longer in South Bend. We have, therefore, concluded to transfer our endeavors elsewhere."

20. Hope, *One Hundred Years*, 372–73. Robert Burns, for his part, doesn't believe the chamber of commerce incident took place, as Hope's book is the only account of it. No mention was made of the stormy meeting in the South Bend papers.

21. Letter from Patrick O'Donnell to Fr. Matthew Walsh, July 9, 1923, UKKK, box 1, folder 2, University of Notre Dame Archives.

22. Letter from Patrick O'Donnell to Albert Erskine, July 12, 1923, UKKK, box 1, folder 2, University of Notre Dame Archives.

23. Letter from Patrick O'Donnell to Fr. Matthew Walsh, December 20, 1923, UKKK, box 1, folder 2, University of Notre Dame Archives.

Chapter 7
D. C. Stephenson's Grab for Power

1. M. William Lutholtz, *Grand Dragon: D. C. Stephenson and the Ku Klux Klan in Indiana* (West Lafayette, IN: Purdue University Press, 1991), 108.

2. Letter from D. C. Stephenson, September 27, 1923, D. C. Stephenson Collection, Indianapolis Historical Society, as quoted in Lutholtz, *Grand Dragon*, 112.

3. Lutholtz, *Grand Dragon*, 127–29.

4. Ibid., 124.

5. Robert E. Burns, *Being Catholic, Being American: The Notre Dame Story*, vol. 1 (Notre Dame, IN: University of Notre Dame Press, 1999), 301.

6. "Klan victory precipitates party fights," *South Bend Tribune*, May 8, 1924, 2. These were the totals reported by the *South Bend Tribune* two days after the primary. The numbers would increase slightly for both men in the final count, but Jackson's margin of victory would stay roughly the same.

7. Lutholtz, *Grand Dragon*, 132.

8. This speech is a work of fictionalization that is based on a number of things D. C. Stephenson wrote and said on the subject of the Indiana Klan and its independence from Atlanta. He actually gave two speeches on May 12, 1924, one early in the day and one late. I have combined them here. Like Lutholtz (*Grand Dragon*, 132–37), I have made the

assumption that Stephenson's first speech, which was not recorded or transcribed, was similar to an article he had written entitled "The Old Man's Answer to Hate Vendors." While the most memorable lines of the speech here can be documented as Stephenson's, I have "connected the dots" and interpolated certain things to make the whole thing read as one speech for the sake of the narrative flow.

9. D. C. Stephenson, "The Old Man's Answer to Hate Vendors," Feightner Papers, Indiana State Library, as quoted in Lutholtz, *Grand Dragon*, 134.

10. Ibid.

11. Lutholtz, *Grand Dragon*, 137.

12. Ibid.

Chapter 8
The Rally and the Riot

1. "Klan is big feature," *South Bend Tribune*, May 6, 1924, 1.

2. "Klan victory precipitates party fights," *South Bend Tribune*, May 8, 1924, 1.

3. "Primary vote is heavy," *South Bend Tribune*, May 6, 1924, 1.

4. "Klan fight at one precinct only feature," *South Bend Tribune*, May 6, 1924, 1.

5. "Klan victory precipitates party fights," 2.

6. Robert E. Burns, *Being Catholic, Being American: The Notre Dame Story*, vol. 1 (Notre Dame, IN: University of Notre Dame Press, 1999), 307.

7. Ibid., 306.

8. "Klan victory precipitates party fights," 1.

9. Fr. J. Hugh O'Donnell and Fr. George Holderith, "Conferences with Chief Lane of the South Bend Police Force in re the Notre Dame student body and the Ku Klux Klan of South Bend," UKKK, box 1, folder 3, University of Notre Dame Archives. This is the report of the two meetings between the priests and Chief Lane. It is signed by both priests. Walsh asked for this written report after the riots, when Chief Lane's accounts of the weekend began to change.

10. *Bulletin of the University of Notre Dame: General Catalogue, 1923–1924* (Notre Dame, IN: University Press, 1924), 376, 56. Various estimates exist as to exactly how many students lived off campus, but I have chosen to go with these numbers.

11. Matthew Walsh, "Bulletin," May 17, 1924, UKKK, box 1, folder 3, University of Notre Dame Archives.

12. "Klan display in South Bend proves failure," *South Bend Tribune*, May 18, 1924, 1.

13. "Rain and city officials halt outbreak peril," *South Bend News-Times*, May 18, 1924, 2.

14. "Klan display in South Bend proves failure," 1.

15. "The city's shame," *South Bend Mirror*, May 24, 1924, 4.

16. "Klan display in South Bend proves failure," 1.

17. Ibid.

18. Ibid., 2.

19. O'Donnell and Holderith, "Conferences with Chief Lane."

20. "Rain and city officials halt outbreak peril," 1.

21. "Klan display in South Bend proves failure," 2.

22. "Rain and city officials halt outbreak peril," 2.

23. "Klan display in South Bend proves failure," 2.

24. "Rain and city officials halt outbreak peril," 2; the detail about the musical instruments being destroyed is from I. I. Probst, interview by the author, September 5, 2002.

25. "Rain and city officials halt outbreak peril," 2.

26. Burns, *Being Catholic, Being American*, 316.

Chapter 9
The Ambush

1. "Klan display in South Bend proves failure," *South Bend Tribune*, May 18, 1924, 1.

2. Ibid.

3. M. William Lutholtz, *Grand Dragon: D. C. Stephenson and the Ku Klux Klan in Indiana* (West Lafayette, IN: Purdue University Press, 1991), 142. Lutholtz describes an account in which Stephenson actually says he came upon Evans and his men waiting for the papal army outside of South Bend.

4. Ibid., 139.

5. "The city's shame," *South Bend Mirror*, May 24, 1924, 1.

6. "Klansmen and opponents in street clash," *South Bend News-Times*, May 20, 1924, 1.

7. "Mayor Seebirt moves toward peace in Klan war; holds meeting with Klansmen and opponents," *South Bend Tribune*, May 20, 1924, 1.

8. Ibid., 2.

9. "Klansmen and opponents in street clash," 1.

10. Ibid., 2. The account of Walsh's speech in the *South Bend Tribune* varies only slightly. Arthur Hope, in his account, embellished the speech by adding a passage in which Walsh points to the Klan headquarters, which wasn't visible from the courthouse, and forms the Notre Dame men up military-style and marches them back to campus.

11. "Mayor Seebirt moves toward peace in Klan war; holds meeting with Klansmen and opponents," 1.

12. "N.D. students enthusiastically pledge selves to law and order," *South Bend News-Times*, UKKK, box 1, folder 4, University of Notre Dame Archives.

13. Ibid.

14. The exact words of the pledge are not recorded, so I modeled my version on a typical temperance pledge of the day.

15. "Notre Dame collegians clash with Kluxers," *St. Paul Daily News*, May 17, 1924, 1, UKKK, box 1, folder 4, University of Notre Dame Archives.

16. "Students rout Klansmen," *Chicago Herald-Examiner*, May 18, 1924, UKKK, box 1, folder 4, University of Notre Dame Archives.

17. H. M. Trausch, *The Truth about the Notre Dame Riot on Saturday, May 17, 1924* (Indianapolis: Fiery Cross Publishing Company, 1924), 3, UKKK, box 1, folder 12, University of Notre Dame Archives.

18. Ibid., 7.

19. "Klan asks ban of Aggie game," *Lansing State Journal*, June 5, 1924, 2, UKKK, box 1, folder 3, University of Notre Dame Archives.

20. Letter from Fr. Matthew Walsh to Fr. J. Hugh O'Donnell, May 20, 1924, UKKK, box 1, folder 3, University of Notre Dame Archives.

21. Letter from Fr. Matthew Walsh to Rev. John C. McGinn, May 27, 1924, CMWA, box 1, folder "Walsh Correspondence 1924," University of Notre Dame Archives.

22. Ibid.

23. Letter from "A Kluxer" to Matthew Walsh, UKKK, box 1, folder 3, University of Notre Dame Archives.

24. Letter from anonymous to M. Walsh, May 20, 1924, UKKK, box 1, folder 3, University of Notre Dame Archives.

25. *The Fiery Cross*, May 30, 1924, UKKK, box 1, folder 1, University of Notre Dame Archives.

Chapter 10
The Ascent of Notre Dame

1. M. William Lutholtz, *Grand Dragon: D. C. Stephenson and the Ku Klux Klan in Indiana* (West Lafayette, IN: Purdue University Press, 1991), 146.

2. Robert E. Burns, *Being Catholic, Being American: The Notre Dame Story*, vol. 1 (Notre Dame, IN: University of Notre Dame Press, 1999), 324.

3. Lutholtz, *Grand Dragon*, 96.

4. Ibid., 148–49.

5. Helen Jackson, *Convent Cruelties; or, My Life in a Convent* (Toledo, OH: Helen Jackson, 1923), 32.

6. Ibid., 6, 104.

7. Ibid., title page.

8. Letter from Pat Emmons to Matthew Walsh, September 16, 1924, UKKK, box 1, folder 3, University of Notre Dame Archives. Walsh's complete handwritten note on the letter is as follows: "King held his meeting in S. Bend. As he was leaving town he was arrested by order of the Klan & charged then with failing to make a split of his collections as he had promised. The matter was adjusted in the law office of Edwin Hunter. M. Walsh, C.S.C."

9. Letter from Matthew Walsh to Charles O'Donnell, October 11, 1924, UKKK, box 1, folder 3, University of Notre Dame Archives.

10. John Heisler, ed., *1999 Notre Dame Football Media Guide* (Notre Dame, IN: University of Notre Dame Sports Information Department, 1999), 391.

11. Burns, *Being Catholic, Being American*, 366.

12. Thomas McAvoy, *Father O'Hara of Notre Dame, the Cardinal-Archbishop of Philadelphia* (Notre Dame, IN: University of Notre Dame Press, 1967), 107, as quoted in Burns, *Being Catholic, Being American*, 373.

13. Burns, *Being Catholic, Being American*, 370.

14. Lutholtz, *Grand Dragon*, 163.

15. William Herschell, *The Smile-Bringer, and Other Bits of Cheer* (Indianapolis: The Bobbs-Merrill Company, 1926), 69–70.

Chapter 11
The Ruin of D. C. Stephenson and the Collapse of the Klan

1. M. William Lutholtz, *Grand Dragon: D. C. Stephenson and the Ku Klux Klan in Indiana* (West Lafayette, IN: Purdue University Press, 1991), page 6 of illustrations.

2. Ibid., 81.

3. Leonard J. Moore, *Citizen Klansmen: The Ku Klux Klan in Indiana, 1921–1928* (Chapel Hill: University of North Carolina Press, 1991), table 3.1, 48–50. The county with the higher percentage was White

County, just north of Lafayette, with nearly 38 percent of its white males in the Klan.

4. Lutholtz, *Grand Dragon*, 223.

5. Ibid., 233.

6. Ibid., 234.

7. Ibid., 273.

8. Ibid., 230.

9. Moore, *Citizen Klansmen*, table 3.1, 48–50.

10. John Duvall, letter to the editor, *Indianapolis Star*, April 25, 1955, as quoted in Moore, *Citizen Klansmen*, 176.

11. Wyn Craig Wade, *The Fiery Cross: The Ku Klux Klan in America* (New York: Oxford University Press, 1998), 246.

12. Robert E. Burns, *Being Catholic, Being American: The Notre Dame Story*, vol. 1 (Notre Dame, IN: University of Notre Dame Press, 1999), 231.

13. University of Notre Dame Faculty Handbook, http://provost.nd.edu/handbook/.

14. Wade, *Fiery Cross*, 253.

15. Ibid., 265.

6. Ibid.

17. Ibid., 273.

18. Ibid., 275.

Chapter 12
The Aftermath

1. Wyn Craig Wade, *The Fiery Cross: The Ku Klux Klan in America* (New York: Oxford University Press, 1998), 235.

2. Knute K. Rockne, *The Autobiography of Knute K. Rockne* (Indianapolis: The Bobbs-Merrill Company, 1931), 273–74, University of Notre Dame Archives.

3. Ibid., 274–75.

4. Burns, *Being Catholic, Being American*, 512. Hope erroneously names the movie *The Spirit of Notre Dame*, the name that Universal gave a revised picture after Rockne's death.

5. Arthur J. Hope, CSC, *Notre Dame: One Hundred Years*, rev. ed. (South Bend, IN: Icarus Press, 1978), 427. There are some discrepancies about the total number of deaths; I believe this is due to the confusion of passengers and crew in the totals.

6. Ibid., 428.

7. Thomas Stritch, *My Notre Dame: Memories and Reflections of Sixty Years* (Notre Dame, IN: University of Notre Dame Press, 1991), 22.

8. I. I. Probst, interview by the author, September 5, 2002.

9. Burns, *Being Catholic, Being American*, 227.

10. Hope, *One Hundred Years*, xii.

11. Senator John F. Kennedy, address to the Greater Houston Ministerial Association (Rice Hotel, Houston, TX, September 12, 1960).

12. "Walsh, ex N.D. president, dies," *South Bend Tribune*, January 19, 1963, 1.

13. Lutholtz, *Grand Dragon*, 313.

14. M. William Lutholtz, *Grand Dragon: D. C. Stephenson and the Ku Klux Klan in Indiana* (West Lafayette, IN: Purdue University Press, 1991), 314.

Epilogue

1. Lisa Miller and David France, "Catholic America: The Trend Report," *Newsweek*, March 4, 2002, 46.

2. "Voting Behaviour in the 2000 Election," History Learning Site http://www.historylearningsite.co.uk/voting_behaviour_2000.htm.

3. Karen S. Peterson, "Refugees battle culture shock," *USA Today*, March 18, 2002, 1D.

4. Mike Borgia, "Admitting Success," *Scholastic*, February 20, 2003, 12–15.

5. Ibid., 14.

BIBLIOGRAPHY

Baepler, Richard. *Flame of Faith, Lamp of Learning: A History of Valparaiso University*. St. Louis, MO: Concordia Publishing House, 2001.

Bulletin of the University of Notre Dame: General Catalogue, 1923–1924. Notre Dame, IN: University Press, 1924.

Burns, Robert E. *Being Catholic, Being American: The Notre Dame Story*. 2 vols. Notre Dame, IN: University of Notre Dame Press, 1999.

Catalogue of the University of Notre Dame: 1902–1903. University of Notre Dame Archives.

"The city's shame." *South Bend Mirror*, May 24, 1924. Read at the Mishawaka Public Library.

Cleckley, Hervey M. *The Mask of Sanity: An Attempt to Clarify Some Issues about the So-Called Psychopathic Personality*. St. Louis, MO: C. V. Mosby Company, 1964.

Connelly, James T. "Notre Dame and the Irish." In *The Encyclopedia of the Irish in America*, edited by Michael Glazier. Notre Dame, IN: University of Notre Dame Press, 1999.

Cook, Fred J. *The Ku Klux Klan: America's Recurring Nightmare*. New York: Julian Messner, 1980.

Coyne, Kevin. *Domers: A Year at Notre Dame*. New York: Viking, 1995.

Cozzens, Donald B. *The Changing Face of the Priesthood: A Reflection on the Priest's Crisis of Soul*. Collegeville, MN: Liturgical Press, 2000.

Daniels, Roger. *Coming to America: A History of Immigration and Ethnicity in American Life*. New York: HarperCollins, 1990.

Diagnostic and Statistical Manual of Mental Disorders (DSM-IV-TR). 4th ed. Text revision. Washington, DC: American Psychiatric Association, 2000.

Dixon, Thomas D. *The Clansman: An Historical Romance of the Ku Klux Klan*. Lexington: University Press of Kentucky, 1970.

The Dome: The Annual of the University of Notre Dame, 1908. University of Notre Dame Archives.

Everett, Susanne. *World War I: An Illustrated History*. Chicago: Rand McNally, 1980.

Goldberg, David J. "Unmasking the Ku Klux Klan: The Northern Movement against the KKK, 1920–1925." *Journal of American Ethnic History* (Summer 1996): 32–49.

"The Great Depression and the New Deal." Gilder Lehrman Institute of American History, University of Houston. http://www.hfac.uh.edu/gl/us34.htm.

Griffith, D. W. *The Birth of a Nation*. VHS. Quebec: Madacy Entertainment, 1997.

Hare, Robert D. *Without Conscience: The Disturbing World of the Psychopaths among Us*. New York: Pocket Books, 1993.

Hare, Robert D. et al. "The Revised Psychopathy Checklist: Descriptive Statistics, Reliability, and Factor Structure." *Psychological Assessment: A Journal of Consulting and Clinical Psychology* 2, no. 3 (1990): 338–41.

Heisler, John, ed. *1999 Notre Dame Football Media Guide*. Notre Dame, IN: University of Notre Dame Sports Information Department, 1999.

Herschell, William. *The Smile-Bringer, and Other Bits of Cheer*. Indianapolis: The Bobbs-Merrill Company, 1926.

Hesburgh, Theodore M. *God, Country, Notre Dame*. With Terry Reedy. New York: Doubleday, 1990.

"History of the 3rd Infantry Division." Grunts.net. http://www.grunts.net/army/3rdid1.html.

"The History of United States Steel Corporation." United States Steel Corporation. http://www.ussteel.com/corp/about.htm.

Hope, Arthur. J., CSC. *Notre Dame: One Hundred Years*. Rev. ed. South Bend, IN: Icarus Press, 1978.

Houghton, Walter C. "Notre Dame in the Early Twenties." University of Notre Dame Alumni Association. http://alumni.nd.edu/~alumpubs/reflections/stpatsbulletin.html.

Howard, Timothy Edward. *A History of St. Joseph County, Indiana.* Vol. 1. Chicago: The Lewis Publishing Company, 1907.

"In Memoriam: Rev. Matthew J. Walsh, C.S.C." *Notre Dame Alumnus,* February–March 1963. University of Notre Dame Archives.

Jackson, Helen. *Convent Cruelties; or, My Life in a Convent.* Toledo, OH: Helen Jackson, 1923.

Jackson, Kenneth T. *The Ku Klux Klan in the City, 1915–1930.* New York: Oxford University Press, 1967.

Jarman, Colin, comp. *The Guinness Book of Poisonous Quotes.* Chicago: Contemporary Books, 1993.

Layden, Joe. *Notre Dame Football A to Z.* Dallas: Taylor Publishing Company, 1997.

Lutholtz, M. William. *Grand Dragon: D. C. Stephenson and the Ku Klux Klan in Indiana.* West Lafayette, IN: Purdue University Press, 1991.

"Military Career of Nathan Bedford Forrest CSA." Sons of Confederate Veterans, Tennessee Division. http://www.tennessee-scv.org/Forrest HistSociety/history.html.

Miller, Lisa, and David France. "Catholic America: The Trend Report." *Newsweek,* March 4, 2002, 46.

Moore, Leonard J. *Citizen Klansmen: The Ku Klux Klan in Indiana, 1921–1928.* Chapel Hill: University of North Carolina Press, 1991.

Morris, Charles R. *American Catholic: The Saints and Sinners Who Built America's Most Powerful Church.* New York: Vintage Books, 1998.

National Center for Education Statistics. *Digest of Education Statistics: 2000.* Washington, DC: U. S. Department of Education, 2000.

Nevel, Jill Suzanne. "Fiery Crosses and Tempers: The Ku Klux Klan in South Bend, Indiana, 1923–1926." Senior history paper, Princeton University, 1977. Read at the Mishawaka Public Library, Mishawaka, Indiana.

O'Connell, Marvin R. *Edward Sorin*. Notre Dame, IN: University of Notre Dame Press, 2001.

"The Peopling of America." The Statue of Liberty–Ellis Island Foundation, Inc. http://www.ellisisland.org/immexp/wseix_5_3.asp?.

Peterson, Karen S. "Refugees battle culture shock." *USA Today*, March 18, 2002, 1D.

Probst, I. I. Interview with author. September 5, 2002.

Reed, Rebecca, and Maria Monk. *Veil of Fear: Nineteenth-Century Convent Tales*. Edited by Nancy Lusignan Schultz. West Lafayette, IN: NotaBell Books, 1999.

Rockne, Knute K. *The Autobiography of Knute K. Rockne*. Indianapolis: The Bobbs-Merrill Company, 1931.

Sandburg, Carl. "The Mayor of Gary." In *Smoke and Steel*. New York: Harcourt, Brace and Howe, 1920.

Scheuer, George. Interview with author. September 4, 2002.

Schlereth, Thomas J. *A Dome of Learning: The University of Notre Dame's Main Building*. Notre Dame, IN: University of Notre Dame Alumni Association, 1991.

———. *A Spire of Faith: The University of Notre Dame's Sacred Heart Church*. Notre Dame, IN: University of Notre Dame Alumni Association, 1991.

Sorin, Edward, CSC. *The Chronicles of Notre Dame du Lac*. Translated by John M. Toohey, CSC. Edited and annotated by James T. Connelly, CSC. Notre Dame, IN: University of Notre Dame Press, 1992.

South Bend News-Times. 1924. Read at the Mishawaka Public Library.

South Bend Tribune. 1923–2002. Read at the Mishawaka Public Library.

Stock, Catherine McNicol. *Rural Radicals: Righteous Rage in the American Grain*. Ithaca, NY: Cornell University Press, 1996.

Stritch, Thomas. *My Notre Dame: Memories and Reflections of Sixty Years*. Notre Dame, IN: University of Notre Dame Press, 1991.

Trausch, H. M. *The Truth about the Notre Dame Riot on Saturday, May 17, 1924*. Indianapolis: Fiery Cross Publishing Company, 1924.

United States Census Data. Researched with the assistance of the analysis tool at the Geospatial and Statistical Data Center, University of Virginia Library. http://fisher.lib.virginia.edu.

"A Very Brief History of the Studebaker Family and Company." Studebaker Family National Association. http://www.studebakerfamily.org/history .html.

Vonada, Damaine. *Notre Dame: The Official Campus Guide*. Notre Dame, IN: University of Notre Dame Press, 1998.

Wade, Wyn Craig. *The Fiery Cross: The Ku Klux Klan in America*. New York: Oxford University Press, 1998.

Walsh, Matthew J. "The Drama and Modern Stagecraft." *Scholastic*, September 26, 1903, 41–45. University of Notre Dame Archives.

———. "Foundation of Universities." *Scholastic*, February 21, 1903, 344–45. University of Notre Dame Archives.

———. "A Leap Year Ride." *Scholastic*, January 31, 1903, 291–92. University of Notre Dame Archives.

———. Manuscript collections. University of Notre Dame Archives.

———. *The Political Status of Catholics in Colonial Maryland*. PhD diss., Catholic University, 1907. University of Notre Dame Archives.

———. "The Shield of Two Colours." *Scholastic*, November 29, 1902, 193–94. University of Notre Dame Archives.

Ward, Geoffrey C. *The Civil War: An Illustrated History*. Based on a documentary filmscript by Geoffrey C. Ward, Ric Burns, and Ken Burns. New York: Alfred A. Knopf, 1990.

INDEX